SAP ABAP Advanced Cookbook

Over 80 advanced recipes with excellent programming
techniques that focus on the Netweaver 7.0 EHP2 and above

Rehan Zaidi

[PACKT] enterprise 88
PUBLISHING   professional expertise distilled

BIRMINGHAM - MUMBAI

SAP ABAP Advanced Cookbook

First published: December 2012

Production Reference: 1191212

Published by Packt Publishing Ltd.
Livery Place
35 Livery Street
Birmingham B3 2PB, UK.

ISBN 978-1-84968-488-0

www.packtpub.com

Cover Image by Artie Ng (artherng@yahoo.com.au)

Credits

Author
Rehan Zaidi

Reviewers
Steffen Macke

Alvaro Tejada Galindo

Alexey Tveritinov

Eric Wildenstein

Acquisition Editor
Rukhsana Khambatta

Lead Technical Editor
Susmita Panda

Technical Editors
Kaustubh S. Mayekar

Kirti Pujari

Copy Editor
Laxmi Subramanian

Project Coordinator
Arshad Sopariwala

Proofreaders
Clyde Jenkins

Lydia May Morris

Kevin McGowen

Stephen Swaney

Indexer
Rekha Nair

Graphics
Aditi Gajjar

Production Coordinator
Shantanu Zagade

Cover Work
Shantanu Zagade

About the Author

Rehan Zaidi has more than 13 years of SAP experience and has been writing about SAP topics since 2001. He co-authored an ABAP programming training manual for a course taught in North America and has written a number of SAP books and articles about ABAP, workflow, HR functional and technical users, and SAP user experiences. Rehan has carried out support and implementation projects involving various areas of ABAP and workflow, and has worked in technical and functional areas of SAP ERP HCM. He holds bachelor and master's degrees in computer science. You may reach Rehan via e-mail at erpdomain@gmail.com.

I am very thankful to my parents, especially my mother, whose prayers are with me all the time. I am grateful to the many friends and well-wishers who have supported and encouraged me both through the duration of this project and throughout my life as a whole.

In the preparation of the book, I would like to thank Rukhsana Khambatta for turning a book idea (that began in my mind) into reality. In addition, I am indebted to the entire team at Packt Publishing, including Susmita Panda, Sai Gamare, Arshad, and others. Last but not least, my thanks to those who reviewed this book and provided me with feedback, especially Steffen Macke for his invaluable suggestions.

I apologize to anyone whom I have failed to mention. There are many people who have helped me in this process and who have encouraged the creation of this book. To all of you, I extend my most heartfelt thanks.

About the Reviewers

Steffen Macke is a Civil Engineer and Software Developer. After several years of work on water supply projects in the Middle East, he's now back in Germany and has joined the software industry.

Maps and Geographic Information Systems (GIS) played a key role in his hydraulic analysis and customer database activities. They served him as an entry point to the world of programming, relational databases, version management systems, and web technology. The complexity of the projects he encountered made him embrace diversity, active communities, and practical approaches. That's why he doesn't have a favorite programming language, operating system, or database management system.

Steffen is actively involved in a number of open source projects, among which the general purpose drawing software Dia is the most popular (http://dia-installer.de). His passion for open source does not mean that he's ignorant to the advantages of commercial software development models, he believes that they're great to make a living. If you're interested in Steffen's views and projects, make sure that you visit his website http://sdteffen.de.

Alvaro Tejada Galindo worked as a Senior ABAP Consultant for 11 years, then he moved to SAP Labs in Montreal where he works as a Development Expert. Besides his SAP background, Alvaro is very proficient in scripting languages like PHP, Python, Ruby, and R and considers himself to be a regular expressions hero.

Alvaro has worked in Peru and Canada for some of the best consultant companies, namely Stefanini IT Solutions, ActualiSap, and Beyond Technologies. Presently, he is working for SAP.

Alvaro has published several programming books on
`http://www.lulu.com/spotlight/blag`.

I would like to thank my wife Milly and my daughter Kiara for all their support while I was doing this book's review.

Alexey Tveritinov graduated from Moscow State University of Informatics and Craftsmanship in 2008. After that he was hired by NVIDIA in a GPU and driver testing team as Junior Software Engineer, where he undertook development of various tools for tests automation and performance measurement. After spending one year at NVIDIA he left the company as his work on the software had finished, and he wasn't involved in other developments.

After that he was hired by a medical company named Trackpore Technology where he developed embedded software for plasmapheresis medical units using Linux and C++.

In 2011, he was hired by SAP CIS as Developer Associate and started to work on implementing the framework for XML reports according to specifications of legal units of Russia, Ukraine, and other CIS countries, without the limitations of DMEE.

I would like to thank Vasily Kovalsky, a teacher at the SAP training center, for his patience and knowledge. In addition, I would like to thank my managers Vadim and Juri for the trust in me and my skills. Also I would like to thank all developers in the GS unit of SAP, who were open to share their knowledge and experience. Also, I would like to thank my girlfriend Olga Tupikina for her patience and understanding while I was working on several projects and had little time to share with her.

Eric Wildenstein is a SAP independent Consultant, who has been working on ERP implementations for blue chip companies in Western Europe and North Africa regions since 1997. He mainly specializes in ABAP Object programming, NetWeaver XI/PI and SAP Business Workflow, providing technical expertise across the core business modules of SAP. Prior to being self-employed in 2000, he worked as an in-house Programmer Analyst on behalf of PricewaterhouseCoopers, U.K. and Andersen Consulting, France, on both SAP R/3 and C/S architectures.

www.PacktPub.com

Support files, eBooks, discount offers and more

You might want to visit www.PacktPub.com for support files and downloads related to your book.

Did you know that Packt offers eBook versions of every book published, with PDF and ePub files available? You can upgrade to the eBook version at www.PacktPub.com and as a print book customer, you are entitled to a discount on the eBook copy. Get in touch with us at service@packtpub.com for more details.

At www.PacktPub.com, you can also read a collection of free technical articles, sign up for a range of free newsletters and receive exclusive discounts and offers on Packt books and eBooks.

http://PacktLib.PacktPub.com

Do you need instant solutions to your IT questions? PacktLib is Packt's online digital book library. Here, you can access, read and search across Packt's entire library of books.

Why Subscribe?

- ▶ Fully searchable across every book published by Packt
- ▶ Copy and paste, print and bookmark content
- ▶ On demand and accessible via web browser

Free Access for Packt account holders

If you have an account with Packt at www.PacktPub.com, you can use this to access PacktLib today and view nine entirely free books. Simply use your login credentials for immediate access.

Instant Updates on New Packt Books

Get notified! Find out when new books are published by following @PacktEnterprise on Twitter, or the *Packt Enterprise* Facebook page.

Table of Contents

Preface

Advanced Business Application Programming (ABAP) is SAP's proprietary 4th Generation Language (4GL). SAP core is written almost entirely in ABAP. ABAP is a high level programming language used in SAP for development and other customization processes. This book covers advanced SAP programming applications with ABAP. It teaches you to enhance SAP applications by developing custom reports and interfaces with ABAP programming. This cookbook has quick and advanced real world recipes for programming ABAP.

It begins with the applications of ABAP objects and ALV tips and tricks. It then covers design patterns and dynamic programming in detail. You will also learn the usage of quality improvement tools such as transaction SAT, SQL Trace, and the code inspector. Simple transformations and its application in Excel downloading will also be discussed, as well as the newest topics surrounding Adobe Interactive Forms and the consumption and creation of Web services. The book comes to an end by covering advanced usage of Web Dynpro for ABAP and the latest advancement in Floorplan Manager.

What this book covers

Chapter 1, *ABAP Objects*, introduces useful recipes related to the object-oriented programming. This will include useful design patterns, the shared memory, and the persistent object concept.

Chapter 2, *Dynamic Programming*, covers facets of dynamic programming as applied in ABAP, such as Dynamic Open SQL and usage of field symbols and references.

Chapter 3, *ALV Tricks*, shows how you can get the most out of ALV programs. Starting with a simple ALV program, we will add code in recipes to fulfill a variety of user requirements.

Chapter 4, *Regular Expressions*, guides you on how you can embed regex programming in your ABAP programs and solve complicated problems in the least possible time and with minimal code.

Chapter 5, *Optimizing Programs*, shows the newer feature of secondary indexes and the transaction SAT (runtime analyzer) along with valuable program optimization tips.

Chapter 6, *Doing More with Selection Screens*, discusses recipes based on less frequently applied functionality within ABAP programs' selection screens, such as the addition of tabstrips and placement of buttons on toolbar. In addition, we will see how to take folder and file names as input, followed by a recipe for writing code in search help exits.

Chapter 7, *Smart Forms – Tips and Tricks*, introduces various recipes based on Smart forms and fulfilling user's form printing requirements in the least possible time.

Chapter 8, *Working with SQL Trace*, provides lesser-known tricks related to the SQL Trace tool. This will include the performance optimization usage of the SQL trace tool as well as the use of finding data source of screen fields.

Chapter 9, *Code Inspector*, shows how to check the quality of custom programs using standard checks, along with the procedure for creating your own checks.

Chapter 10, *Simple Transformations*, discusses in detail the Simple Transformation language and the representation of data variables in it, the application for Excel download format will also be shown.

Chapter 11, *Sending E-mail Using BCS Classes*, covers the classes of the Business Communication Service (BCS) for e-mail generation. This chapter will cover everything from simple e-mails for SAP users to Internet e-mail addresses, and also the procedure for adding attachments of various formats.

Chapter 12, *Creating and Consuming Web Services*, covers the step-by-step procedure for the creation of Web services based on an ABAP function module using the Inside-Out approach. The steps required to create a consumer of the Web service will also be shown.

Chapter 13, *SAP Interactive Forms by Adobe*, shows how to create both print and interactive forms using the SAP Interactive forms technology. A number of scenarios such as Offline form processing will also be covered.

Chapter 14, *Web Dynpro for ABAP*, shows how to create simple and advanced Web Dynpro for ABAP (WD4A) applications. The advanced topics related to the Web Dynpro components will also be covered.

Chapter 15, *Floorplan Manager*, covers newer features of the Floorplan Manager design used for creating Web Dynpro applications quickly. Both the configuration and coding for useful Floorplans will also be covered.

What you need for this book

ECC 6 system with Netweaver 7.02 or higher. A trial version of ABAP Netweaver 7.02 or higher will also suffice.

Who this book is for

SAP Developers and Consultants who have at least a basic knowledge of ABAP.

Conventions

New terms and **important words** are shown in bold. Words that you see on the screen, in menus or dialog boxes for example, appear in the text like this: "clicking the **Next** button moves you to the next screen".

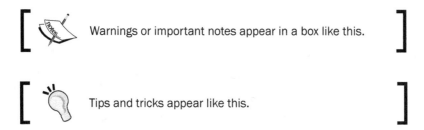

Warnings or important notes appear in a box like this.

Tips and tricks appear like this.

Reader feedback

Feedback from our readers is always welcome. Let us know what you think about this book—what you liked or may have disliked. Reader feedback is important for us to develop titles that you really get the most out of.

To send us general feedback, simply send an e-mail to feedback@packtpub.com, and mention the book title in the subject of your message.

If there is a topic that you have expertise in and you are interested in either writing or contributing to a book, see our author guide on www.packtpub.com/authors.

Customer support

Now that you are the proud owner of a Packt book, we have a number of things to help you to get the most from your purchase.

Downloading the example code

You can download the example code files for all Packt books you have purchased from your account at http://www.packtpub.com. If you purchased this book elsewhere, you can visit http://www.packtpub.com/support and register to have the files e-mailed directly to you.

Errata

Although we have taken every care to ensure the accuracy of our content, mistakes do happen. If you find a mistake in one of our books—maybe a mistake in the text or the code—we would be grateful if you would report this to us. By doing so, you can save other readers from frustration and help us improve subsequent versions of this book. If you find any errata, please report them by visiting http://www.packtpub.com/support, selecting your book, clicking on the **errata submission form** link, and entering the details of your errata. Once your errata are verified, your submission will be accepted and the errata will be uploaded to our website, or added to any list of existing errata, under the Errata section of that title.

Piracy

Piracy of copyright material on the Internet is an ongoing problem across all media. At Packt, we take the protection of our copyright and licenses very seriously. If you come across any illegal copies of our works, in any form, on the Internet, please provide us with the location address or website name immediately so that we can pursue a remedy.

Please contact us at copyright@packtpub.com with a link to the suspected pirated material.

We appreciate your help in protecting our authors, and our ability to bring you valuable content.

Questions

You can contact us at questions@packtpub.com if you are having a problem with any aspect of the book, and we will do our best to address it.

1
ABAP Objects

In this chapter, we start with recipes for ABAP objects. This chapter is designed to provide useful recipes related to the storage of ABAP objects in shared memory and the database (persistent objects), as well as some useful design patterns. In this chapter, we will look at ways of:

- ▸ Creating a shared memory object
- ▸ Creating a persistent object
- ▸ Creating classes based on factory methods
- ▸ Creating classes based on singleton design pattern
- ▸ Creating classes based on adapter pattern

Introduction

This chapter explores recipes related to ABAP objects. Two useful features of the object-oriented ABAP are storage options in the shared memory as shared objects, and in the database as objects of persistent classes. The details about both the prerequisites as well as the necessary steps needed to created shared memory-enabled objects and persistent objects will be discussed later in this chapter.

Moreover, design patterns are very important in object-oriented programming. In this chapter, we will see how to implement three of them using ABAP objects, namely the adapter, `singleton`, and the factory design. We will create a class with a `factory` method design. Later, we will show how this class may be modified in order to behave like a singleton class. Finally, we will see how an object of one class may be converted to that of another using an adapter class. The examples are kept simple in order to emphasize on the design pattern concept.

For this chapter, we assume that the reader has basic knowledge of the ABAP objects, and is familiar with the class-builder transaction.

Creating a shared memory object

This recipe shows how to store the instances of your classes in the shared memory of the application server. A number of programs may access these objects that reside on the application server shared memory.

Two classes are necessary for shared memory, namely the `area` class and the `area root` class. The `root` class is necessary for storing (encapsulating) the data that are to be stored in the shared memory. An `area` class may comprise of various instances that may consist of a number of versions.

An important concept shown in this recipe is the `CREATE OBJECT` statement with the addition `AREA HANDLE`. This will create the object in the application server that is shared memory pointed to by the area handle `myarea`.

Getting ready

Prior to writing the code for storing objects in shared memory, an `area root` class must be created and a shared memory area be defined using transaction `SHMA`.

The steps required for creating a root class are:

1. Call transaction `SE24`; enter a suitable name to your `root` class, as shown in the following screenshot. On the **Properties** tab, we need to make sure that the `Shared-Memory` checkbox is switched on.

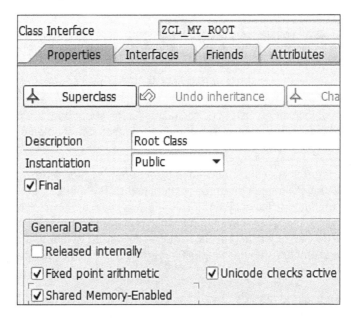

Downloading the example code

You can download the example code files for all Packt books you have purchased from your account at http://www.packtpub.com. If you purchased this book elsewhere, you can visit http://www.packtpub.com/support and register to have the files e-mailed directly to you

2. We have named it ZCL_MY_ROOT. We will then define two **Instance Attributes**, **NUMBER** and **NAME**, having private visibility, as shown in the following screenshot:

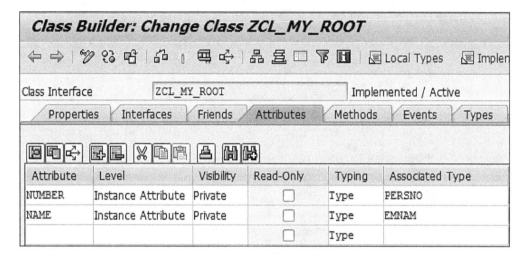

3. Two suitable methods, **SET_DATA** and **GET_DATA**, are also added to the class. The **SET_DATA** method contains code that imports number and name and assigns to the attributes **NUMBER** and **NAME** of the class. The **GET_DATA** method does just the opposite, that is, it exports the **NUMBER** and **NAME** attribute for a given shared memory object.

4. Next, the shared memory area should be created. This is done via transaction SHMA.

5. Enter a suitable name and click on the **Create** button. We have typed the name
ZCL_MY_EMP_AREA. On the screen that appears, enter the description of the area.
Also, enter the name of the root class created earlier in the **Root Class** field. You
may leave the **Client-Specific Area** checkbox unchecked as it is not required for our
recipe. Now, save your entries. Refer to the following screenshot:

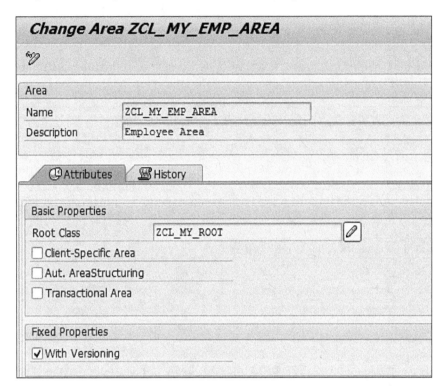

6. This will also generate an area class by entering the same name
ZCL_MY_EMP_AREA.

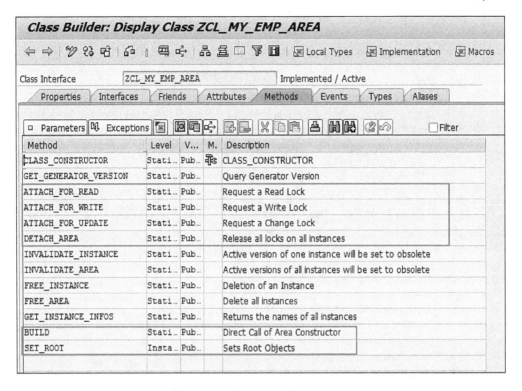

7. This area class will contain the necessary methods used for reading, changing, and creating the `area`, such as **ATTACH_FOR_UPDATE**, **ATTACH_FOR_READ**, and **ATTACH_FOR_WRITE**.

How to do it...

For creating the set of code that writes object's contents to the shared memory, follow these steps:

1. Two object references `my_handle` and `my_root` are defined, one for `area` class and the other for `root` class.

2. The static method `attach_for_write` of the `area` class `zcl_my_emp_area` is called.

3. The `CREATE OBJECT` with the area handle, `my_handle` must then be called.

4. The root and the created area instance must be linked using the `set_root` method of the handle.

5. The `set_data` method is called with the relevant number and name.

6. The `detach_commit` method of the `area` class is then called.

```
data : my_handle  type ref to zcl_my_emp_area  .
data : my_root type ref to zcl_my_root.

try .
    CALL METHOD zcl_my_emp_area=>attach_for_write
      EXPORTING
        inst_name = 'INST_NAME'
      RECEIVING
        handle    = my_handle.

    CREATE OBJECT my_root area handle my_handle.

    CALL METHOD my_handle->set_root
      EXPORTING
        root = my_root.

    CALL METHOD my_root->set_data
      EXPORTING
        number = '00000024'
        name   = 'John Reed'.

    CALL METHOD my_handle->detach_commit.

  catch cx_shm_attach_error.
    write :/ 'Error in Writing to Area' .
endtry.
```

How it works...

In the shared memory-writing program, the statements collectively make the writing of object in the shared memory. Let us see how the program code works.

An area instance version needs to be created before any data may be written in the shared memory on the application server. The `attach_for_write` static method is used for this purpose and returns a handle to the area instance created in the application server memory. This imposes `write` lock on the version.

The `CREATE OBJECT` statement is then called with the name of the created handle. This creates a `root` object in the `area` instance of the shared memory. The link between the `area` instance and the `root` class is created using the `set_root` method. The `set_data` method is then called for the root reference `my_root` and supplied with the name and number of the employee, which are then stored in the shared area. Finally, the `detach_commit` method is called and the `write` lock is released.

Once the program has run successfully, you may see the created object in the shared memory using the shared memory transaction SHMM. This will appear as your **area** class name **ZCL_MY_EMP_AREA**. Refer to the following screenshot:

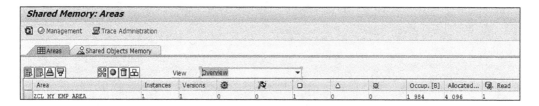

Double-click on the name of area to view the details, as shown in the following screenshot:

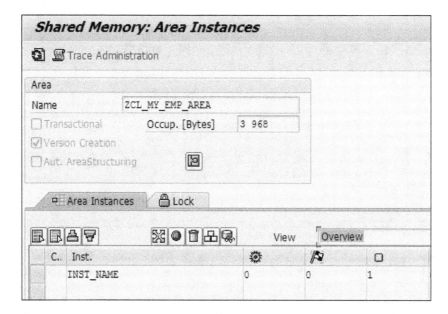

There's more...

The read program is somewhat similar. However, instead of the attach_for_write method used earlier, we will use attach_for_read. The same instance name is passed and the handle is received. The method imposes a read lock on the area instance. Then, the get_data method of the root object is called using the area handle, my_handle. This returns the employee name and number stored earlier into the variables name and number respectively.

Finally, the `detach` method is called and the `read` lock is released.

```
data : my_handle type ref to zcl_my_emp_area   .
data : my_root type ref to zcl_my_root.
data : number type persno.
data : name type emnam.

try.

    CALL METHOD zcl_my_emp_area=>attach_for_read
      EXPORTING
        inst_name = 'INST_NAME'
      RECEIVING
        handle    = my_handle.

    CALL METHOD my_handle->root->get_data
      IMPORTING
        number = number
        name   = name.

    CALL METHOD my_handle->detach.

  catch cx_shm_attach_error.
    write :/ 'Error in reading from area'.
endtry.

write :/ name, number.
```

While creating the shared memory area, if we select the **Transactional Area** checkbox, the area becomes transactional. In this case, the modifications to the `area` instance versions are not active immediately after the call of `detach_commit` method. Rather, they become active when the next database commit is executed.

See also

▸   http://help.sap.com/saphelp_nw73ehp1/helpdata/en/4a/035233f1bd0
    88ce10000000a421937/frameset.htm

Creating a persistent object

ABAP objects provide a persistent object service that allows the developer to store objects in the database. The values of the attributes of the object are stored in appropriate fields of the database table specified. This recipe shows how to define `persistent` classes and then how to call them in your application programs.

Getting ready

Prior to storing objects in the database, a suitable database table with the name
ZEMP_TABLE is created to store the values of the objects' attributes. Two fields are defined,
NUMBER1 and **NAME** (the field name **NUMBER** was not allowed, so **NUMBER1** has been
used as the field name). Refer to the following screenshot:

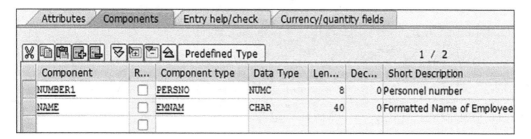

How to do it...

Once the database table is defined, a persistence class must be defined. In order to define
persistent classes, follow these steps:

1. Call transaction SE24. Enter a suitable name of the persistent class to be created.
    We will create a class by entering the name ZCL_MY_PERSIST. Enter the name in
    the **Class** field and click on the **Create** button.

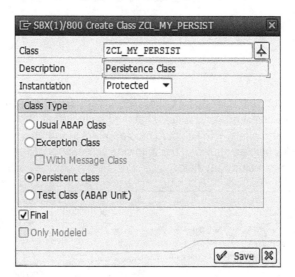

2. Enter a suitable description in the field provided. Make sure that the **Persistent Class** indicator is selected, and click on **Save**.

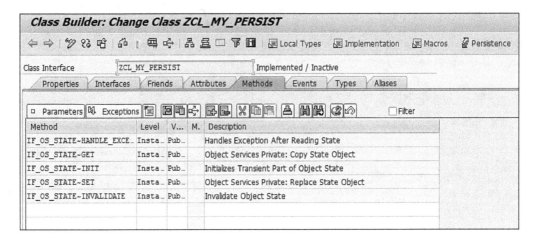

3. The programmer may only modify the methods HANDLE_EXCEPTION and INIT.

4. Click on the **Persistence button**. Then, enter the name of the table that was created for storage of data(in our case, we will enter the name ZEMP_TABLE). Refer to the following screenshot:

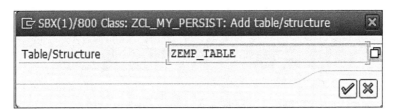

5. This will take you to the mapping editor. The lower part of the screen will show **Table/Fields**. Double-click each of the field that is to be included and stored as attributes of the persistent class. The selected field appears in the area earlier (for example, the **NUMBER1** field as shown in the following screenshot). Click on the **Set attribute values** button to include the field.

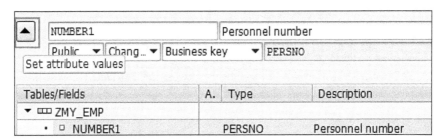

6. This will transfer the selected field in the topmost area of the editor.

7. Similarly, the **NAME** field must be included.

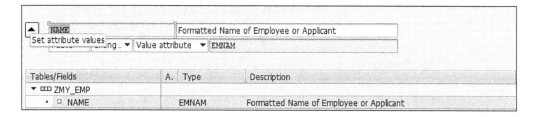

8. All the mapped fields will appear at the top area of the mapper. The **Number1** field will appear as a business key, as show in the following screenshot:

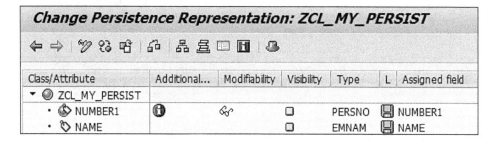

9. Upon activation of the `persistence` class, the system asks for activation of the `actor` class as well. Click on **Yes**, as shown in the following screenshot:

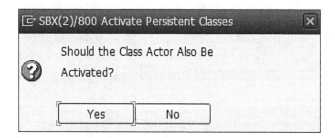

10. The class ZCL_MY_PERSIST is created and necessary methods needed for the persistence service are included. An actor class is also created with the class. The agent class has been generated by the name ZCA_MY_PERSIST. There is one base agent class generated as a result. In total, three classes are generated, the persistent class, the agent class, and the base class of the agent.

Object Type Name	Short description
ZCA_MY_PERSIST	Agent Persistence Class
ZCB_MY_PERSIST	Base agent Persistence Class
ZCL_MY_PERSIST	Persistence Class

11. The class ZCL_MY_PERSIST contains methods for setting and getting the values of the attributes **NAME** and **NUMBER1**. Note that no **SET** method is generated for the **key** field, in our case **NUMBER1**.

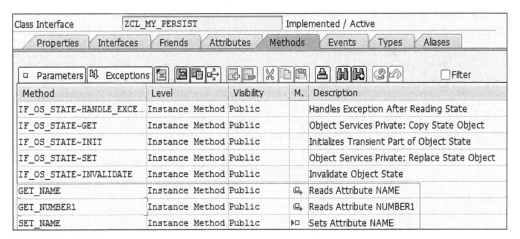

12. The agent class provides number of useful methods related to the persistent property. Important methods, such as create_persistent, delete_persistant, and get_persistent are provided. The methods are implemented in the superclass zcb_my_persist of the agent class zca_my_persist.

Class Builder: Class ZCB_MY_PERSIST Display

← → | 🖉 📇 📑 ◎ | 📇 | 🖥 📑 | 🖧 📇 ▭ 🖽 | 📇 📇 | Pattern | Pretty Printer | Signature

Ty.	Parameter	Type spec.	Description
▶□	I_NAME	TYPE EMNAM OPTIONAL	Persistent Attribute
▶□	I_NUMBER1	TYPE PERSNO	Business Key
⏏,	VALUE(RESULT)	TYPE REF TO ZCL_MY_PERSIST	Newly Generated Persistent Object
🗐	CX_OS_OBJECT_EXISTING		Object Services Exception

Method	CREATE_PERSISTENT	Active

How it works...

During the generation of the `persistent` class `zcl_my_persist`, two additional classes are generated. These are the `actor` (agent) and the `base agent` classes having the names `zca_my_persist` and `zcb_my_persist` respectively. The `base agent` class is generated as abstract (that is, no instance can be constructed from it), and cannot be modified. It is created in a separate pool class from `zcl_my_persist`. The `agent` class `zca_my_persist` may be extended, as well as the loading and saving methods may be modified.

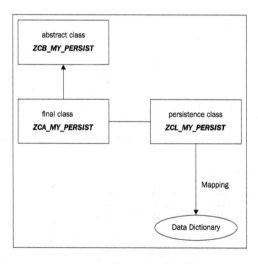

The instantiation mode of the `persistence` class may be set as abstract or protected. In our recipe, we have chosen the instantiation mode as protected (which means that only instances may be created from within the class or its subclasses). However, making the instantiation mode of a `persistent` class as protected makes the generated `base agent` class a friend of the `persistent` class (in the world of ABAP objects, a friend or its subclasses may create instances of the class in question).

The coding for this recipe declares two references, `emp` and `agent`, to the `persistent` class `zcl_my_persist` and the `agent` class `zca_my_persist`, respectively. Next, the `static factory` method `agent` is called for the class `zca_my_persist` (agent class). The reference returned is stored in the variable `agent`.

The `agent` class contains the method `create_persistent` required for storing the data into the database (this is analogous to the concept of insertion in database table).

The most important part is the calling of the `create_persistent` method that is passed the number and name that is to be stored. The employee with the number `00000017` and name `John Reed` is created and reference is returned in `emp`. Finally, the `COMMIT WORK` method stores the data of the `emp` object into the table created earlier in this recipe. One row with the number and a name is added to the table `ZEMP_TABLE`.

```
DATA: emp TYPE REF TO zcl_my_persist ,
      agent TYPE REF TO zca_my_persist ,
      number TYPE persno ,
      name TYPE emnam.
number = '00000017'.
name   = 'John Reed'.
agent = zca_my_persist=>agent .
TRY .
    CALL METHOD agent->create_persistent
    EXPORTING
        i_number1 = number
        i_name    = name
    RECEIVING
        result    = emp.
    COMMIT WORK.
  CATCH cx_root.
ENDTRY.
```

For reading the stored value related to the employee number `00000017`, a number variable is declared and assigned the value `00000017`. The static method agent of the `zca_my_persist` class is called in order to get a reference to the `agent`. The `get_persistent` method is then called and the number (in our case, `00000017`) is passed. This method returns the entire object emp pertaining to the employee number. You may then call the `get_name` method of the `zcl_my_persist` class for the emp object in order to retrieve the employee name.

```
number = '00000017'.
agent = zca_my_persist=>agent .

CALL METHOD agent->get_persistent
   EXPORTING
      i_number1 = number
   RECEIVING
      result    = emp.

CALL METHOD emp->get_name
   RECEIVING
      result = name.
WRITE :/ name.
```

See also

- http://help.sap.com/saphelp_nw73ehp1/helpdata/en/06/
  f23c40638d11d4966d00a0c94260a5/content.htm

- http://help.sap.com/saphelp_nw73ehp1/helpdata/en/49/
  e560e26149088fe10000000a421937/content.htm?frameset=/en/49/
  e8807d7cf0088ce10000000a421937/frameset.htm

Creating classes based on factory methods

One important design pattern that is used in object-oriented ABAP is the factory design. This allows you to create objects of a particular class either via a `factory` class or via `factory` method defined within the class. The emphasis of this recipe is to design a class that supports the creation of its objects via a `factory` method, rather than direct instantiation outside the class via `CREATE OBJECT` statement.

A `factory` method is a static method that creates and then returns (as a parameter) a reference to the object of the class it belongs to. The code for the creation of the object is contained within the `factory` method. This recipe shows the factory design. You may further modify to enhance the structure in order to suit your needs

We have referred to the coding of the standard `cl_salv_table` class factory method for creating the class shown in this recipe. The class created in this recipe will be used in the subsequent recipes of singleton and adapter design pattern.

Getting ready

For the sake of this recipe and the ones that follow, we will focus on an employee and name example. The class will encapsulate an eight-character number (in numeric form) for the employee number `00000014` and a 30-character field for the employee name. For example, there can be an employee `John Reed` with number. This will be stored in the private attributes of the class as `Name` and `Number`.

How to do it...

For creating a class as a **factory** method design, follow these steps:

1. Create a class definition for `fac_meth_class` in the program. The `factory` method is a static method for the class and is defined via `CLASS-METHODS`. The class definition contains the addition `create private` in order to stop the instantiation of the class from outside via `CREATE OBJECT`. A constructor is defined that allows setting the value of the number and the employee name.

```abap
CLASS fac_meth_class DEFINITION create private.
  PUBLIC SECTION.
    CLASS-METHODS factory IMPORTING number TYPE persno
                                    employee_name TYPE smnam
                          EXPORTING employee_obj TYPE REF TO fac_meth_class.
    METHODS    constructor IMPORTING number TYPE persno
                                     employee_name TYPE smnam.
  PRIVATE SECTION.
    DATA  employee_no TYPE persno.   """ eight digit employee number numeric type
    DATA  employee_name TYPE smnam.  """ name in (lastname firstname) format

ENDCLASS.                    "fac meth class DEFINITION
```

2. The private attributes employee number and name are defined, as it is based on the dictionary data elements `persno` and `smnam` respectively.

3. The static method `factory` imports the name and number of the employee to be created and returns the employee object `employee_obj` of the object reference `fac_meth_class`. The constructor takes as input the number and the employee name.

4. The implementation of the `fac_meth_class` object reference is then created. The code for the `factory` and the `constructor` is written here. The `factory` method receives the number and the name of the employee to be created. It includes the `CREATE OBJECT` statement for creation of the employee object.

```abap
CLASS fac_meth_class IMPLEMENTATION.
  METHOD factory.
    CREATE OBJECT employee_obj EXPORTING number        = number
                                         employee_name =  employee_name.

  ENDMETHOD.                        "factory


  METHOD constructor.
    me->employee_no   = number .
    me->employee_name =  employee_name.
    WRITE : / ' Employee created having number' , number ,
              'and name ' , employee_name.
  ENDMETHOD.                        "constructor

ENDCLASS.                        "fac meth class IMPLEMENTATION
```

5. The constructor assigns the number and employee name to the corresponding private attributes of the newly constructed object. A WRITE statement is also included that outputs the name and number of the successful created employee.

6. Finally, the call for the factory method is included. The static method of the fac_meth_class=>factory object is included and passed with the number and name of the employee to be created. A code shows two such method calls for object references emp1 and emp2, that is, employee 00000012 and 0000014.

```
DATA :     emp TYPE REF TO fac_meth_class .
DATA :     emp2 TYPE REF TO fac_meth_class .
DATA :     number TYPE persno.
DATA :     name TYPE smnam  .

number    = '00000012'.
name = 'Fernandes John'.

CALL METHOD fac_meth_class=>factory
  EXPORTING
     number          = number
     employee_name = name
  IMPORTING
     employee_obj   = emp.

number    = '00000014'.
name = 'Reed John'.
CALL METHOD fac_meth_class=>factory
  EXPORTING
     number          = number
     employee_name = name
  IMPORTING
     employee_obj   = emp2.
```

How it works...

When the program calls the static factory method, the code within the factory method is called for each of the two objects emp1 and emp2. The factory method triggers CREATE OBJECT statement, which creates a new object and calls the constructor.

The constructor is called twice, once for each of the two instantiated objects emp1 and emp2. This prints the message successful creation for emp1 and emp2.

```
Employee created having number 00000012 and name  Fernandes John
Employee created having number 00000014 and name  Reed John
```

Creating classes based on singleton design pattern

A `singleton` class is a class that can have only one instance at a time. Any attempt to create a second or more instances should not be allowed. This recipe shows how to create a class based on the singleton design.

Getting ready

We will use the same class created in the last recipe of `factory` method. We will make few changes to the class so that we can prevent the creation of multiple instances of the class. We will make a copy of the class (program) shown in the previous recipe and modify it. The name of the copy is `singleton_class`.

How to do it...

For creating a `singleton` class, follow these steps:

1. Make sure the CREATE PRIVATE addition is included in the `singleton` class definition.

2. Within the definition, a static attribute `number_of_instances` having type `integer` is added to the private section.

```
CLASS singleton_class DEFINITION CREATE PRIVATE .
  PUBLIC SECTION.
    CLASS-METHODS factory IMPORTING number TYPE persno
                                    employee_name TYPE smnam
                          EXPORTING employee_obj TYPE REF TO singleton_class.
    METHODS    constructor IMPORTING number TYPE persno
                                     employee_name TYPE smnam.

  PRIVATE SECTION.
    DATA  employee_no TYPE persno.    """  type n
    DATA  employee_name TYPE smnam.   """  last name first and
    CLASS-DATA : number_of_instances TYPE i .
ENDCLASS.
```

3. The implementation of the class is then written. The `factory` method has to be slightly modified in order to force the `singleton` characteristic.

```
CLASS singleton_class IMPLEMENTATION.
  METHOD factory.
    IF number_of_instances EQ 0.
      CREATE OBJECT employee_obj EXPORTING number   = number
                                           employee_name =  employee_name.
      number_of_instances = 1.
    ELSE.
      WRITE : / ' Only one object instantiation allowed'.
    ENDIF.
  ENDMETHOD.                        "factory

  METHOD constructor.
    me->employee_no  = number .
    me->employee_name =  employee_name.
    WRITE : / ' Employee created having number' , number ,
             'and name ' , employee_name.
  ENDMETHOD.                        "constructor

ENDCLASS.
```

4. In the implementation of the `singleton` class, the `factory` method now contains an `IF` statement that first checks the number of instances already there when the `factory` call is made. If the first instance is being created (that is, `number_of_instances` equals 0), the employee object is created and `number_of_instances` is set as 1. An `ELSE` condition is included to output a message if one instance already exists.

```
DATA :    obj TYPE REF TO singleton_class .
DATA :    number TYPE persno.
DATA :    name TYPE smnam   .

number   = '00000012'.
name = 'Fernandes John'.

CALL METHOD singleton_class=>factory
  EXPORTING
    number         = number
    employee_name = name
  IMPORTING
    employee_obj  = obj.


DATA :    obj2 TYPE REF TO singleton_class .
number   = '00000014'.
name = 'Reed Jon'.

CALL METHOD singleton_class=>factory
  EXPORTING
    number         = number
    employee_name = name
  IMPORTING
    employee_obj  = obj2.
```

How it works...

Similar to the previous recipe, we try to instantiate two objects emp1 and emp2, having number 0000012 and 00000014 respectively. However, in our singleton class, we have added an attribute number_of_instances, which keeps track of the number of class instances that already exist. Upon creation of the first object, the factory method increments this static attribute to 1. On the second object creation attempt, the IF statement does not allow the CREATE OBJECT statement to be called a second time. The result is that the second object is not created. No further attempts of object creation will be allowed. Rather, a message saying that only one object instantiation is allowed is outputted for the second object creation attempt.

```
Employee created having number 00000012 and name   Fernandes John
Only one object instantiation allowed
```

See also

▶ http://www.abaptutorial.com/abap-singleton-design-pattern/

Creating classes based on adapter pattern

Another important design pattern is the adapter design. As the name suggests, the adapter design is used for conversion of one object into another object belonging to a different class. An adapter class will have a method that takes as input the object reference that is to be converted and outputs it into the other object reference format.

We have referred to the cl_salv_tree_adapter standard class while making of this recipe.

Getting ready

In order to demonstrate the adapter, we need two classes (input class and output class). The input class will be the fac_meth_class created earlier. For the output, we will create another class fac_meth_class2. This will serve as the class, into the format of which the input object will be converted.

```
CLASS fac_meth_class2 DEFINITION.
  PUBLIC SECTION.
    METHODS   constructor IMPORTING number TYPE char8
                                    employee_name TYPE emnam.
  PRIVATE SECTION.
    DATA  employee_no TYPE char8.  """ employee number in character format
    DATA  employee_name TYPE emnam. """ name in (lastname firstname) format

ENDCLASS.

CLASS fac_meth_class2 IMPLEMENTATION.
  METHOD constructor.
    me->employee_no  = number .
    me->employee_name =  employee_name.
    WRITE : / ' Converted: Employee created having number' , number ,
              'and name ' , employee_name.
  ENDMETHOD.                    "constructor

ENDCLASS .                      "fac meth class2 IMPLEMENTATION
```

It is without a `factory` method for sake of simplicity. It contains employee number and employee name but the format of these two is different from the classes shown in the previous recipes. The employee name of this class is based on data element `emnam`, whereas the number is a character without zeros having length as eight. The name is of the form (`firstname lastname`), meaning `John Reed` will be stored as `John Reed` and not Reed John as in the previous recipes. The constructor outputs the message, `Converted employee created`.

We will use the same class used previously as the input object for the adapter method.

How to do it...

For creating a `singleton` class, follow these steps:

1. Create a deferred definition of the `adapter` class `adapter_meth_class` that we are going to create in the next step.

2. Specify the `adapter_meth_class` as a friend of our `fact_meth_class` class in the definition via the `FRIENDS` addition.

```
CLASS adapter_meth_class DEFINITION DEFERRED .

CLASS fac_meth_class DEFINITION CREATE PRIVATE FRIENDS adapter_meth_class .
  PUBLIC SECTION.
    CLASS-METHODS factory IMPORTING number TYPE persno
                                    employee_name TYPE smnam
                          EXPORTING employee_obj TYPE REF TO fac_meth_class.
    METHODS   constructor IMPORTING number TYPE persno
                                    employee_name TYPE smnam.
  PRIVATE SECTION.
    DATA  employee_no TYPE persno.   """ eight digit employee number numeric type
    DATA  employee_name TYPE smnam. """ name in (lastname firstname) format

ENDCLASS.                    "fac meth class DEFINITION
```

3. The `adapter` class is then defined. It contains a `static adapter` method adapter that imports an object based on `fac_meth_class` and returns one in the `fac_meth_class2` format.

```
CLASS adapter_meth_class DEFINITION   .
  PUBLIC SECTION.
    CLASS-METHODS :  adapter IMPORTING
                              employee_form1 TYPE REF TO fac_meth_class
                            EXPORTING
                              employee_form2 TYPE REF TO fac_meth_class2.

ENDCLASS.
```

4. The implementation of the `adapter` class is then created. It contains the code of the `adapter` method. The `adapter` method will convert the incoming number of the employee from numeric to character format. In addition, the name of the employee is converted to the `firstname lastname` format. The new object based on the second class `fac_meth_class2` is then created and returned as an exporting parameter of the method.

```
CLASS adapter_meth_class IMPLEMENTATION.
  METHOD adapter.
    DATA : number TYPE char8,
           lastname(40),
           firstname(40),
           name TYPE emnam.

    WRITE employee_form1->employee_no TO number NO-ZERO.
    CONDENSE number NO-GAPS.
    SPLIT employee_form1->employee_name AT space INTO lastname firstname .
    CONCATENATE firstname lastname INTO name SEPARATED BY space.

    CREATE OBJECT employee_form2 EXPORTING number     =   number
                                           employee_name = name.

  ENDMETHOD.                          "factory
```

5. While calling the `adapter` method, you first create an object based on the `fac_meth_class` class that is a `factory` method (for illustrative purpose), similar to the previous recipe for the object reference EMP. This is then passed on to the `static adapter` method of the `adapter_meth_class`. The `adapter` class returns the converted object in the second format.

```
DATA :     emp TYPE REF TO fac_meth_class .
DATA :     emp_converted TYPE REF TO fac_meth_class2.
DATA :     number TYPE persno.
DATA :     name TYPE smnam   .

number   = '00001234'.
name = 'Reed John'.

CALL METHOD fac_meth_class=>factory
  EXPORTING
    number         = number
    employee_name = name
  IMPORTING
    employee_obj  = emp.

CALL METHOD adapter_meth_class=>adapter
  EXPORTING
    employee_form1 = emp
  IMPORTING
    employee_form2 = emp_converted.
```

How it works...

When the program calls the static method adapter of the class adapter_meth_class , the
code in the adapter method is executed. The adapter method calls the necessary code
for converting the number into the character format and any zeros are removed from the
number. In addition, the SPLIT statement is called for converting name of the employee in
the (first name last name) format such as converting Reed John into John Reed. Finally the
CREATE OBJECT is called in order to create the object in the converted class format . This
triggers the constructor for the converted class fac_meth_class2 that outputs the message
"Converted: Employee Created having number 1234" and name John Reed. Since we called
the factory method of the original fac_meth_class before the adapter method call, the original
constructor was also called and message printed also.

```
Original : Employee created having number 00001234 and name  Reed John
Converted: Employee created having number 1234     and name  John Reed
```

See also

▸ Design Patterns in Object-Oriented ABAP published by SAP-Press

2

Dynamic Programming

In this chapter, we will cover recipes related to dynamic programming. This chapter is designed to provide useful recipes related to field symbols and data references, as well as dynamic SQL and ABAP code generation. In this chapter, we will look at the ways of:

- ▸ Using field symbols and data references to print database table contents
- ▸ Applying dynamic Open SQL
- ▸ Dynamic program generation

Introduction

This chapter explores recipes related to dynamic programming. Dynamic programming is a very vast topic. It may be simply defined as a technique whose behavior/effect is only evident at execution time. There are many facets of dynamic programming with ABAP. These include generic programming such as dynamic source code generation. Also specifying parts of the Open SQL statements (clauses) dynamically using string variables, and the creation of data objects based on a type known only at runtime are within the dynamic programming landscape. When using dynamic programming, we may also sometimes need to determine the data type of data objects at runtime. This is called **Runtime Type Identification** (**RTTI**).

The ABAP language provides a number of features/options for making programs dynamic or to avoid hardcoding of values. We will start with application of field symbols and references. As an example, we will create a program that will take as input the name of a table and print its contents.

Also we will look at some of the ways in which dynamic SQL may be applied to fulfill simple requirements. We will also cover the option of generating ABAP programs at runtime using the `INSERT REPORT` statement.

The examples are kept simple in order to emphasize on the dynamic programming concept. We assume that the reader is familiar with basics of `SELECT` statement, the `CREATE DATA` statement and the concept of field symbols, and the `ASSIGN` statement. Also, the knowledge of the `cl_abap_datadescr` classes is assumed. Moreover, the knowledge of downcasting (widening cast) is also important.

See also

▶ http://help.sap.com/abapdocu_731/en/abendynamic_prog_technique_guidl.htm

Using field symbols and data references to print database table contents

Field symbols and references are an important combination for dynamic programming. Data references are addresses of data objects stored in reference variables. Field symbols are placeholders, or symbolic representations of these data objects.

This recipe shows how to print all the contents of a particular database table (the name of which is only known at runtime). For simplicity sake, we will only focus on the main logic pertaining to dynamic programming. In addition to data references and field symbols, we will also see some dynamic SQL statement application.

Getting ready

The code will let you create a small data browser program that will take as input the database table name whose contents are to be read, and the number of rows and columns (fields) to be displayed. The output displays the table's field names as column headers along with the data stored in the table.

The knowledge of the `describe_by_data` method of the `cl_abap_structdescr` class and widening (downcasting) will also be used.

How to do it...

For creating a program that prints the contents of an entered SAP table name, follow these steps:

1. Declare parameters for inputting the name of the table whose data is to be accessed. Also we take as input the number of rows and columns (fields) that are to be displayed.

```
parameters : myt_name(30) default 'LFA1',
             rows type i,
             columns type i.
```

2. Declare field symbols for the internal table, the table row, and the table fields. In addition, data reference variables for internal table and the structure are defined.

```
data : tab_reference type ref to data,
       struc_reference type ref to data.

field-symbols : <my_struc> type any,
                <my_field> type any,
                <my_itab> type any table.
```

3. We place a small `check` statement to make sure the program runs only when the `columns` value entered by the user is equal to one or more.

```
check columns ge 1.
```

4. Next, we create the data objects using the `create data` statement. We then dereference and assign them to placeholders (field symbols) respectively. If the table name entered by the user is wrong, a `cx_sy_create_data_error` exception is generated, and therefore need to catch it in our coding using the `catch` statement.

```
try .
    create data tab_reference type standard table of (myt_name)
            with non-unique default key.
    assign tab_reference->* to <my_itab>.

    create data struc_reference  type (myt_name) .
    assign struc_reference->* to <my_struc>.

""""""""""""  code for steps 5- 8 to be added here
"""""""""""""

    catch cx_sy_create_data_error.
      write :/ 'Wrong Table Name'.
endtry.
```

5. Then, the `SELECT` statement is written in order to fetch the data. The name from the parameter is used as the table name and read into the internal table pointed by field symbol `my_itab`. The number of rows are also specified based on user input.

```
SELECT * FROM (myt_name) INTO TABLE <my_itab> UP TO rows ROWS.
```

6. The description of the created row structure (pointed by `my_struc`) of the internal table is then read using the `describe_by_data` statement. An object reference `descr` to the class `cl_abap_structdescr` is declared. Then, the static method `describe_by_data` of the `cl_abap_typedescr` class is called and returned to the `descr` variable. The operator (`?=`) is used for downcasting. (As the `cl_abap_typedescr` class is an abstract class and returns a reference to the description object `cl_abap_typedescr`).

```
DATA : descr TYPE REF TO cl_abap_structdescr.
descr ?= cl_abap_typedescr=>describe_by_data( <my_struc> ).
```

7. As each column (field) of the database table is represented as a row in the component `components` of the `descr` object, a loop is run on it. Only the number of columns entered by the user is read using the `from 1 to columns`.

8. A `positions` internal table `position` is also created that will hold the position (starting position) of each column displayed on the screen. The length of each field is used for finding the next field position. Also included is the code for printing the table column header.

```
data : begin of positions occurs 0 ,
          position type i ,
       end of positions.

data : end_position type i.
data : wa_key type line of abap_compdescr_tab

positions-position = 1 .
loop at descr->components into wa_key from 1 to columns.
  write at positions-position '|'.
  if wa_key-length lt 10.
    wa_key-length = 10.
  endif.
  write : wa_key-name.
  append positions.
  positions-position = wa_key-length + positions-position .
endloop.
end_position = positions-position + 1.
write at end_position '|'.
```

9. Then, the main part for reading the contents of the table is written. The loop is then run at the data internal table pointed to by field symbol `my_itab`. A do loop is also run for each row which used the `assign` statement for each field value. The table `positions` value is read for getting the correct position of the corresponding field column.

```
loop at <my_itab> into <my_struc>.
  new-line.
  do columns times.
    read table positions index sy-index.
    assign component sy-index of structure <my_struc>
      to <my_field>.
    if sy-subrc eq 0.
      write at positions-position '|'.
      write : <my_field> .
    else.
      exit.
    endif.
    write : at end_position '|'.
  enddo.
endloop.
new-line.
uline at 1(end_position).
```

How it works...

In the data browser program, the statements read any table name entered by the user and the number of rows and columns entered, and then display the relevant data from the table. Let us see how the program code works.

The parameters statement displays the selection screen to the user, and takes as input the table name and the table rows and columns.

Simple Data Browser

Table Name	T511
Table Rows to be Read	6
Columns to be Shown	6

The static method describe_by_data of the cl_abap_typedescr class provides the description object pertaining to the structure passed.

The widening cast method is used to store the returned object in the descr variable of cl_abap_structdescr type (as the cl_abap_typedescr class is the super class of cl_abap_structdescr and cl_abap_typedescr is an abstract class).

The descr object contains a component internal table components. A loop is then carried out on the components table in order to print the name of the table fields as columns headers. The length of the field is also taken into consideration. For example, if the table T511 is entered, the length and names of the various table fields exists in DESCR->COMPONENTS. The position table is also filled within this loop in order to store the appropriate positions of the each. This will be later used so that the correct data is printed under the corresponding column header (field name).

Table	DESCR->COMPONENTS			
Table Type	Standard Table[23x4(72)]			
Li...	LENGTH[I(4)]	DECIMALS[I(4)]	TYPE_KIND[C(1)]	NAME[C(30...
1	6	0	C	MANDT
2	4	0	C	MOLGA
3	8	0	C	LGART
4	16	0	D	ENDDA
5	16	0	D	BEGDA
6	20	0	C	ABTYZ

Finally, the main loop is run. The loop is carried out on the internal table, which contains all the rows of the database table in question. For each row of the table, the do loop is run. within the do loop, the components (fields) of the table row are processed and assigned to the field symbol <my_field>. The do loop is run the number of times equal to the number of table fields asked by the user. The value of the field is then outputted. Once all required fields have been processed, the do loop is exited. Within the do loop, the positions table filled earlier is read in order to get the correct position where a particular cell is to be positioned.

Simple Data Browser

MANDT	MOLGA	LGART	ENDDA	BEGDA	ABTYZ
800	01	/28F	12/31/9999	01/01/1901	1111111111
800	01	/2RR	12/31/9999	01/01/1901	1111111111
800	01	/453	12/31/2001	01/01/1900	111
800	01	/453	12/31/9999	01/01/2002	111
800	01	/454	12/31/2001	01/01/1900	111
800	01	/454	12/31/9999	01/01/2002	111

Total Columns Shown	6
Total Rows Shown	6

The positions table along with the uline statements lets you give the box shape to the output.

See also

► `http://help.sap.com/saphelp_nw04/helpdata/en/fc/` `eb3860358411d1829f0000e829fbfe/content.htm`

► `http://help.sap.com/saphelp_nw2004s/helpdata/en/fc/` `eb3145358411d1829f0000e829fbfe/frameset.htm`

Applying dynamic Open SQL

The Open SQL statement components may be specified statically or dynamically. This applies to database read statement SELECT, as well as data manipulation statements such as INSERT and UPDATE. The primary emphasis of this recipe will be on dynamic specifications of the various components of the SELECT statement. The previous recipe saw some usage of the dynamic SQL in the SELECT statement, where the table name, the target area internal table (pointed to by a field symbol), and the number rows to read using UP TO addition were specified dynamically. In addition to these, the GROUP BY, the ORDER BY, and WHERE conditions may be specified dynamically.

In this recipe, we will create a program that will take input from the user and create dynamic specifications for the where condition and the order by clause. (For simplicity's sake we emphasize on the dynamic where and order by clauses and keep the table name as spfli).

Getting ready

We will create a program that will contain a selection screen, which will allow you to take input from the user. We will create two blocks on the selection screen, namely Where and Order by.

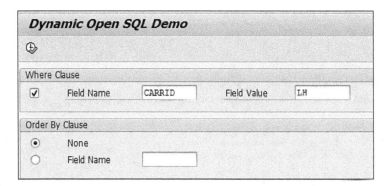

The table to be considered for this example is spfli. The **Where Clause** block has one checkbox (WHERE1) used for specifying the component of the WHERE condition. Also for the **Order By Clause**, we have two radio buttons—orderby1 and orderby2.

How to do it...

For creating a program based on dynamic SQL, follow these steps:

1. Declare two string variables `where_cond` and `order_by` for specification of the dynamic `where` condition and `order by` criteria, respectively.

```
data : order_by type string.
data : where_cond type string.
```

2. Next, the `if` statements are added for checking the options selected by the user. In this part, we will make sure that the correct criteria/condition is filled in the defined string variables.

```
if orderby2 eq 'X'.
   order_by = ordby_f.
endif.
```

3. For the ORDER BY criteria, if the user selects the first option (orderby1—no sorting), no code is added/executed. If the user has entered the sort criteria on the screen (field `ordby_f`) using the second radio button (orderby2), the entered name is assigned to the `order_by` string.

4. Similarly, for the **Where Clause** formulation, the checkbox selection is checked. If the checkbox is selected, the entered field name (`field1`) is concatenated with EQ and the value entered (`value1`).

```
if where1 eq 'X'.
   concatenate field1 'EQ value1' into where_cond
   separated by space .
endif.
```

5. Finally, the most important portion is added. The `select` statement is written using the string variables, `where_cond` and `order_by`. We make sure that `select` is not executed if `where_cond` is empty (using a `check` statement).

```
check where1 eq 'X'.
data: ex_ref type ref to cx_sy_dynamic_osql_error.
data: message_text type string.

try .
    select * from spfli into table t_spfli
      where (where_cond)
      order by (order_by).
    loop at t_spfli into wa_spfli.
      write :/  wa_spfli-carrid ,
                wa_spfli-connid,
                wa_spfli-countryfr,
                wa_spfli-cityfrom,
                wa_spfli-airpfrom,
                wa_spfli-countryto,
                wa_spfli-cityto,
                wa_spfli-airpto,
                wa_spfli-fltime.

    endloop.

  CATCH cx_sy_dynamic_osql_error into ex_ref.
    message_text = ex_ref->get_text( ).
    write: / message_text.
endtry.
```

6. The data is read and stored in the `t_spfli` internal table, and outputted to the user using the `loop` and `write` statements.

7. It is also necessary to `catch` the `cx_sy_dynamic_osql_error` exception in case the `select` statement's `where` conditions and `order by` sort criteria are incorrect. Any exception occurring is caught, and the relevant message text is written using the exception class `cx_sy_dynamic_osql_error`.

How it works...

In the dynamic Open SQL program, there is one `select` statement executed that prints and fetches the data that is to be read from the database. The program checks the input entered by the user. If the `where` condition variable is empty, the program does not display any records from the table.

Suppose the user enters values for `field1` and the `value1`.

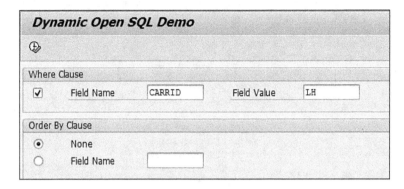

Then, after the execution of the `if` statements related to the `where` condition, the `where_cond` variable will contain the corresponding criteria to be passed to the `select` statement.

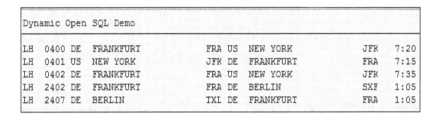

The `value1` variable is passed on to the `where` condition and the system, at runtime, evaluates their values in order to get the correct data from the database.

Similarly for the `order by` criteria, when the user specifies none as the sorting by, an empty string is passed to the `select` statement. This has no effect on the sorting, and the data is displayed as residing in the database table.

There's more...

We may use field symbols and references as shown in the previous recipe in conjunction with the code of this recipe in order to make the program work for any database table.

See also

- http://virtualforge.com/tl_files/Theme/Presentations/HITB2011.pdf
- http://help.sap.com/saphelp_nw2004s/helpdata/en/8f/35de1718944eb8a1462cf6362cc8b8/content.htm

Dynamic program generation

The ABAP language also allows the creation of ABAP programs at runtime. An `INSERT REPORT` statement may be used for creating a new program specified by the a name in the statement. Dynamic program generation should only be used when there is no alternate option.

Also, you may generate a subroutine pool using a `GENERATE` subroutine pool statement. A subroutine pool is generated, and is of a temporary nature. The subroutines in the pool may be called from within the generation program.

On the other hand, the programs created via the `INSERT REPORT` statement are permanent and overwrite any prior existing programs with the same name. Within the generation program, the new program may be called via a `SUBMIT` statement.

Getting ready

We will use the concepts of dynamic program generation in order to show how a simple requirement may be solved. We will take as input two program names. The code of the first program will be read and then any comments or unwanted blank lines will be removed and a new program will be created by the name specified on the input screen.

How to do it...

1. Two parameters, `origprog` and `newprog`, are declared for taking the input names of the existing and converted program respectively.

    ```
    parameters: origprog type sy-repid,
                newprog type sy-repid.
    ```

2. Internal tables, `itab` and `itab2`, are also declared for storing the source code of the original program and converted program respectively. These are based on `string` type. A work area of `string` type is also declared along with a temporary variable `tempwa`.

    ```
    data: itab type table of string,
          itab2 type table of string,
          wa type string,
          tempwa type string.
    ```

3. The `read report` is then used with the original program name and the internal table, `itab`. We will check the value of `sy-subrc` in order to proceed further.

```
read report origprog into itab.
check sy-subrc eq 0.
```

4. The `LOOP` statement is then added for reading `itab` into `wa`. The `APPEND` statement is used in conjunction with the `IF` and `SPLIT` statements in order to process all non-blank lines without having asterisk at the beginning. The `SPLIT` statement splits the source code line under consideration at the occurrence of a quotation mark (`"`). The work area, `wa`, contents are then appended to the internal table, `itab2`.

```
LOOP AT itab INTO wa.
  IF not wa is initial and wa(1) NE '*'.
    SPLIT wa AT '"' INTO wa tempwa.
    APPEND wa TO itab2.
  ENDIF.

ENDLOOP.
```

5. The `SELECT SINGLE` statement is then written in order to check `newprog` in `trdir` table.

```
SELECT SINGLE * FROM trdir WHERE name EQ newprog.
```

6. If the return code value is not equal to zero (0), the `insert report` statement is added and on success a message **Program Converted by Name** message is displayed. If the insert fails, a message **Program Conversion failed** message is displayed.

   If the return code value after the SELECT statement is equal to 0, the message saying that a program having the desired destination program name already exists, is displayed.

```
if sy-subrc ne 0.
  insert report newprog from itab2.
  if sy-subrc eq 0.
    write : / ' Program Converted by Name ', newprog.
  else.
    write : / ' Program Conversion failed'.
  endif.
else.
  write : /
  'Program not converted since destination program already exists'.
endif.
```

How it works...

The program statements collectively allow the conversion of a program. The new converted program is free from all types of comments and blank lines.

Let us see how the program works.

The selection screen displays two fields for taking input for **Original Program** that is to be converted and **New Program** that is to be generated.

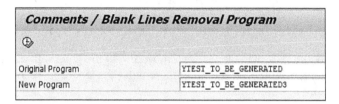

For example, we can enter the **Original Program** value as YTEST_TO_BE_GENERATED whereas the new converted program is YTEST_TO_BE_GENERATED3.

```
Report              YTEST_TO_BE_GENERATED              Active
 1    ⊟ *&-----------------------------------------------------
 2    │ *& Report   YTEST_TO_BE_GENERATED
 3    │ *&
 4    │ *&-----------------------------------------------------
 5    │ *&
 6    │ *&
 7    └ *&-----------------------------------------------------
 8
 9      REPORT  ytest_to_be_generated.
10
11
12    ⊟ *  this is a comment
13    └ * this is a omment
14
15      START-OF-SELECTION.
16
17        WRITE :/' Hello World'. ""this is comment
18
19      END-OF-SELECTION.
```

The code of the **YTEST_TO_BE_EXECUTED** program is read into the **itab** internal table using the READ REPORT statement.

Internal table	itab
13	

13	* this is a omment
14	
15	START-OF-SELECTION.
16	

The loop is then run, and any blank lines are removed. Also the lines with asterisk (*****) are removed, and anything written after the quotation mark (") is ignored. The new lines are appended to the **itab2** internal table.

Internal table	itab2
1	

1	REPORT ytest_to_be_generated.
2	START-OF-SELECTION.
3	WRITE :/' Hello World'.
4	END-OF-SELECTION.

The last step is to check the trdir table's program directory. The SELECT statement checks the table to see if a program already exists with the new program name entered by the user. If a program already exists, a message is displayed saying "Program not converted since destination program already exists". This is necessary to avoid overwriting of the existing program. If the name is unique, the INSERT REPORT statement is called and the new program is generated.

YTEST_TO_BE_GENERATED3	Active

```
report   ytest_to_be_generated.
start-of-selection.
   write :/' Hello World'.
end-of-selection.
```

There's more...

While using the `insert` statement, the `CX_SY_WRITE_SRC_LINE_TOO_LONG` exception may occur if the program line to be inserted is too long. We may catch the exception using the `try` and `catch` statements as shown in the following screenshot:

```
try .
    select single * from trdir where name eq newprog.

    if sy-subrc ne 0.
      insert report newprog from itab2.
      if sy-subrc eq 0.
    else.
      write : /
      'Program not converted since destination program already exists'.
    endif.


  catch CX_SY_WRITE_SRC_LINE_TOO_LONG.
    write / 'Error: Program line too long'.
endtry.
```

See also

- ▶ http://help.sap.com/abapdocu_731/en/abendynamic_prog_technique_guidl.htm

- ▶ http://help.sap.com/abapdocu_70/en/ABAPSYNTAX-CHECK_FOR_ITAB.htm

- ▶ ABAP Keyword Documentation available at http://help.sap.com/abapdocu_702/en/abenabap.htm

- ▶ SAP Advanced ABAP Course BC402

- ▶ Determining the Attributes of Data Objects available at http://help.sap.com/saphelp_470/helpdata/en/fc/eb3145358411d1829f0000e829fbfe/content.htm

3

ALV Tricks

In this chapter, we will see recipes related to the ABAP List Viewer (ALV). Also, we will look at ways of:

- ▶ Setting ALV columns as key columns and making zero amount appear as blank
- ▶ Removing columns from display and layout
- ▶ Enable Adding Layout toolbar buttons
- ▶ Adding Hotspot to columns
- ▶ Adding your own buttons to ALV toolbar
- ▶ Adding checkboxes to columns

Introduction

This chapter explores recipes related to the ALV displays. We will start with a simple requirement with basic ALV displays. We will then enhance the basic ALV program by hiding few columns from display as well as from the initial layout. We will then see a recipe showing how to save user-specific layouts. Adding buttons to standard ALV toolbars will be shown, along with checkboxes and hotspots displayed within ALV columns.

For this chapter, I assume that the reader has basic knowledge of the ABAP objects, the ALV object model, and is familiar with basic ALV creation using `CL_SALV_TABLE`. Also, the reader should have knowledge of creating and changing of GUI status, and should have knowledge of `Ranges` and `Select-Options`.

For the sake of this chapter, we will make a simple example that will display data into an ALV format. This will be used in all the recipes mentioned in this chapter.

```
TYPES : BEGIN OF TY_PA0008,
          PERNR TYPE PERSNO,
          SUBTY TYPE SUBTY,
          BEGDA TYPE BEGDA,
          ENDDA TYPE ENDDA,
          AEDTM TYPE AEDAT,
          UNAME TYPE AENAM,
          BET01 TYPE PAD_AMT7S,
          WAERS TYPE WAERS,
        END OF TY_PA0008.
DATA    WA_PA0008 TYPE  TY_PA0008.
DATA    IT_PA0008 TYPE STANDARD TABLE OF TY_PA0008.
DATA    MYALV TYPE REF TO CL_SALV_TABLE.
DATA    MYFUNCTIONS TYPE REF TO CL_SALV_FUNCTIONS_LIST.
DATA    MYCOLUMNS TYPE REF TO CL_SALV_COLUMNS_TABLE.
START-OF-SELECTION.
  SELECT * FROM PA0008 INTO CORRESPONDING FIELDS
              OF TABLE IT_PA0008 UP TO 15 ROWS.
  TRY.
      CALL METHOD CL_SALV_TABLE=>FACTORY
        IMPORTING
          R_SALV_TABLE = MYALV
        CHANGING
          T_TABLE      = IT_PA0008.
    CATCH CX_SALV_MSG.
  ENDTRY.
  MYCOLUMNS = MYALV->GET_COLUMNS( ).
  MYCOLUMNS->SET_OPTIMIZE( ).
  MYFUNCTIONS = MYALV->GET_FUNCTIONS( ).
  MYFUNCTIONS->SET_ALL( ).
  CALL METHOD MYALV->DISPLAY.
```

In this example, we declared a data structure type containing simple important fields of table PA0008. We then declared an internal table and a work area based on this type.

We selected 15 rows from the table PA0008 and stored them in the internal table.

The factory method is then called of the class CL_SALV_TABLE for instantiating the ALV object. The GET_COLUMNS method is called in order to get the columns object of the ALV. The SET_OPTIMIZE method of the columns object is used to optimize the column width.

Likewise, the GET_FUNCTIONS method provides access to the ALV's functions' objects. We then set all the functions using SET_ALL method. Finally, ALV is displayed using the DISPLAY method.

Simple ALV Example

PersNo.	SType	Start Date	End Date	Changed on	Changed by	Amount	Currency
2	0	09/12/2011	10/11/2011	09/12/2011	STUDENT001	0.00	EUR
2	0	10/12/2011	12/31/2011	10/12/2011	STUDENT003	1,500.00	EUR
2	0	01/01/2012	12/31/9999	10/14/2011	STUDENT003	1,000.00	EUR
29	0	09/13/2011	12/31/9999	09/13/2011	STUDENT001	0.00	EUR
35	0	09/16/2011	12/31/9999	09/16/2011	STUDENT003	15,000.00	EUR
55	0	01/04/2011	12/31/9999	10/17/2011	STUDENT001	50,000.00	EUR
56	0	01/04/2011	12/31/9999	10/17/2011	STUDENT001	800.00	EUR
57	0	01/05/2011	12/31/9999	10/17/2011	STUDENT001	25.00	EUR
62	0	01/01/2012	12/31/9999	11/11/2011	STUDENT001	0.00	EUR
67	0	11/29/2011	12/31/9999	11/29/2011	STUDENT060	0.00	EUR
68	0	12/01/2011	12/31/9999	12/01/2011	STUDENT060	2,500.00	EUR
69	0	01/01/2003	12/31/9999	09/17/2003	HOLDERM	0.00	GBP
70	0	01/01/2003	12/31/9999	09/17/2003	HOLDERM	0.00	GBP
71	0	01/01/2003	12/31/9999	09/30/2003	HOLDERM	0.00	GBP
72	0	01/01/2003	12/31/9999	09/30/2003	HOLDERM	0.00	GBP

Note that until this point, the ALV toolbar does not have a layout save button. No fields are defined as keys (no blue colour). The **Amount** column displays **0.00** and not blank in case the value is initial. No hotspots or checkboxes are enabled in the columns. In the next set of recipes, we will see systematically how each of these options may be added.

See also

> ► `http://wiki.sdn.sap.com/wiki/display/ABAP/ALV+Grid+Report+-+wit`
> `h+Object+Oriented+SALV+Classes`

Setting ALV columns as key columns and making zero amount appear as blank

This recipe is comprised of two subrecipes:

We will see how the personnel number (PERNR) column may be set as key with blue colour. In addition, how a particular column **Amount**, where a zero amount is shown as **0.00**, may be made to appear blank.

How to do it...

For making the above adjustments, proceed as follows:

1. Declare a column variable with reference to the class `cl_salv_column_table`.

2. Next, use the `get_column` method of the `mycolumns` object pointing to the columns of the ALV in order to get the reference to the column PERNR. We will then use the `set_key` method to set the PERNR column as the key column.

3. Similarly, the `get_column` method is called for the **Amount** column BET01. The `set_zero` method is called to convert the zeros to blanks while outputting the BET01 column. It is necessary that the value space (' ') is passed to the `set_zero` method.

```
   data : mycolumn type ref to cl_salv_column_table.
try.
  mycolumn ?= mycolumns->get_column( 'PERNR' ) .
  mycolumn->set_key( ) .

  mycolumn ?= mycolumns->get_column( 'BET01' ) .
  mycolumn->set_zero( ' ' ) .

  catch CX_SALV_NOT_FOUND.

endtry.
```

4. The code fragment was added before the ALV display method but after the assignment to `mycolumns` statement followed by the `factory` method `call`.

How it works...

We already had the reference to the entire set of ALV columns within the variable `mycolumns`. For each of the two columns, PERNR and BET01, the single column object reference was required. This was done through usage of the `get_column` method. Methods `set_key` and `set_zero` were then called and appropriate values passed for parameters (if necessary) for setting the key column and removal of zeros respectively.

Any exception raised due to wrong name supplied to the `get_column` method is caught using the TRY .. ENDTRY and CATCH statements. The exception that was addressed was CX_SALV_NOT_FOUND. We can add a suitable MESSAGE statement after the `catch` statement to output a message in case an error arises, which is not been shown in the previous screenshot:

PersNo.	SType	Start Date	End Date	Changed on	Changed by	Amount
2	0	09/12/2011	10/11/2011	09/12/2011	STUDENT001	
2	0	10/12/2011	12/31/2011	10/12/2011	STUDENT003	1,500.00
2	0	01/01/2012	12/31/9999	10/14/2011	STUDENT003	1,000.00
29	0	09/13/2011	12/31/9999	09/13/2011	STUDENT001	
35	0	09/16/2011	12/31/9999	09/16/2011	STUDENT003	15,000.00
55	0	01/04/2011	12/31/9999	10/17/2011	STUDENT001	50,000.00
56	0	01/04/2011	12/31/9999	10/17/2011	STUDENT001	800.00
57	0	01/05/2011	12/31/9999	10/17/2011	STUDENT001	25.00
62	0	01/01/2012	12/31/9999	11/11/2011	STUDENT001	
67	0	11/29/2011	12/31/9999	11/29/2011	STUDENT060	
68	0	12/01/2011	12/31/9999	12/01/2011	STUDENT060	2,500.00
69	0	01/01/2003	12/31/9999	09/17/2003	HOLDERM	
70	0	01/01/2003	12/31/9999	09/17/2003	HOLDERM	
71	0	01/01/2003	12/31/9999	09/30/2003	HOLDERM	
72	0	01/01/2003	12/31/9999	09/30/2003	HOLDERM	

Note the change in the **PersNo.** and the **Amount** column.

See also

▸ http://scn.sap.com/thread/752043

Removing columns from display and layout

By default, all columns that are defined in the internal table IT_PA0008 are displayed in the ALV output. This recipe will now show how we will remove columns from ALV output.

There are two ways of doing this. We can remove columns from the initial layout. In this case, we can still bring them back to display by choosing the **Change Layout** option. On the other hand, you may remove columns totally, so that they are not even available in the layout.

In this recipe, we will see how the **SUBTYPE** (SUBTY) column is made invisible, and the **Changed on** (AEDTM) column to be removed from initial output but still available in the layout.

How to do it...

For making the SUBTY and AEDTM columns disappear, follow these steps:

1. We will use the same mycolumn variable used earlier referring to the class CL_SALV_COLUMN_TABLE. For each column, we will use the get_column method to get a reference to the respective column.

2. For the SUBTY column, we will use the set_technical method for removing it from the display (and also from the layout).

3. For the AEDTM column, we will use the set_visible method of the class CL_SALV_COLUMN_TABLE. We will pass the value FALSE to the method.

```
mycolumn ?=  mycolumns->get_column( 'SUBTY' ) .
mycolumn->set_technical( 'X' ) .

mycolumn ?=  mycolumns->get_column( 'AEDTM' ) .
mycolumn->set_visible( IF_SALV_C_BOOL_SAP=>FALSE ) .
```

How it works...

The set_technical method is used for making the column as technical. This means that the column is set as a technical column and not displayed in the output, and is not available for display through the **Change layout** options.

On the other hand, we have made the AEDTM column (**Changed On**) invisible from the initial display using the set_visible method of the CL_SALV_COLUMN_TABLE class.

Both the columns are not displayed in the new output.

PersNo.	Start Date	End Date	Changed by	Amount	Currency
2	09/12/2011	10/11/2011	STUDENT001		EUR
2	10/12/2011	12/31/2011	STUDENT003	1,500.00	EUR
2	01/01/2012	12/31/9999	STUDENT003	1,000.00	EUR
29	09/13/2011	12/31/9999	STUDENT001		EUR
35	09/16/2011	12/31/9999	STUDENT003	15,000.00	EUR
55	01/04/2011	12/31/9999	STUDENT001	50,000.00	EUR
56	01/04/2011	12/31/9999	STUDENT001	800.00	EUR
57	01/05/2011	12/31/9999	STUDENT001	25.00	EUR
62	01/01/2012	12/31/9999	STUDENT001		EUR

When the user selects **Change Layout**, only the **Changed on** column is available for inclusion in the output. The SUBTY column is totally unavailable for display.

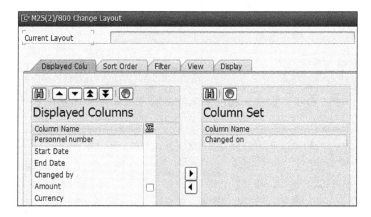

Enable Adding Layout toolbar buttons

Up to this point, the output of the ALV does not allow the user to save changes made to layout. In this recipe, we will add coding that will allow saving user-specific layouts, load layouts, as well as specify a default layout.

How to do it...

For enabling layout saving, follow these steps:

1. We declare two variables and also, an object reference to the class `cl_salv_layout`. In addition, a key is defined based on the type `salv_s_layout_key`.

2. The `get_layout` method is then used to get the layout object for the ALV.

3. The `set_key` method is called for the layout object `mylayout`. The `mykey` structure having the report name `sy-repid` is passed to this method.

4. Next, the `set_save_restriction` method is called. It is passed the static attribute `RESTRICT_USER_DEPENDANT` of the interface `if_salv_c_layout`.

5. Finally, the `set_default` layout method is called with the value `'X'`, as shown in the next screenshot.

```
data mylayout type ref to cl_salv_layout.
data mykey type salv_s_layout_key.

mylayout = myalv->get_layout( ).
mykey-report = sy-repid.
mylayout->set_key( mykey ).
mylayout->set_save_restriction( if_salv_c_layout=>RESTRICT_USER_DEPENDANT ).
mylayout->set_default( 'X' ) .
```

6. The code is added before the `ALV` display method call shown in the first screenshot of this chapter.

How it works...

In this recipe, we declared a layout variable based on the `cl_salv_layout` class. An essential step is to set the key of the layout object and passing the name of the program. This is done using the `set_key` method.

Next, for enabling the **Save layout** button, the `set_save_restriction` method is used. Based on the value passed on to the method, the system determines whether the user is allowed to save layout as user-specific, user-unspecific, or without any restrictions. Three possible constant values may be passed.

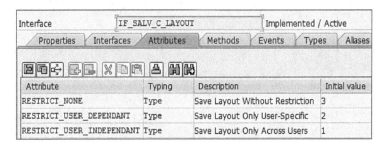

Since our requirement was to enable user to store layout as **User-Specific**, we used `RESTRICT_USER_DEPENDANT` constant attribute of the interface `if_salv_c_layout`.

Finally, we wanted the **Default** setting checkbox to be enabled so that the user may save a particular layout as his or her default. For this reason, the `set_default` method was called with the value `'X'`.

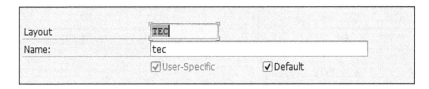

The next time the user executes the report, his or her default layout is loaded and data displayed in that layout format.

See also

- http://www.sapgeek.net/2011/10/sap-abap-select-layout-of-alv-through-selection-screen/
- http://forums.sdn.sap.com/thread.jspa?threadID=1001363

Adding Hotspot to columns

It may also be required to display hotspots (similar to hyperlinks) for an entire column in the ALV display. Clicking a particular hotspot cell will take the user to another detail screen. In this recipe, we will add hotspot functionality to the `PERNR` column.

How to do it...

We will see how a particular column may be made to appear as a hotspot. We will also add the necessary code that is needed to carry out the steps needed for the hotspot selection. Proceed as follows:

1. We get access to the PERNR column and call the set_cell_type method for it. Then, we pass the hotspot static constant attribute of the if_salv_c_cell_type interface to it.

```
mycolumn ?=  mycolumns->get_column( 'PERNR' ) .
mycolumn->set_cell_type( if_salv_c_cell_type=>hotspot ) .
```

2. Next, we define the class myhotspot. Within the class definition, we create a static public method on_click_hotspot that will be called when a hotspot cell is clicked. This imports the row and column pertaining to the selection.

```
class myhotspot definition.
  public section.
    class-methods on_click_hotspot FOR EVENT link_click
      OF cl_salv_events_table IMPORTING row column .

endclass.
```

3. Within the implementation of this class, we read the row from the table IT_PA0008 that the user has selected. The necessary details are read from table PA0008 using a SELECT statement. The function module HR_INFOTYPE_OPERATION is then called in order to display the details of the employee Infotype 0008 record in display mode of transaction PA20.

```
class myhotspot implementation.
  method on_click_hotspot.
    clear wa_pa0008.
    read table it_pa0008 index row into wa_pa0008.

    data : p0008 type p0008.
    select single * from pa0008 into corresponding fields of p0008
                             where pernr eq wa_pa0008-pernr
                             and begda eq wa_pa0008-begda
                             and endda eq wa_pa0008-endda.

    CALL FUNCTION 'HR_INFOTYPE_OPERATION'
      EXPORTING
        INFTY         = '0008'
        NUMBER        = p0008-pernr
        VALIDITYEND   = p0008-endda
        VALIDITYBEGIN = p0008-begda
        RECORD        = P0008
        OPERATION     = 'DIS'
        DIALOG MODE   = '2'
      EXCEPTIONS
        OTHERS        = 0.

  endmethod.

endclass.
```

4. Finally, the SET HANDLER statement is called in order to link the static method on_click_hotspot of the class myhotspot to the ALV. Before that, we get the handle to the events object of the ALV using the get_event method.

```
DATA: myevents TYPE REF TO cl_salv_events_table.
myevents = myalv->get_event( ).
SET HANDLER myhotspot=>on_click_hotspot FOR myevents.
```

The previous code will make sure that the on_click_hotspot method is called when the user clicks a particular cell of PERNR.

How it works...

The **Pers.No** column is displayed as underlined and selectable through a hotspot, as shown in the following screenshot:

PersNo.	Start Date	End Date	Changed by
2	09/12/2011	10/11/2011	STUDENT001
2	10/12/2011	12/31/2011	STUDENT003
2	01/01/2012	12/31/9999	STUDENT003
29	09/13/2011	12/31/9999	STUDENT001
35	09/16/2011	12/31/9999	STUDENT003

When the user clicks a particular row displayed as a hotspot within the PERNR column, the method on_click_hotspot is triggered. Within the method, the importing parameters row and column contain the number of the selected row and the column name (PERNR) respectively.

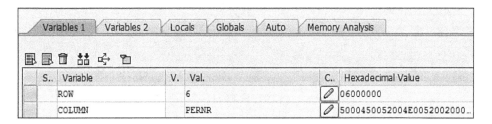

The code written within the on_click_hotspot method is then executed. The corresponding record is read from the table IT_PA0008 using the READ statement. The SELECT statement is used for reading additional information related to the employee selected. This information is then passed on to the function module HR_INFOTYPE_OPERATION with other Displays parameters in order to display the record in transaction PA20 (Display Master Data) transaction.

See also

- ▸ http://help-abap.zevolving.com/2008/09/salv-table-8-add-handle-hotspot/

- ▸ http://www.sapfans.com/forums/viewtopic.php?f=13&t=158570

- ▸ Standard SAP demo programs SALV_DEMO_TABLE_EVENTS and SALV_DEMO_TABLE_SIMPLE

Adding your own buttons to ALV toolbar

The standard ALV toolbar provides a number of useful functions. However, depending on the requirement, you may be asked to add new buttons to the ALV toolbar. This recipe will show how to add your own buttons to the ALV toolbar and then writing appropriate coding to be executed when the user presses the button.

We will add a new button saying **View Summary** to the toolbar. Upon clicking, the total number of displayed records will be shown (for purpose of illustration).

Getting ready

For creating your own toolbar buttons, we need to make a copy of the GUI status displayed in the original ALV program. We will then make changes to the copied status. Proceed as follows:

1. For finding out the program whose GUI status is currently being called, generate the output of the ALV program and then select the menu option **System | Status..**. On the dialog that appears, we will use the values shown in the **Program (GUI)** and **GUI status** fields. The GUI status being used is ALV_TABLE_STANDARD residing in the program having name SAPLSALV_METADATA_STATUS.

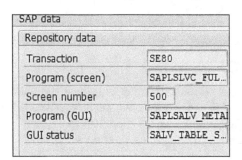

SAP data	
Repository data	
Transaction	SE80
Program (screen)	SAPLSLVC_FUL...
Screen number	500
Program (GUI)	SAPLSALV_METAI
GUI status	SALV_TABLE_S...

2. We will copy this GUI status from the respective standard SAP program into our program. This may be done by using transaction SE80.

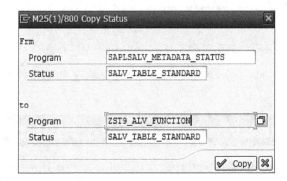

In the next section, we will see how new buttons are added.

How to do it...

We will see how to add new buttons and adding appropriate coding. Proceed as follows.

1. Use transaction SE80 to see the various components of your program. The newly copied status **SALV_TABLE_STANDARD** is shown under the **GUI Status** node.

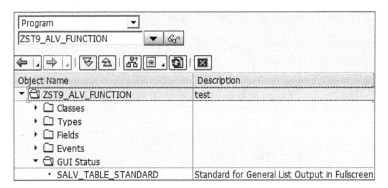

2. Double-click the GUI status name to display its contents in the right-hand pane. From the section of toolbar buttons, we will remove the **INFO** button item, as it is not needed, and add our own function **SUMM** having the display text **View Summary**, as shown in the following screenshot:

Items 1 - 7	&ETA	&EB9	&REFRESH	
Items 8 - 14	&OUP	&ODN	&ILT	&ILD
Items 15 - 21	&RNT_PREV		&VGRID	&VEXCEL
Items 22 - 28	%PC	%SL	&GRAPH	
Items 29 - 35		SUMM View Su...		&CRB

3. Next, we will call the method `set_screen_status` of the class `cl_salv_table` and pass it the name of our program `SY-REPID` and the newly created status `SALV_TABLE_STANDARD`.

```
call method myalv->set_screen_status
    exporting
        pfstatus = 'SALV_TABLE_STANDARD'
        report   = sy-repid.
```

4. We will then create a class by the name `summbutton` (we can also use the existing class for hotspot created in a previous _Adding hotspots to columns_ recipe). In the definition, a static method `on_button_press` is defined that responds to the triggering of the ALV event `added_function`. The method has an importing parameter `e_salv_function` that provides the function code of the selected customer function.

```
class summbutton definition.
  public section.
    class-methods on_button_press FOR EVENT added_function
      OF cl_salv_events_table IMPORTING e_salv_function .
endclass.
```

5. Next, the implementation of the method is created. Within the `on_button_press` method, we check to see if the `SUMM` function button has been pressed. If found true, we then calculate the number of lines in the table `IT_PA0008`, then concatenate the line numbers with appropriate text and display in an information message.

```
class summbutton implementation.
  method on_button_press.
    data   lines type i.
    data   text type string.
    if e_salv_function eq 'SUMM'.
      describe table it_pa0008 lines lines.
      text = lines.
      concatenate text 'records are displayed' into text
        separated by space.
      message i208(00) with text.
    endif.
  endmethod.
endclass.
```

6. Finally we use the `SET HANDLER` statement to link the static method `on_button_press` of the class `newbutton` with the events object `myevents`. This will make sure the clicking on the **New** button triggers the execution of the `on_button_press` method.

```
SET HANDLER summbutton=>on_button_press FOR myevents.
```

How it works...

Calling the `set_screen_status` method results in the display of our newly created GUI status having the button **View Summary**. The method is called in order to make sure that instead of the standard GUI status, our newly created GUI Status is shown.

PersNo.	Start Date	End Date	Changed by	Amount	Currency
2	09/12/2011	10/11/2011	STUDENT001		EUR
2	10/12/2011	12/31/2011	STUDENT003	1,500.00	EUR
2	01/01/2012	12/31/9999	STUDENT003	1,000.00	EUR

The **CL_SALV_EVENTS_TABLE** class contains an **ADDED_FUNCTION** event that is raised when our added button is pressed.

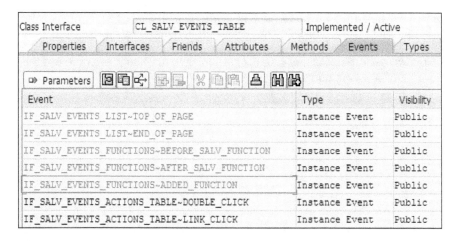

We registered this event with the static method `on_button_press` of our class `newbutton` using `SET HANDLER` statement.

Upon clicking the **View Summary** button, the code of the `on_button_press` method is called. We make sure in the method that the code is run only when the function code supplied by importing variable `e_salv_function` contains `SUMM`. If that is the case, the number of lines determined in the internal table are displayed using a `MESSAGE` statement.

For adding icons in the toolbar button, refer to the SAP documentation at `http://help.sap.com/saphelp_nw04/helpdata/en/d1/801d43454211d189710000e8322d00/frameset.htm`.

There's more...

The work so far done looks fine, but has a small problem. Clicking on the **View Summary** button will give the entire set of rows in the internal table `IT_PA0008`, irrespective of taking into account any filter applied.

We will now refine the recipe in order to read the filters, the column names included on which the filters have been applied, and the selection options specifying the filter values. At the end, we will delete the rows from `IT_PA0008` that do not adhere to the filter criteria (so that the row count is correct). The example may then be refined later for deletion of filters, and so on.

The code that will be added will be within the IF statement (checking the function code) just before the DESCRIBE statement. The code is divided into three parts:

1. First, we declare necessary variable pertaining to ALV filters. We then use the get_filters method in order to read the filter objects.

```
""""" step  1
DATA: myfilters_obj TYPE REF TO cl_salv_filters,
      myfilter_obj  TYPE REF TO cl_salv_filter.
data : myfilters_tab TYPE salv_t_filter_ref.
data : myfilters_struc  type salv_s_filter_ref.

myfilters_obj = myalv->get_filters( ).
myfilters_tab = myfilters_obj->get( ).
```

2. The get method of the cl_salv_filters class is then called in order to fetch the internal table myfilters_tab specifying the column names on which filter has been specified. The **R_FILTER** component of this table row is a reference to the class CL_SALV_FILTER, which contains the values, entered at the filter screen.

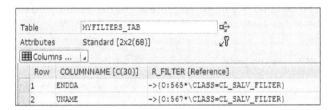

Table	MYFILTERS_TAB	
Attributes	Standard [2x2(68)]	
Columns ...		
Row	COLUMNNAME [C(30)]	R_FILTER [Reference]
1	ENDDA	->{O:565*\CLASS=CL_SALV_FILTER}
2	UNAME	->{O:567*\CLASS=CL_SALV_FILTER}

3. Next, a loop is run at this internal table and the details of the r_filter object are fetched.

```
""""" step 2
TYPES: BEGIN OF ty_range,
         column TYPE string,
         range TYPE RANGE OF string,
       END OF ty_range.
data : filter_conditions_table  TYPE salv_t_selopt_ref,
       filter_conditions   TYPE REF TO cl_salv_selopt,
       final_range_table TYPE STANDARD TABLE OF ty_range,
       final_range_struc  TYPE ty_range,
       ws_temp LIKE LINE OF final_range_struc-range.

loop at myfilters_tab into  myfilters_struc.
  final_range_struc-column = myfilters_struc-columnname.
  CLEAR final_range_struc-range.
  filter_conditions_table = myfilters_struc-r_filter->get( ).

  LOOP AT filter_conditions_table INTO filter_conditions.
    ws_temp-sign   = filter_conditions->get_sign( ).
    ws_temp-option = filter_conditions->get_option( ).
    ws_temp-low    = filter_conditions->get_low( ).
    ws_temp-high   = filter_conditions->get_high( ).
    INSERT ws_temp INTO TABLE final_range_struc-range.
  ENDLOOP.
  INSERT final_range_struc INTO TABLE final_range_table.
endloop.
```

4. We run a loop at the `myfilters_tab` method and get the filter conditions object for each column. The `get_sign`, `get_option`, `get_low`, and `get_high` methods of the class `cl_SALV_SELOPT` is used for getting the sign, option, low, and high values of the filter condition respectively. These are added to the `range` table of the `final_range_struc`. Finally, the `final_range_struc` contents are inserted into the internal table `final_range_table`. The purpose of this step is to form a final range table named `final_range_table`, which will provide us with the name of each column specified in the filter definition, along with the filter values in the form of `range` table.

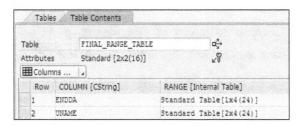

5. As you can see the user had specified two fields **ENDDA** and **UNAME** in the filter criteria. For the **UNAME** field, two filter values are specified, that is, **UNAME = HOLDERM** and **UNAME = STUDENT060**.

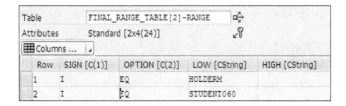

6. We will keep the third step simple, and will run a loop at the final range table which will delete from the main `IT_PA0008` internal table those records that violate any of the filter criteria.

```
loop at final_range_table into final_range_struc.
  case final_range_struc-column.
    when 'PERNR'.
      delete it_pa0008 where not pernr in final_range_struc-range.
    when 'SUBTY'.
      delete it_pa0008 where not subty in final_range_struc-range.
    when 'BEGDA'.
      delete it_pa0008 where not begda in final_range_struc-range.
    when 'ENDDA'.
      delete it_pa0008 where not endda in final_range_struc-range.
    when 'AEDTM'.
      delete it_pa0008 where not aedtm in final_range_struc-range.
    when 'UNAME'.
      delete it_pa0008 where not uname in final_range_struc-range.
  endcase.
endloop.
```

Once this additional code is added, the internal table `IT_PA0008` will take into account any applied filter. Thus, the correct values will be shown by the **View Summary** button.

The code shown may be written more efficiently and elegantly using field symbols. Since the table contains fewer entries and for the sake of simplicity, field symbols were not used.

See also

▶ `http://wiki.sdn.sap.com/wiki/display/Snippets/Get+set+of+filter ed+values+from+CL_SALV_TABLE`

Adding checkboxes to columns

In this recipe, we will see how we can display checkboxes in a column in the ALV output. The user may select a checkbox and switch it on or off. Then, based on his or her selection, a button may be pressed and function executed. The primary emphasis of this recipe will be the display of checkboxes within a column and the coding to set it as on or off.

Getting ready

For this recipe, we will make a copy of the simple ALV program that was created in the beginning of the chapter. We will then add the checkbox-related coding to this copy.

How to do it...

For adding a checkbox column to your ALV program, follow these steps:

1. Add a new field `CHECKBOX` to the type `TY_PA0008` defined in your program. The position of the field will determine the position of this column in the ALV display. We will place it at the end.

```
types : begin of ty_pa0008,
          pernr type PERSNO,
          subty type subty,
          begda type begda,
          endda type endda,
          aedtm type AEDAT,
          uname type AENAM,
          bet01 type PAD_AMT7S,
          waers type waers,
          checkbox type c,
        end of ty_pa0008.
```

2. Then, use the `get_column` method to get access to the CHECKBOX column. We will set the long , medium, and short texts of this column as `Checkbox`. The most important step is to set the cell type of this column to a checkbox using the method `set_cell_type`. The constant static attribute `checkbox_hotspot` of the interface `if_salv_c_cell_type` is passed.

```
data : mycolumn type ref to cl_salv_column_table.
try.
    mycolumn ?= mycolumns->get_column( 'CHECKBOX' ) .
    mycolumn->set_medium_text( 'Checkbox').
    mycolumn->set_long_text( 'Checkbox').
    mycolumn->set_short_text( 'Checkbox').
    mycolumn->set_cell_type( if_salv_c_cell_type=>checkbox_hotspot ) .
  catch CX_SALV_NOT_FOUND.
endtry.
```

3. A new class `mycheckbox` is defined, the definition of which contains a static method `on_click_checkbox` defined for the `link_click` event for the ALV events. This method imports the row and column of the user selection.

```
class mycheckbox definition.
  public section.
    class-methods on_click_checkbox FOR EVENT link_click
      OF cl_salv_events_table
      IMPORTING row column.
endclass.
```

4. Next, the implementation of the `mycheckbox` method is created. As already mentioned, this method is triggered when the user clicks on a particular checkbox for any row of the displayed ALV table. The `read` statement is used to determine which particular row's checkbox has been clicked. The `IF` statement checks whether the checkbox field of the row in consideration is already on or off (meaning equal to `'X'` or space). Depending on the current value, the value of the checkbox field is changed. A `MODIFY` statement is used to change the internal table `IT_PA0008`. Finally, the `refresh` method of the ALV object is called.

```
class mycheckbox implementation.
  method on_click_checkbox.
    clear wa_pa0008.
    read table it_pa0008 index row into wa_pa0008.
    if wa_pa0008-checkbox is initial.
      wa_pa0008-checkbox =  'X'.
    else.
      clear wa_pa0008-checkbox.
    endif.
    modify it_pa0008 from wa_pa0008 index sy-tabix.
    myalv->refresh( ).
  endmethod.
endclass.
```

5. The SET HANDLER statement is used to register the static method on_click_checkbox method of the mycheckbox class for the ALV events.

```
DATA: myevents TYPE REF TO cl_salv_events_table.
myevents = myalv->get_event( ).
SET HANDLER mycheckbox=>on_click_checkbox FOR myevents.
```

How it works...

When the program is run, the set_cell_type method results in the CHECKBOX column to be displayed with editable checkboxes. The set_short_text, set_medium_text, and set_long_text methods display the heading of this column as **Checkbox**.

PersN...	SType	Start Date	End Date	Changed on	Changed by	Amount	Currency	Checkbox
2	0	09/12/2011	10/11/2011	09/12/2011	STUDENT001	0.00	EUR	☐
2	0	10/12/2011	12/31/2011	10/12/2011	STUDENT003	1,500.00	EUR	☑
2	0	01/01/2012	12/31/9999	10/14/2011	STUDENT003	1,000.00	EUR	☐
29	0	09/13/2011	12/31/9999	09/13/2011	STUDENT001	0.00	EUR	☐

When the user clicks a particular checkbox, the on_click_checkbox method is executed. The READ statement gets the selected row using the parameter row. If the value of the CHECKBOX field of the selected row is found to be initial (meaning, checkbox off), it is assigned 'X' (that is, switched on). Otherwise, if it is already on, the CHECKBOX field is cleared (that is, switched off).

The table IT_PA0008 that is linked to ALV display is modified in order to reflect the user's selection. Finally, the refresh method is called to display the new state of the checkboxes on the user screen.

There's more...

Apart from the CHECKBOX display, there are other possibilities of a particular column. For the set_cell_type method, the various possible values supplied for the value parameter and the relevant output is shown as follows:

Value Paramter of set_cell_type	Output
0	TEXT
1	CHECKBOX
2	Button
3	DROPDOWN
4	Link
5	Hotspot

See also

- ▸ http://sites.google.com/site/ruslimchang/handle-checkbox-in-alv-object-model

4
Regular Expressions

In this chapter, we will see recipes related to regular expressions as used in ABAP. We will look at:

- ▶ Using regex as an IF statement
- ▶ Removal of characters from a string
- ▶ Converting date into internal date type
- ▶ Validation of format (telephone number)
- ▶ Removing repeated words from text string
- ▶ Inserting commas in an amount string
- ▶ Removing comments from program code
- ▶ Interpreting HTML stream

Introduction

As of release 7.0, ABAP supports regular expressions based on POSIX standard 1003.2. Regular expressions may be specified after the addition REGEX within the FIND and REPLACE statements.

An entire description of the topic constitutes a book by itself. However, the most important and commonly used regular expressions requirements will be discussed.

In the introduction, we will cover important operators used in regular expression processing within ABAP. These will be used in the various recipes mentioned in this chapter. We will then see recipes for writing programs that uses regular expressions for pattern matching, validation as well as conversion and extraction of data from a given text stream. Throughout the chapter, the terms "Regular Expression" and "Regex" will be used interchangeably.

In addition to `FIND` and `REPLACE` statements, SAP provides classes `CL_ABAP_REGEX` and `CL_ABAP_MATCHER` for regex processing. However, the coding in the recipes will comprise regular expressions used within `FIND` and `REPLACE` statements.

For this chapter, I assume that the reader has basic knowledge of the regular expressions, and is familiar with basic `FIND` and `REPLACE` statements. We will use the `DEMO_REGEX` standard program screenshots for illustration, where required.

For more information on regex, see the following link:

`http://help.sap.com/abapdocu_70/en/ABENREGULAR_EXPRESSIONS.htm`

Regular expressions

A regular expression comprises literals and operators. The operators are special characters used for a particular purpose and have special meanings when we need to search for any pattern within a text stream. Before the recipes, we will have a look at some useful operators available in ABAP for regular expressions.

Operator	Purpose
.	Dot matches a single character.
?	Denotes either no or a single occurrence of a character or set of characters.
*	Denotes any number of occurrences (0, 1, or more) of a character or a set of characters.
+	Matches one or more occurrence of a character or set of characters.
\<	Matches start of a word.
\>	Matches end of a word.
^	Used for denoting negation when used with box brackets, as well as the start of line marker.
?=	Used as a preview condition.
?!	Used as a negated preview condition.
\1, \2	Used for placeholders for subgroup registers (also called the back-referencing operator). For replacement, $1 and $2 represent the subgroup registers in the replacement string (this will be discussed in a recipe ahead).
$	Denotes end of a line.
\d	Denotes a digit (0-9).
\w	Denotes an alphanumeric character.
\u	Matches a single alphabet.

All the three operators (`*`, `+`, and `?`) must be used after a character or a character sequence specification. The box brackets denote the possible characters that may occur in a string. On the other hand, the round brackets denote a specific set of characters in a given sequence to be matched. For example, the `regex [01]?` will match 0 or 1. The expression `[01]*` will match 01, 11 0101, and so on. On the other hand, `(01)*` will match 01, 0101, or blank. (Also, `\w+` denotes one or more alphanumeric characters.)

The special characters that are used in regex may also need to be searched in a given text. For searching them, we must precede them with a backslash (Escape Character for special characters). Some of the examples are shown in the following table:

Searching for special characters
\.
\+
\"
\?
\$
\^
\(
\)
\[
\]

These are then treated as literals rather than operators.

The `?=` is a preview condition. For example, if we write regex in the form `a(?=s)`, the expression behaves like an IF statement condition. The pattern *a* will be matched only if the following substring matches the condition specified by *s*.

There is a difference between `^` when used within box brackets `[]` and round brackets `()`. When the `^` operator is used in box brackets, it represents the characters not included in the text to be matched. For example, `[^ab]` will match all strings that do not include a and b, such as cd, ch, hh, and so on. Whereas, `^` when used with round brackets (or without it) specifies the beginning of a string. For example, `^(ab)` or `^ab` will match all strings starting with ab, such as abc, abd, abbbbb, and so on.

For simplicity's sake, our examples will contain the regex specified within the `FIND` or `REPLACE` statements. In this case, any error in the regex is identified by the syntax checker, as shown in the following screenshot along with the exact position on which the error has occurred (so in this chapter, no error handling will be shown).

```
Report              ZST9_REGEX_DATE_TO_INT_FORMAT    Inactive

    10
    11
    12      data : mydate(10).
    13      start-of-selection.
    14
    15        mydate = '20120101'.
    16        replace first occurrence of regex '(*\d{4})(\d{2})(\d{2})'
    17                  in mydate with '$3/$2/$1'.
    18      write :/ 'Converted date is', mydate.


  🔍 ✏ 🗙 ⊘
  Syntax error

  Description                                                        Row    Type
  Program ZST9_REGEX_DATE_TO_INT_FORMAT                              16     ⊘○○
  Regular expression '(*\d{4})(\d{2})(\d{2})' is invalid in character
  position 2
```

For error handling, however, the `CX_SY_REGEX` class within the `TRY` and `CATCH` statements may be used, if required.

For `replace` statement, when the replace has been done successfully, the return code `SY-SUBRC` value is equal to `0`. This may be used for checking the success of the `replace` statement.

Using regex as an IF statement

In this recipe, we will write a simple program that will function as an `if` statement. A simple `find regex` statement will be used.

Getting ready

We will first write an `if` statement that will check if the value of a parameter variable `field1` has the value equal to `ABC`, `DEF`, or `CDE`. In case the value is equal to any of the three, the message **Field Value is Valid** is displayed. We will then see the equivalent regex.

```
parameters    field1 type c length 3 lower case.

if field1 eq 'ABC' or
   field1 eq 'CDE' or
   field1 eq 'DEF' .
  write :/ 'Field Value is Valid'.
else.
  write :/ 'Wrong Field Value'.
endif.
```

How to do it...

For replacing the if statement with find regex statement, proceed as follows:

1. Instead of the if statement, we will write a find regex statement along with the regex ' [ABC|CDE|DEF] '.

2. After the statement, the sy-subrc is checked, and the appropriate messages are written.

```
find regex '[ABC|CDE|DEF]' in field1.
if sy-subrc eq 0.
  write :/ 'Field Value i Valid'.
else.
  write :/ 'Wrong Field Value'.
endif.
```

How it works...

We have used an OR (|) operator within the find statement. A match is found if the value of the three-character field1 is equal to any of the three values specified. In this case, sy-subrc is equal to zero, and the success message is then displayed.

There's more...

Suppose we need to ignore the case. Say the input is to be compared such that there is no difference between ABC, abc, and ABc. In such a case, we may simply add ignoring case to the statement, as shown in the following screenshot:

```
find regex '[ABC|CDE|DEF]' in field1 ignoring case.
```

Removal of characters from a string

In this recipe, we will see how special characters and blanks may be removed from a text string comprising of a telephone number. We will create a program that will take as input the number containing blank spaces and special characters such as +, (, and).

The `replace` statement along with suitable regular expressions will be used. Various regular expressions may work in this case. We will see two such expressions in this recipe.

How to do it...

For meeting the mentioned requirement, proceed as follows:

1. Declare a parameter by the name `number`, consisting of 20 characters.
2. The `replace all occurrences` is added having the regular expression [^\d].

```
parameters : number type c length 20.

start-of-selection.

replace all occurrences of regex '[^\d]'
        in number with '' .
write :/ number.
```

How it works...

The solution is based on searching all non-digit characters in the string and replacing them with blank. The negated operator (^) is used within the box brackets and the \d denotes the digits. We have used all occurrences, as this will replace all non-digits.

Suppose the user enters the number having + and parentheses and blank spaces.

NUMBER	+67 (345) 8888888888

This will remove all special characters, as well as spaces, and will only display numbers.

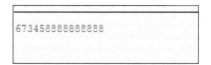

673458888888888

There's more...

Alternately, you may also use [0-9] in place of \d. The regex will be then be written as '[^0-9]'. In addition, it is important to include regex in the replace statement. Otherwise, instead of searching the pattern within the text, the system searches for [^\d] or [^0-9] in the text, and the desired results will not be achieved.

Converting date into internal date type

As already mentioned, regular expressions are useful for converting data into the required format. One good example is the conversion of a date stored in internal format into display format, and vice versa. For example, a date may be available as 20120101 and we need to format it in the form 01/01/2012, and so on. In this recipe, we will see how a single statement of replace may be used to carry out this task. For this recipe, we assum that input date is in the correct internal format.

How to do it...

For carrying out the previously mentioned conversion, proceed as follows:

1. First, declare a variable mydate having a length of 10 characters. A date having the internal format date is then assigned to this variable. The same variable will be used for storing the converted date.

2. The replace statement having the regex '(\d{4})(\d{2})(\d{2})' is used, along with the replacement '$3/$2/$1'.

3. The converted date is then outputted on the screen.

```
data : mydate(10).
start-of-selection.

  mydate = '20120101'.
  replace first occurrence of regex '(\d{4})(\d{2})(\d{2})'
          in mydate with '$3/$2/$1'.
  write :/ 'Converted date is', mydate.
```

How it works...

We have used three subgroups in the formation of the regular expression. The \d refers to digits and the number given in curly brackets specifies the length of the various date components (4 for year, 2 for month and the date). The three subgroups are specified using parentheses.

Within the `replace` statement, the subgroup placeholders are used. It specifies the format in which the date is to be outputted (the year followed by a forward slash, then the month, then another forward slash, and finally the date). For the input date, `20120101`, following are the values in each of the subgroup registers:

- ▸ Subgroup register 1 denoted by $1: 2012
- ▸ Subgroup register 2 denoted by $2: 01
- ▸ Subgroup register 3 denoted by $3: 01

In this case, the date after the `replace` statement and the `write` statement is shown in the following screenshot:

```
Converted date is 01/01/2012
```

Validation of format (telephone number)

In this recipe, we will see how to use the back-referencing operator in order to validate telephone numbers. Suppose telephone numbers in a certain city follow the rule: a number must be of exactly eight digits, and the first and second digit must be the same.

For example, the valid numbers of the city may be `44005600`, `88008700`, and so on. If the number entered starts with a zero or has length less than eight, an error should be displayed. We will see how a short validation program may be written.

How to do it...

For creating the program that checks the validity of a telephone number according to the given criteria, proceed as follows:

1. Declare a parameter having the name `tel_no` with eight characters.
2. We then use the `find regex` statement to search for the pattern `([1-9])\1[0-9]{6}` in the telephone number entered by the user.
3. The `if` statement is then used for checking the return code. For `sy-subrc`, having the value `0`, the message `Number is Valid` is displayed.

```
parameters : tel_no type char8.

start-of-selection.
  find regex '([1-9])\1[0-9]{6}' in tel_no .
  if sy-subrc eq 0.
    write: /' Number is Valid'.
  else.
    write :/ ' Number is Invalid'.
  endif.
```

How it works...

There are two parts of the regular expression that we created, that is, the regex for the first two digits and then for the remaining six digits. Let us look at this in detail.

The requirement is that the first and second number cannot be a zero. So, we have specified the range [1-9] and not [0-9] for the first number. We want the first number to be part of the first subgroup and hence the parenthesis is used. The first digit of the phone number that matches the [1-9] part of the regex is stored in the first subgroup register. This value may be addressed using the back-referencing operator \1. (Since, in this case, we have one subgroup, the corresponding placeholder for the value stored in the first register is \1). Since the first and the second number must match, we use \1 in place of the second digit.

The next part is comparatively simple. For the remaining six digits of the telephone may include zeros as well, we use the [0-9] range along with the length of 6 specified in curly brackets.

The find regex statement tries to find the given regex in the eight-character telephone number. In case, a match is found, the return code sy-subrc equals 0, so we input the message Number is Valid.

Removing repeated words from text string

In this recipe, we will use the start and end of word operators along with the subgroup register placeholders in order to write a program that will remove adjacent duplicate words from a text string. For example, from the text 'this this is is a repeated text text 11 11', the duplication of words will be removed and the new text 'this is a repeated text 11' is given as the output.

How to do it...

In order to create a repeated word removal program, proceed as follows:

1. Declare the textstream string. Then assign some text to it that has repeated words in it.

2. A replace all occurrences statement is then written with the regular expression (\<\w+\>) \1. The replacement key is '$1'.

3. The if statement is then used for checking the return code. For sy-subrc having the value 0, the message Number is Valid is displayed.

```
data : textstream type string.

start-of-selection.

  textstream = 'this this is a repeated text text 11 11'.

  replace all occurrences of regex '(\<\w+\>) \1'
   in textstream with '$1' ignoring case.

  write :/ textstream.
```

How it works...

The regex used in this recipe is different from that used in the previous one. Since we require searching of duplicate words rather than single characters, we will use the start and end word operators. We used \w+ so that all words comprising of alphanumeric characters will be found searched and then replaced. In order to find out repeated adjacent words (set of characters surrounded by blank space) we used parenthesis for the first subgroup and then the back-referencing operator \1 to find out repetition. It is also necessary to include a space between the subgroup in brackets and the \1 (since we are dealing with words).

The replace statement uses the placeholder $1, referring to the first subgroup register. In other words, via the replace statement, we are actually telling the system to first find the occurrence of two adjacent words, and then replace this found duplicate with a single word that is the one stored in the first subgroup register (thus removing duplicates).

For the example shown in the code, the string outputted after removal of adjacent duplicates is shown in the following screenshot:

```
this is a repeated text 11
```

Inserting commas in an amount string

In this recipe, we will see how a small program may be written to take as input an amount string, and insert commas in it after every thousand (that is, every three digits from right). This is interesting because the normal search of a pattern within a text is from the left.

We will use the preview condition and the negated preview condition, along with subgroups in order to find a solution. Please note that one such example appears on the `help.sap.com` site under business warehouse routines that has been slightly modified for this recipe.

How to do it...

For creating a program for comma insertion within an amount string, follow the following steps:

1. Declare a parameter `amount` of type character and length `10`. We can increase the length for a larger amount, keeping provision for the commas.

2. The `REPLACE` statement with the addition `ALL OCCURENCES` and `REGEX '(\d) (?=(\d{3})+(?!\d))'` and replace substring `'$1,'`.

3. A `write` statement is then used to output the convert amount.

```
parameters: amount type c length 10.

start-of-selection.

  REPLACE ALL OCCURRENCES OF
  REGEX '(\d)(?=(\d{3})+(?!\d))' IN amount WITH '$1,'.

  write: 'Amount with added commas is' , amount.
```

How it works...

We have used subgroups in conjunction with the preview condition. The first subgroup denoted by `(\d)` is matched for digits within the number which subsequent numbers meet the condition specified by `(\d{3})+(?!\d)`. (We may also write `[0-9]` in place of `\d`).

The preview condition finds all numbers that are followed by one or more sequence of three digits after it starting from the left. (For this reason, the `(\d{3})+` has been used.) For example, we look for digits that are followed by three, six, or nine digits. (The negated preview condition ensures that only those numbers are matched, which have multiples of exactly three digit numbers after them.)

In case any such digit is matched, it is replaced using the register subgroup placeholder $1 followed by a comma. Suppose we choose 10000 as the input number, the first zero is the matched digit (and in this case) the only match. This is replaced by the zero itself followed by a comma. The match is shown in red in the following screenshot (output taken from DEMO_REGEX_TOY program):

The output of the program is shown in the following screenshot:

Amount with added commas is 10,000

If 100 is entered, the condition does not meet, so no matches are found. That is why no commas are inserted in the amount 100 at any position. Since a big amount may require more than one comma, we use the REPLACE ALL OCCURRENCES addition.

Removing comments from program code

In this recipe, we will see how we can use the replace statement in conjunction with a suitable regex in order to remove comments from a program. For the sake of this recipe, we assume that the program whose comments are to be removed is syntactically correct. Similar to program created for the *Dynamic program generation* recipe in *Chapter 2, Dynamic Programming*, the program for this recipe will remove all statements beginning with a asterisk (*) or all parts following a line after an inverted comma (").

Getting ready

For this recipe, we will make a copy of the program created in *Chapter 2, Dynamic Programming*, that reads the source code of a program specified by user input. In the previous program, we used two internal tables and used a loop at the first table itab to delete comments. For this recipe, we will replace the loop with one replace statement and use only one table that is the first internal table itab. The code of the original program is read in the table from which comments are removed.

How to do it...

For adjusting the program, proceed as follows:

1. The main part of the new portion is a `replace` statement. This replace statement contains `(^\*.*)|([^\"]*)(\"*.*)` as the regular expression. The replace statement is with the addition `in table` and with the substring `$2`.

2. A `delete` statement is then used for deleting all blank rows from the internal table.

```
replace all occurrences of regex '(^\*.*)|([^\"]*)(\"*.*)'
 in table itab with '$2' ignoring case.
delete itab where table_line is initial.
```

How it works...

There are three subgroups used in this recipe. An OR condition is used for separating the first subgroup from the other two. Let us consider the two subgroups.

▶ `(^\*.*)`: This part tries to match lines having the first character an asterisk (`*`) that is, an entire line commented. The match found is stored in subgroup register 1.

▶ `([^\"]*)(\"*.*)`: This pattern tries to divide a given program line into two parts, the first with set of characters without a double quote (`"`) followed by the part that begins with a inverted comma (`"`). The first part before the inverted comma is stored in subgroup register 2 and is denoted by `$2`.

Since we do not require lines beginning with an asterisk and the part followed by the inverted comma, the placeholders `$1` and `$3` are not used in the `replace` statement. Only the second subgroup register has been used in the `replace` statement. This trims the comments from the code.

If a line starting with an asterisk (`*`) is reached, the second register is empty, so the entire code line is replaced by blank space. If a line having some code and then comments starting with inverted comma is reached, we only pick up the code part.

We finally call the `delete` statement in order to remove any blank lines from the program's internal table.

(For simplicity's sake, we have specified three subgroups with parenthesis, the third parentheses subgroup may be omitted also, without affecting the functioning of the code).

Interpreting HTML stream

In this recipe, we will see how an HTML code may be read and interpreted using regular expressions. We will create a program that will read an HTML stream in a string and will display the tag names along with the content of the tags. The FIND and replace statements are used together with a do loop. (This recipe will focus on reading tags beginning with <tag> and ending with <\tag>).

How to do it...

For creating a program for interpreting HTML code, follow the steps shown in the following steps:

1. Declare three strings by the name htmlstream, tagcontents, and tagname.

2. We then assign a suitable HTML code to the htmlstream variable.

3. Within a do loop, a FIND REGEX statement is added that finds tag names and their contents. The regex used in this case for matching an HTML tag is '<(\u\w*) [^>]*>(.*)</\1>'.

4. Once a tag is processed, a replace all occurrences statement is used for replacing the tag with '$$$'.

5. The tag name and tag contents are printed.

6. Once all the tags are processed, the exit statement is executed.

```
data : htmlstream type string.
data : tagcontents type string.
data : tagname type string.

htmlstream   =
'<html> <h1> this is heading 1 </h1> <h2> this is heading 2 </h2></html>'.

do .
  FIND REGEX '<(\u\w*)[^>]*>(.*)</\1>' in htmlstream IGNORING CASE
             SUBMATCHES tagname tagcontents.
  replace all occurrences of tagname in htmlstream with '$$$'.
  if sy-subrc ne 0.
    exit.
  endif.
  write :/ tagname ,' --->' ,  tagcontents .
enddo.
```

How it works...

We have used ignoring case since the tag names may start with upper or lowercase such as H1 or h1. The regular expression searches for tags starting with a <, then followed by a single alphabet (denoted in regex by \u), followed by zero or more alphanumeric characters. After this, an optional substring (comprising of all characters except for a > may be found, followed by a > character. This will match HTML tag names such as H1, H2, HTML, or html. The tag name without the special characters < and > is assigned to a subgroup that is then available in the submatch variable tagname. The start and end of the tag is checked using the back-referencing operator \1. Note that in this case, the forward slash / is part of the HTML code denoting the end of the tag. The content of a particular tag is read into the submatch variable tagcontents.

The find statement finds all the tags. Once a tag is processed, we replace the tag name as $$$ in order to avoid it to be found by the find statement another time. On the next do loop pass, the next tag is matched and contents are read.

Using a WRITE statement, all the tag names and tag contents are printed on screen. The output is shown in the following screenshot:

```
html  ---> <h1> this is heading 1 </h1> <h2> this is heading 2 </h2>
h1    --->  this is heading 1
h2    --->  this is heading 2
```

Once all the tags are processed, the sy-subrc condition of being not equal to zero is met and the loop is exited.

See also

- http://help.sap.com/saphelp_erp2005/helpdata/en/42/9d6ceabb211d73e10000000a1553f6/frameset.htm

- http://help.sap.com/abapdocu_702/en/abenregex_search.htm

- http://www.sdn.sap.com/irj/scn/go/portal/prtroot/docs/library/uuid/03a52be5-0901-0010-9da4-e9d5f8c5ce1c?QuickLink=index&overridelayout=true

- http://help.sap.com/abapdocu_702/en/abenregex_syntax_operators.htm

- http://www.sdn.sap.com/irj/scn/go/portal/prtroot/docs/library/uuid/866072ca-0b01-0010-54b1-9c02a45ba8aa?QuickLink=index&overridelayout=true

5

Optimizing Programs

In this chapter, we will see recipes related to program optimization. We will look at:

- Using transaction SAT to find problem areas
- Creation of secondary indexes in database tables
- Adding hints in SELECT clause
- Secondary indexes for internal tables
- Hashed table for single read access
- Replacing for all entries construct with Ranges

Introduction

An entire description of the topic constitutes a book by itself. However, we will see some useful and important techniques, as well as some new tools and concepts that are important for developers for program optimization. There are two main techniques—optimizing database statements, particularly SELECT statements and the optimizing ABAP code particularly internal table's access. We will see useful recipes related to both the optimization of database statements as well as internal tables.

We will start with some general rules necessary for optimization. We will start with a recipe showing the usage of transaction SAT for measuring performance of report programs. Then, we will see in detail the steps required in creating secondary indexes for database tables in order to boost performance of queries used in the concerned program. We will then see how hints may be used in programs within SELECT statements, so that a particular index may be used by the system. Finally, we will see how the FOR ALL ENTRIES construct may be replaced with ranges table. The usage of hashed internal tables as well as the new concept of secondary indexes for internal tables will be discussed in separate recipes.

For this chapter, I assume that the reader has basic knowledge of SELECT statements and database concepts and internal tables, as well as basic optimization techniques. For the better understanding of the information in this chapter, the reader should know which database would be used in his or her project and know some tricks specific to the database.

Before starting with the recipes, let us see some rules for program optimization:

- Do not use asterisk (*) in SELECT statements. It means not to select unnecessary columns from database.

- Do not use nested SELECT statements. Rather use subqueries or inner joins.

- Create views when multiple tables' data is required.

- Appropriate and complete WHERE clause conditions should be written.

- Using FOR ALL ENTRIES within SELECT statements when multiple tables are involved. Also check that the FOR ALL ENTRIES tables are not empty. Otherwise, all records in the underlying table will be accessed that will drastically affect the performance.

- Using Aggregate functions within SELECT clause such as AVG, MIN, MAX, COUNT(DISTINCT col), and COUNT(*) rather than calculating them yourselves in programs.

- Avoiding SELECT or SELECT SINGLE within a loop.

- Usage of hashed tables where a single record within the table is to be searched.

- Usage of secondary index for internal tables.

For more examples of the previously discussed items, see the **Tips and Tricks** screen of transaction SAT. For doing so, you need to call transaction SAT. Then press the ▦ Tips & Tricks button on the toolbar.

Using transaction SAT to find problem areas

In this recipe, we will see the steps required to analyze the execution of any report, transaction, or function module using the transaction SAT.

Getting ready

For this recipe, we will analyze the runtime of a standard program RIBELF00 (Display Document Flow Program). The program selection screen contains a number of fields. We will execute the program on the order number (aufnr) and see the behavior.

How to do it...

For carrying out runtime analysis using transaction SAT, proceed as follows:

1. Call transaction SAT. The screen appears as shown:

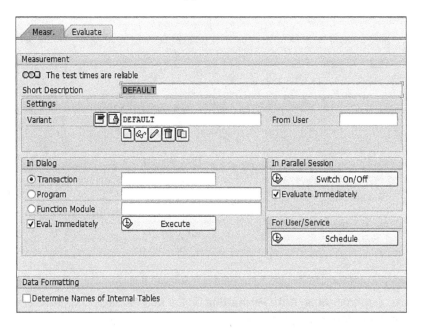

2. Enter a suitable name for the variant (in our case, YPERF_VARIANT) and click the **Create** button below it. This will take you to the **Variant** creation screen.

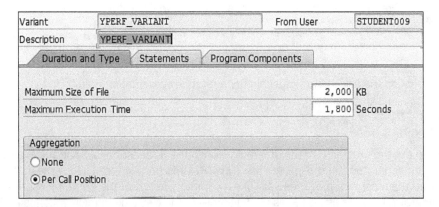

3. On the **Duration and Type** tab, switch on **Aggregation** by choosing the **Per Call Position** radio-button.

4. Then, click on the **Statements** tab. On the **Statements** tab, make sure **Internal Tables**, the **Read Operations** checkbox and the **Change Operations** checkbox, and the **Open SQL** checkbox under **Database Access** are checked.

Processing Blocks	Database Accesses
☑ Methods	☑ Open SQL
☑ Events (ABAP Objects)	☑ Native SQL
☑ Function Modules	☑ Contexts
☑ Subroutines	☐ Database-Related Operations
Screen	**Data Transfer**
☑ Flow Logic	☑ EXPORT/IMPORT
☑ Formatting for frontend	☑ DATASET
☑ Modules	
☑ Message Handling	**Miscellaneous**
	☑ Additional ABAP Statements
Internal Tables	☑ Statistics
☑ Read Operations	☐ Kernel Runtime Adminstration
☑ Change Operations	☑ C calls

5. Save your variant. Come back to the main screen of SAT.

6. Make sure that within **Data Formatting** on the initial screen of SAT, the checkbox for **Determine Names of Internal Tables** is selected.

7. Next, enter the name of the program that is to be traced in the field provided (in our case, it is RIBELF00). Then click the ⊕ Execute button.

8. The screen of the program appears as shown. We will enter an order number range and execute the program.

9. Once the program output is generated, click on the *Back* key to come back to program selection screen.

10. Click on the *Back* key once again to generate the evaluation results.

How it works...

We carried out the execution of the program through the transaction SAT and the evaluation results were generated. On the left are the **Trace Results** (in tree form) listing the statements/events with the most runtime. These are like a summary report of the entire measurement of the program. They are listed in descending order of the **Net** time in microseconds and the percentage of the total time. For example, in our case, the **OPEN CURSOR** event takes 68 percent of the total runtime of the program.

| Desktop 1 | Hit List | DB tables | Profl. | Times |

Profile: Trace Results

Profile	Selection	Number	Net [mircosec]	Net [%]
▼ 🗀 Runtime Measurement		397,351	37,544,498	100.00
▼ 🗀 Not Assigned	☐	397,351	37,544,498	100.00
• 》 OPEN CURSOR	☐	15,885	25,572,034	68.11
• 》 FETCH	☐	16,110	4,841,607	12.90
• 》 SELECT SINGLE	☐	24,652	4,164,245	11.09
• 》 PERFORM	☐	126,622	1,148,561	3.06
• 》 LOOP AT	☐	26,366	364,276	0.97
• 》 CALL FUNCTION	☐	18,470	275,437	0.73
• 》 CALL C	☐	7,919	267,716	0.71
• 》 Load Report	☐	102	232,759	0.62
• 》 READ TABLE	☐	61,866	226,971	0.60
• 》 Load Dynpro	☐	6	77,233	0.21
• 》 INSERT	☐	37,215	72,090	0.19
• 》 APPEND	☐	30,850	59,431	0.16
• 》 Load CUA Objects	☐	6	55,551	0.15
• 》 System Event	☐	3,901	39,243	0.10
• 》 PERFORM (ext)	☐	4,395	27,780	0.07
• 》 PAI Dynpro	☐	7	19,861	0.05
• 》 DELETE	☐	6,104	16,626	0.04
• 》 CALL SCREEN	☐	2	16,445	0.04

Selecting the **Hit List** tab will show the top time consumer components of the program. In this example, the access of database tables **AFRU** and **VBAK** takes most of the time.

Hit List

Hits	Gross [mircosec]	Net [mircosec]	Gross [%]	Net [%]	Statement/Event
3,043	9,909,801	9,909,801	26.37	26.39	Open Cursor AFRU
3,043	9,595,758	9,595,758	25.53	25.56	Open Cursor VBAK
3,692	2,357,589	2,357,589	6.27	6.28	Open Cursor JEST
3,692	2,269,879	2,269,879	6.04	6.05	Select Single JSTO
3,043	1,574,522	1,574,522	4.19	4.19	Open Cursor AUFM
3,043	1,294,445	1,294,445	3.44	3.45	Open Cursor VBEP
649	1,205,983	1,205,983	3.21	3.21	Select Single VIQMEL
3,692	1,130,753	1,130,753	3.01	3.01	Fetch JEST
3,043	995,902	995,902	2.65	2.65	Fetch AUFM
3,043	928,195	928,195	2.47	2.47	Fetch VBEP
3,043	882,760	882,760	2.35	2.35	Fetch AFRU
3,043	860,107	860,107	2.29	2.29	Fetch VBAK
1	680,984	680,984	1.81	1.81	Open Cursor VIAUFKST
19,609	305,907	305,907	0.81	0.81	Select Single TJ02T
45	257,639	257,639	0.69	0.69	Call C C_DD_READ_FIELD

Double-clicking any item in the **Trace Results** window on the left-hand side will display (in the **Hit List** area on the right-hand pane) details of contained items along with execution time of each item. From the **Hit List** window, double-clicking a particular item will take us to the relevant line in the program code. For example, when we double-click the **Open Cursor VBAK** line, it will take us to the corresponding program code.

```
Include          MIBELF01                              Active
   1687    *          -->P_AUFNR              pm order                           *
   1688    *--------------------------------------------------------------------*
   1689  ⊟ FORM GET_SALES_ORDERS TABLES    P_SALES_ORDER_TAB STRUCTURE G_SALESDOC
   1690                          USING      P_AUFNR.
   1691
   1692    | SELECT * FROM VBAK
   1693        INTO CORRESPONDING FIELDS OF TABLE P_SALES_ORDER_TAB
   1694        WHERE VBELN IN S_VBELN5
   1695        AND    VBTYP = 'L'
   1696        AND    AUFNR = P_AUFNR
   1697        AND    KUNNR IN S_KUNNR5
   1698        AND    BSTNK IN S_BSTNK5
   1699        AND    ERDAT IN S_ERDAT5
   1700        AND    ERNAM IN S_ERNAM5.
   1701
```

We have carried out analysis with **Aggregation** switched on. The switching on of **Aggregation** shows one single entry for a multiple calls of a particular line of code. Because of this, the results are less detailed and easier to read, since the hit list and the call hierarchy in the results are much more simplified.

Also within the results, by default, the names of the internal table used are not shown. In order for the internal table names to appear in the evaluation result, the **Determine Names** checkbox of **Internal tables** indicator is checked.

As a general recommendation, the runtime analysis should be carried out several times for best results. The reason being that the DB-measurement time could be dependent on a variety of factors, such as system load, network performance, and so on.

Creation of secondary indexes in database tables

Very often, the cause of a long running report is full-scan of a database table specified within the code, mainly because no suitable index exists. In this recipe, we will see the steps required in creating a new secondary index in database table for performance improvement. Creating indexes lets you optimize standard reports as well as your own reports. In this recipe, we will create a secondary index on a test table ZST9_VBAK (that is simply a copy of VBAK).

How to do it...

For creating a secondary index, proceed as follows:

1. Call transaction SE11. Enter the name of the table in the field provided, in our case, ZST9_VBAK. Then click the **Display** button. This will take you to the **Display Table** screen.

2. Next, choose the menu path **Goto | Indexes**. This will display all indexes that currently exist for the table.

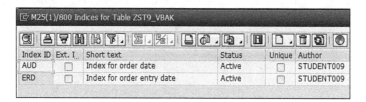

3. Click the **Create** button 🗋 ▾ and then choose the option **Create Extension Index**.

4. The dialog box appears. Enter a three-digit name for the index. Then, press *Enter*.

5. This will take you to the extension index maintenance screen. On the top part, enter the short description in the **Short Description** field provided.

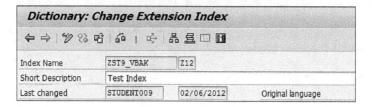

6. We will create a non-unique index so the **Non-unique index** radio button is selected (on the middle part of the screen).

7. On the lower part of the screen, specify the field names to be used in the index. In our case, we use **MANDT** and **AUFNR**.

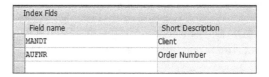

Index Flds	
Field name	Short Description
MANDT	Client
AUFNR	Order Number

8. Then, activate your index using keys *Ctrl + F3*. The index will be created in the database with appropriate message of creation shown below **Status**.

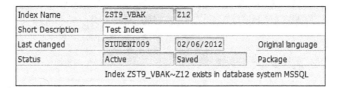

Index Name	ZST9_VBAK	Z12	
Short Description	Test Index		
Last changed	STUDENT009	02/06/2012	Original language
Status	Active	Saved	Package
	Index ZST9_VBAK~Z12 exists in database system MSSQL		

How it works...

This will create the index on the database. Since we created an extension index, the index will not be overwritten by SAP during an upgrade. Now any report that accesses ZST9_VBAK table specifying MANDT and AUFNR in the WHERE clause, will take advantage of index scan using our new secondary index.

There's more...

It is recommended by SAP that the index be first created in development system and then transport to quality, and to the production system. Secondary indexes are not automatically generated on target systems after being transported. We should check the status on the **Activation Log** in the target systems, and use the **Database Utility** to manually activate the index in question.

A secondary index, preferably, must have fields that are not common (or as much as uncommon as possible) with other indexes. Too many redundant secondary indexes (that is, too many common fields across several indexes) on a table has a negative impact on performance. For instance, a table with 10 secondary indexes is sharing more than three fields. In addition, tables that are rarely modified (and very often read) are the ideal candidates for secondary indexes.

See also

▶ http://help.sap.com/saphelp_erp2005/helpdata/EN/85/685a41cdbf80 47e10000000a1550b0/content.htm

- http://help.sap.com/saphelp_nw04/helpdata/en/cf/21eb2d446011d1
  89700000e8322d00/frameset.htmhttp://docs.oracle.com/cd/ SELECT
  clause E17076_02/html/programmer_reference/am_second.html

- http://forums.sdn.sap.com/thread.jspa?threadID=1469347

Adding hints in SELECT clause

If there are many indexes that contain common fields (or for any other reason), the database optimizer cannot decide the right index to be used for a particular query, and then use a wrong index that may not be of optimal performance. From SAP Release 4.5, hints can be provided using the %_HINTS parameter. In this recipe, we will see the syntax for specifying HINTS within your SELECT clause in order for a particular index to be used by the database optimizer. We will see how the hints may be specified when the underlying database is MS SQL Server.

Getting ready

In this recipe, we will have a small program that runs a SELECT statement on the table ZST9_VBAK. We will use the index (Z12) that we created in the previous *Creating Secondary Indexes in Database Tables* recipe.

How to do it...

For creating the program containing the SELECT clause with the HINT parameter, proceed as follows:

1. A parameter P_AUFNR is declared for taking as input an order number.
2. Next, a data variable myvbeln is defined.
3. A SELECT statement is then written. The addition %_HINTS followed by the database name, the table, and table index name is made to the SELECT clause.

```
parameters: p_aufnr type ZST9_VBAK-aufnr.
data : myvbeln type ZST9_VBAK-VBELN.

SELECT  VBELN into myvbeln
     FROM  ZST9_VBAK
     WHERE  aufnr eq p_aufnr
  %_HINTS MSSQLNT 'TABLE ZST9_VBAK ABINDEX(Z12)'.
  write :/ MYVBELN.
endselect.
```

How it works...

It is a very simple addition. There is a special syntax used for specifying the name of the database index to be used for the particular SELECT statement. The name of the index we used can be taken from the index name as defined in the ABAP Dictionary. The table name and the index name are specified within TABLE <tablename> ABINDEX(<suffix>). The syntax should be proper because other than the database name check, the syntax checker does not check the index name. Therefore, if a wrong index is used, the corresponding query will not give a syntax error but the desired results will not be achieved.

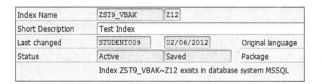

Index Name	ZST9_VBAK	Z12	
Short Description	Test Index		
Last changed	STUDENT009	02/06/2012	Original language
Status	Active	Saved	Package
	Index ZST9_VBAK~Z12 exists in database system MSSQL		

There's more...

In our case, we use MSSQLNT as the database name. However, you may use other database names such as ADABAS, AS400, DB2, DB6, INFORMIX, MSSQLNT, and ORACLE (depending on what is applicable to your underlying database). The code pertaining to the HINT parameter of one database may differ from that of another.

For example, if we have an ORACLE database, the same Z12 index may be specified in the SELECT statement in the following manner:

```
SELECT  VBELN into myvbeln
     FROM  ZST9_VBAK
     WHERE  aufnr eq p_aufnr
     %_HINTS ORACLE 'INDEX("ZST9_VBAK" "ZST9_VBAK~Z12")'.
  write :/ MYVBELN.
endselect.
```

Note the database name added along with the changed format for index specification.

See also

► http://blogs.msdn.com/b/saponsqlserver/archive/2011/08/31/how-to-integrate-sql-server-specific-hints-in-abap.aspx

Secondary indexes for internal tables

In this recipe, we will see the new concept of secondary keys/index within internal tables. This lets you optimize your programs when accessing data residing within an internal table.

Getting ready

In this recipe, we will create a program that will store all data of table VBAK into an internal table. Then we will use the secondary key in order to fetch a record pertaining to a given order number, aufnr. The primary emphasis of this recipe is on the definition and usage of a secondary key for internal tables.

How to do it...

For creating a program using secondary index in internal tables, follow the steps below:

1. We first declare a type ty_vbak based on the database table vbak. We create two keys for this table type. The first is a non-unique primary key having vbeln as the key field. We also create a non-unique sorted secondary key sec_key having one field aufnr. An internal table it_vbak is defined based on the type ty_vbak. In addition, a work area wa_vbak is declared for the table it_vbak. It is always better in terms of performance to use field symbols rather than work areas. In this example, for simplicity's sake and since the performance gain is minimal, work areas have been used.

   ```
   types ty_vbak type standard table of vbak
      with non-unique key primary_key components vbeln
      with non-unique sorted key sec_key components aufnr.

   data : it_vbak type ty_vbak.
   data : wa_vbak type line of ty_vbak.
   ```

2. Next, all records from table vbak are read into table it_vbak.

3. Then, the read table statement is used to read the row of internal table it_vbak pertaining to aufnr 503002 using the secondary key sec_key.

   ```
   select * from vbak into table it_vbak.
   read table it_vbak into wa_vbak
   with key sec_key components aufnr = '000000503002'.

   write :/ wa_vbak-vbeln.
   ```

How it works...

In the table type definition, we specified a non-unique sorted secondary key (based on `aufnr`) along with the primary key. For the `read` statement, we also specify that the secondary key `sec_key` is to be used when searching in internal table `it_vbak` the row corresponding to `aufnr` 503002. Since the secondary key is used, the `aufnr` field is first searched in the secondary index `sec_key`. A faster binary search is used since it is a sorted index. The row number of the actual internal table `it_vbak` containing the `aufnr` 503002 field is then determined. Once this number is known, the relevant row is read and values assigned to the structure `wa_vbak`. The `vbeln` field is then printed. Had no secondary index been specified, a sequential search through the internal table `it_vbak` would have been used, which was very time consuming.

Hashed table for single read access

In this recipe, we will create a program that will use a `hashed` table and a standard table for accessing and displaying employee data from two tables PA0003 and PA0006. There may be many solutions to this requirement. We will use `SELECT` clause and `hashed` tables.

Getting ready

In this recipe, we create a program that will take as input personnel number and then print the last payroll run date of the employee (from PA0003) and the permanent residence address (subtype 1) stored in the `STRAS` field of the table PA0006. For simplicity's sake, only one data field of each table has been shown.

How to do it...

For creating the program, proceed as follows:

1. We define `select-options` for taking input of personnel number.

   ```
   tables : pernr.
   select-options : s_pernr for pernr-pernr.
   ```

2. Next, we define a type `ty_payroll` based on payroll infotype fields `pernr` and `abrdt`. A structure and a hashed table based on this type are also defined. The hashed table has a unique key `pernr`.

```
types: begin of ty_payroll,
          pernr   type pa0003-pernr,
          abrdt   type pa0003-abrdt,
       end    of ty_payroll.

data: wa_payroll   type ty_payroll,
         it_payroll type   hashed table of ty_payroll
             with unique key pernr.
```

3. Similarly, an address type `ty_address` is defined, along with a structure and internal table.

```
types: begin of ty_address,
          pernr   type pa0006-pernr,
          stras   type pa0006-stras,
       end    of ty_address.

data: wa_address   type ty_address,
         it_address   type standard table of ty_address      .
```

4. We then write two `select` statements. The first reads `PA0003` for all personnel numbers specified and the date of last payroll run (`abrdt`). The second `select` statement is used to read all the `stras` addresses corresponding to permanent address type (`subty` = 1) valid at the system date.

```
select pernr ABRDT from pa0003
   into table it_payroll where pernr in s_pernr.

select pernr stras into table it_address from pa0006
        where pernr in s_pernr
        and subty eq '1'
        and begda le sy-datum
        and endda ge sy-datum.
```

5. Finally, a loop is run on the addresses internal table `it_address`. Within the loop, the `read table` statement is used for reading the payroll table `it_payroll` (the hashed table) for each of the personnel number processed. Within the loop, the personnel number, `abrdt` date, and the address field `stras` are displayed. We have used field symbols instead of work areas, in conjunction with `loop` and `read` statements for better performance.

```
field-symbols : <fs_address> type ty_address,
                <fs_payroll> type ty_payroll.

loop at it_address assigning <fs_address>.
  read table it_payroll with table key
    pernr = <fs_address>-pernr assigning <fs_payroll>.
  write:/ <fs_payroll>-pernr,<fs_payroll>-abrdt,
          <fs_address>-stras.
endloop.

write :/ sy-dbcnt.
```

How it works...

Two internal tables `it_address` and `it_payroll` are defined. `it_payroll` is a hashed table. We read data from both the database tables PA0003 and PA0006 into the internal tables `it_payroll` and `it_address` respectively. We need to print each employee number and the corresponding data from each of the two tables.

Therefore, a loop is carried out on the internal table `it_adrress` and within the loop, a `read table` is used to read the hashed table, the row corresponding to the employee number in question. Since it is a single entry access from the internal table `it_payroll` which is a hashed table with the value corresponding to the hash key (`pernr`) being passed, the `read` statement is very quick. All the values that we need are there within the loop after the `read` statement. These values are then outputted using a `write` statement.

See also

▶ http://help.sap.com/saphelp_nw70/helpdata/en/fc/
  eb35de358411d1829f0000e829fbfe/content.htm

Replacing for all entries construct with Ranges

In this recipe, we will see how we can replace `for all entries` within a `select` statement with ranges in the `where` clause. The ranges maybe used to improve performance. This two-table example is just for illustrative purpose and comparison. You may apply the concepts to other tables and fields. You may or may not further refine this based on your requirement.

Getting ready...

We will create a simple program that uses the `for all entries` addition in the `select` statement for the two tables `cobk` and `coep`. We declare two internal tables `t_header` and `t_line_items`. The `t_header` table contains one field for the `belnr` document number, whereas the items table `t_line_items` has three fields `belnr`, `period` (period), and `amount wtgbtr` (amount).

We first select up to 35,000 numbers from table `cobk` into the internal table `t_header` based on the code `kokrs` equal to `1000`. Next, the table `coep` is read for `kokrs 1000` and for all document numbers contained in table `t_header` using the `for all entries` addition. The data is read and stored in table `t_line_items`. We also make sure that the `for all entries` table is not empty.

```
data : t_header type standard table of co_belnr.
types : begin of ty_line_items,
               belnr type co_belnr,
               perio type co_perio,
               wtgbtr type WTGXXX,
         end of ty_line_items.

data : t_line_items type standard table of ty_line_items.

start-of-selection.

  select belnr from cobk into table t_header
       up to 35000 rows where kokrs eq '1000'.

  select distinct belnr perio wtgbtr from coep
     into corresponding fields of table t_line_items
     for all entries in t_header
     where kokrs eq '1000' and
     belnr eq t_header-table_line.
```

How to do it...

In this recipe, we will see how we can improve the performance of the code by replacing the `for all entries` construct with a range of document numbers. For this, we need to add some additional code before the second `select` statement.

For forming ranges of document numbers, we will use the function module
`WLF_CREATE_RANGE_FOR_WBELN`. You may copy or write your own code as well
but since we have both the number used having same length and type (character 10),
the function module `WLF_CREATE_RANGE_FOR_WBELN` may be used. The steps for
writing the additional code for forming ranges are shown as follows:

1. We declare one range table `r_header` based on the type `WBELN_RAN_ITAB`.
   The structure of `WBELN_RAN_ITAB` is shown as follows:

Component	Typing Method	Component Type	Data Type	Length
SIGN	Types	▾ RALDB_SIGN	CHAR	1
OPTION	Types	▾ RALDB_OPTI	CHAR	2
LOW	Types	▾ WBELN_LF	CHAR	10
HIGH	Types	▾ WBELN_LF	CHAR	10

2. In addition, a `temp_header` variable is declared based on the type `WBRK_KEY_ITAB`
   (our function module will accept this type).

3. We then sort the table `t_header` and assign the `t_header` table to our
   `temp_header` internal table.

4. The function module `WLF_CREATE_RANGE_FOR_WBELN` is then called. We pass the
   `temp_header` variable to the function module for exporting parameter `it_wbeln`.
   The function module creates the ranges from the values in the `temp_header` table
   and returns the range in the table `r_header`.

5. Finally, the `select` statement is written with the `for all entries` part replaced
   with the ranges `r_header`.

```
data : r_header TYPE  WBELN_RAN_ITAB.
data : temp_header  type WBRK_KEY_ITAB.

sort t_header.
temp_header = t_header.

CALL FUNCTION 'WLF_CREATE_RANGE_FOR_WBELN'
   EXPORTING
     IT_WBELN      = temp_header
   CHANGING
     CT_WBELN_RAN = r_header.

refresh t_line_items.
select distinct belnr perio wtgbtr from coep
    into corresponding fields of table t_line_items
    where kokrs eq '1000' and
    belnr in r_header.
```

How it works...

Let us now see how the additional code works. The document numbers are passed to the
function module. The various numbers (in our case `35000`) are used for creating ranges
and returned in the table `r_header`.

Row	SIGN [C(1)]	OPTION [C(2)]	LOW [C(10)]	HIGH [C(10)]
1	I	BT	0000000014	0000000016
2	I	BT	0000000019	0000000058
3	I	BT	0000000062	0000000063
4	I	EQ	0000000067	
5	I	BT	0000000070	0000000111
6	I	EQ	0000000113	
7	I	BT	0000000115	0000000117
8	I	BT	0000000119	0000000146
9	I	BT	0000000246	0000000258
10	I	BT	0000000260	0000000271

Table: R_HEADER
Attributes: Standard [1085x4(46)]
Columns ...

The `r_header` table is then used in the `select` statement for reading data from table `coep`. This technique works best when the document numbers passed to the function modules are close together, so that less rows exists in the ranges table.

The efficiency of the `Ranges` code may be easily demonstrated. We use the `GET RUNTIME` statement to find out the relative runtime of other various program segments (such as original `select` statement part, the function module call, and the `select` statement using the `Ranges` table). The following are the runtimes (in microseconds) displayed on the screen:

```
Runtime before For All Entries Statement            0
Runtime After For All Entries Statement     1,323,378
Runtime after ranges function module        1,554,917
Runtime After Select Statement with Range   1,855,031
```

The `t_header` table contains 35,000 rows. It can be clearly seen that the time taken by the `select` statement with `for all entries in` clause is 1.3 seconds. The function module consumes 0.23 seconds, whereas the `select` statement having the `Range` table takes 0.3 seconds. Hence, the combined time for our replacement code is 0.53 seconds (0.23 + 0.30) seconds. This is faster than the 1.3 seconds taken by the original `select` statement using the `for all entries` clause.

See also

▸ http://help.sap.com/saphelp_nw04/helpdata/en/9f/
  db994235c111d1829f0000e829fbfe/content.htm

▸ http://www.sdn.sap.com/irj/scn/index?rid=/library/uuid/
  d0c750c1-7d04-2e10-8492-a11b9219371d

▸ http://help.sap.com/saphelp_nw04/helpdata/en/cf/21eb2d446011d18
  9700000e8322d00/frameset.htm

6
Doing More with Selection Screens

In this chapter, we will see recipes related to enhancing report selection screens. We will look at:

- ▶ Adding tabstrips and listboxes to the report selection screens
- ▶ Adding toolbar buttons on the selection screen
- ▶ Changing screen fields on radio button selection
- ▶ Taking desktop folder and filename as input
- ▶ Coding search help exits for creating better F4 helps

Introduction

There are three types of screens within the SAP R/3 system, namely dialog screens, list, and the selection screen. Selection screens are used for taking input from the user. They are formed by using ABAP statements without the screen painter. A selection screen may comprise of input fields, checkboxes, radio buttons, tabstrips, and list boxes.

This chapter explores useful recipes that will help you in building better selection screens for your programs as well as allow the addition of certain features for improving the user experience. We will start with the first recipe that will show how to add toolbar buttons to your program's selection screen. Then, we will see how tabstrips and list boxes may be added on screens. Next, a recipe that will show how radio button inputs may be used to hide or unhide other screen fields.

We will also see how standard function modules may be used to provide a browsing facility to the user and take as input names of folder and files residing on his or her desktop. Finally, we will have a recipe detailing the steps required to create search help exits.

We assume that the reader has knowledge of basic selection screen concepts and the usage of selection screen blocks. Also, the familiarity with the `screen` table is recommended.

See also

- ► `http://help.sap.com/saphelp_nw04/helpdata/en/e4/2adbec449911d19 49c0000e8353423/frameset.htm`

- ► For more information about the `screen` table, refer to the link `http://help.sap. com/abapdocu_70/en/ABAPLOOP_AT_SCREEN.htm`

Adding tabstrips and listboxes to report selection screens

Within selection screens, tabstrips and listboxes may be displayed without the need of knowing or using the screen painter. This may be done using a few ABAP statements. In this recipe, we will see how tabstrips and listboxes may be added to selection screens. We will create a program that will contain a tabstrip containing two tabs, each containing a listbox representing country names. By default, we will have **USA** displayed on the first tab and **Canada** on the second.

How to do it...

For creating tabstrips and listboxes, follow the following steps:

1. We create two **Text Symbols**, **001** and **002**, that are to be used in the subsequent steps.

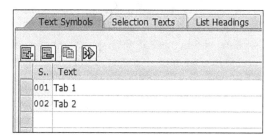

2. First, we define a selection screen `100` as the subscreen. Within the subscreen we define a block that contains a listbox. On the subscreen, we will create a listbox for country that will, by default, show `US` (USA) as the country. The subscreen will be shown in the first tab of the tabstrip that we will be defined in a later step.

```
selection-screen begin of screen 100 as subscreen.
selection-screen begin of block block1 with frame title text-001.
PARAMETERS country TYPE pa0002-GBLND
                    AS LISTBOX VISIBLE LENGTH 20
                    USER-COMMAND COUN
                    DEFAULT 'US'.

selection-screen end of block block1.
selection-screen end of screen 100.
```

3. Similarly, we define another subscreen 101, within which we create another parameter input displayed as a listbox having length 20. The default value we have for this listbox is CA, that is Canada. The user command code, COU2, is defined for this listbox.

```
selection-screen begin of screen 101 as subscreen.
selection-screen begin of block block2 with frame title text-002.
PARAMETERS country2 TYPE pa0002-GBLND
                    AS LISTBOX VISIBLE LENGTH 20
                    USER-COMMAND COU2
                    DEFAULT 'CA'.
selection-screen end of block block2.
selection-screen end of screen 101.
```

4. Finally, the tabstrip (tabbed block containing two tabs) is defined. The two tabs are assigned to the subscreens 100 and 101 defined earlier.

```
selection-screen begin of tabbed block t1 for 20 lines.
selection-screen tab (20) tab1 user-command ucomm1 default screen 100.
selection-screen tab (20) tab2 user-command ucomm2 default screen 101.
selection-screen end of block t1.
```

5. For the two tabs, the system creates character fields with the same names, that is, tab1 and tab2. Within the initialization event, the tab1 and tab2 fields are assigned the texts, **Tab1** and **Tab2**, using the text-001 and text-002 text symbols defined earlier.

```
initialization.
  tab1 = 'Tab 1'.
  tab2 = 'Tab 2'.
```

How it works...

The coding creates a tabstrip having two tabs with the text **Tab1** and **Tab2** respectively. Each tab page is assigned a subscreen that contains a listbox having country as the input field. When the user clicks on a particular tab title, the elements in that subscreen become active and are displayed. The **COUNTRY** field is defined using the **GBLND** field of the PA0002 table. We specified US as the default value for the listbox on the first tab. The text for US, that is **United States**, is displayed in the first tab.

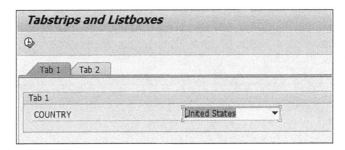

For the second tab, the country Canada is displayed by default. The user may choose the country of his choice.

See also

- ▶ http://wiki.sdn.sap.com/wiki/display/ABAP/ABAP-
  Creating+Tabs+in+Report+program

- ▶ http://help.sap.com/saphelp_nw04/helpdata/en/00/
  deb23789e95378e10000009b38f8cf/content.htm

Adding toolbar buttons on selection screen

In this recipe, we will see how toolbar buttons (and their relevant click code) may be added to selection screens. In this recipe, we will create a program that will display a selection screen having three toolbar buttons, each of which when clicked, takes us to a different transaction.

How to do it...

For adding buttons on your selection screen toolbar, proceed as follows:

1. First, declare the dictionary structure, sscrfields.

2. Here we define buttons with function keys 1, 2, and 3 using the
   selection-screen statement.

3. Also, an integer `abc` is defined.

```
tables : sscrfields.

selection-screen function key 1.
selection-screen function key 2.
selection-screen function key 3.

parameters : abc type i.
```

4. Within the `initialization` event, the respective texts for the buttons are assigned to the `functxt_01`, `functxt_02`, and `functxt_03` fields of the structure `sscrfields`.

```
initialization.
  sscrfields-functxt_01  = 'ABAP Editor' .
  sscrfields-functxt_02  = 'Object Navigator'.
  sscrfields-functxt_03  = 'Business Workplace'.
```

5. Next, within the `at selection-screen` event, we check the value of the field `sscrfields-ucomm`. The FC01, FC02, and FC03 values represent the button-click event of the first, second, and third buttons respectively. We call the respective transactions, SE38, SE80, and SBWP, for each button-click.

```
at selection-screen.
  case sscrfields-ucomm.
    when 'FC01'.
      call transaction 'SE38'.
    when 'FC02'.
      call transaction 'SE80'.
    when 'FC03'.
      call transaction 'SBWP'.
  endcase.
```

How it works...

We will now see how the coding works in displaying the toolbar buttons along with the necessary button text, and how the respective transactions are called after button-click events.

The `selection-screen` statements' coding and the initialization creates the three toolbar buttons and the relevant texts, **ABAP Editor**, **Object Navigator**, and **Business Workplace**. The function code `FC01`, `FC02`, and `FC03` are assigned to the three buttons. When any of the buttons are pressed, the `at selection-screen` event is called. The value of the field `sscrfields-ucomm` is checked. Depending on which button, the **UCOMM** field is automatically populated with `FC01`, `FC02`, or `FC03`. After checking the value, the relevant transaction code is called via the `call transaction` statement and the user is taken to the appropriate transaction.

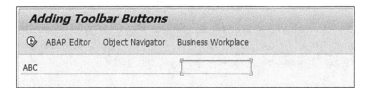

See also

▶ `http://www.saptraininghouse.com/2011/adding-buttons-on-application-toolbar-of-selection-screen/`

Changing screen fields on radio button selection

In this recipe, we will see how input fields may be hidden and shown, based on the input of the radio buttons. We will create a program having a selection screen containing a group of two radio buttons and an integer field. We will then add the code that will hide or display the integer field based on which a radio button is selected.

How to do it...

For creating the program, proceed as follows:

1. First, three radio buttons `show`, `no_show`, and `no_input`, are defined. These are assigned to the radio button group `g1`. The user command, `INT1`, is assigned.

2. Next, an integer is defined with the addition, `modif id INT`.

```
parameters: show radiobutton group g1 user-command INT1,
            no_show radiobutton group g1, """ FCODE INT1
            no_input radiobutton group g1.

parameters : integer type i modif id INT.
```

3. The `AT SELECTION-SCREEN output` event is then defined. A loop is run at the `screen` table. Within the loop, the `group1` of each screen element is checked for `INT`. In addition, if `show` is equal to `X`, the `active` field is set as `1` (active). If `no_show` is equal to `X`, the `active` field is set as `0` (inactive). In case `no_input` equals to `X`, the `input` field is set as `0` (non-editable). Finally, the `modify screen` statement is used to set the values in the `screen` table. (Though `screen` is an internal table, we can't use `loop at screen` with the `WHERE <XXX>` variant).

```
AT SELECTION-SCREEN output.

    loop at screen.
        if screen-group1 eq 'INT' and show eq 'X'.
          screen-active =  1.
            modify screen.
        elseif screen-group1 eq 'INT' and no_show eq 'X'.
          screen-active =  0.
          modify screen.
          elseif screen-group1 eq 'INT' and no_input eq 'X'.
              screen-input =  0.
          modify screen.
        endif.

    endloop.
```

How it works...

The code that we wrote displays three radio buttons and an integer field on the screen.

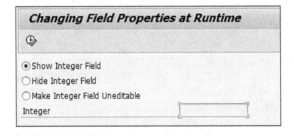

By default, the **Show Integer Field** radio button is selected. When the **Hide Integer Field** radio button is selected, the integer field disappears. The **Hide Integer Field** radio button or **Make Integer Field Uneditable** radio button selection triggers the `at selection screen output` event. A loop is then run on each screen element, but we are only interested in the one that has the `group1` field assigned the value `INT` (as we assigned `INT` for the integer field using the `modify id` addition). We will also check which radio button (**Show Integer Field, Hide Integer Field**, or **Make Integer Field Uneditable**) is set. If the **Hide Integer Field** radio button is on, the integer field is set as inactive (and thus made invisible).

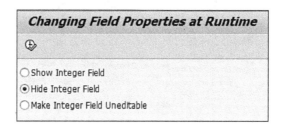

If the **Make Integer Field Uneditable** radio button is set, the `input` field is set as `0`, that is, the input is not allowed, thus making the field uneditable for the user.

When the user selects the **Show Integer Field** radio button, the integer field is set as active and displayed again to the user.

Taking desktop folder and filename as input

In this recipe, we will create a small program that will take as input a folder name and filename(s) from the user. Both standard function modules, as well as classes, may be used for this purpose.

In the main part of this recipe, we will use the function modules, `TMP_GUI_BROWSE_FOR_FOLDER` and `TMP_GUI_FILE_OPEN_DIALOG`. In addition to the browsing capability, the user may also create a new folder while entering a folder. The file's function module lets you select multiple files from your local directory.

The *There's more...* section of this recipe will show an equivalent based on the object oriented approach. The methods, `directory_browse` and `file_open_dialog`, of the class `cl_gui_frontend_services` will be used.

How to do it...

For taking input of folder and files, proceed as follows:

1. First, two parameter input fields are declared for the `folder` and `filename`, having a length of `80` and `50` characters respectively.

```
parameters : folder type c length 80.
parameters : filename type c length 50 .
```

2. Then, we will write the code within the `at selection-screen on value-request` event for the folder. We call the function module `TMP_GUI_BROWSE_FOR_FOLDER`. The window title parameter is passed to the relevant text, `Choose the folder of your choice`.

```
at selection-screen on value-request for folder.

  call function 'TMP_GUI_BROWSE_FOR_FOLDER'
    exporting
      window_title    = 'Choose the folder of your choice'
      initial_folder  = folder
    importing
      selected_folder = folder
    exceptions
      cntl_error      = 1
      others          = 2.
```

3. Similarly, we will call the function module `TMP_GUI_FILE_OPEN_DIALOG` for `at selection-screen on value-request` for the `filename` field. We will pass a suitable window title to the function module. The importing parameter, `rc`, returns the number of files selected by the user. The parameter `multiselection` is used for controlling whether multiple files may be specified by the user. We will keep this as (`' '`) meaning only one file may be specified. The filename and the complete path is returned in the table parameter `file_table` of the function module. As the user will provide one filename, we use a `read table` statement in order to read the first record, that is the filename and path specified by the user.

```
at selection-screen on value-request for filename.

  data : number_of_files type i.
  data : file_names_tab type STANDARD TABLE OF SDOKPATH .
  data : wa_names_tab type SDOKPATH .


  call function 'TMP_GUI_FILE_OPEN_DIALOG'
    exporting
      window_title    = 'Enter the File names'
      multiselection  = ' '
    importing
      rc              = number_of_files
    tables
      file_table      = file_names_tab
    exceptions
      cntl_error      = 1
      others          = 2.

  read table file_names_tab into wa_names_tab index 1.
  filename = wa_names_tab.
```

How it works...

When the program is run, two input value fields for `folder` and `filename` are displayed. When the folder input help is selected, the folder dialog box is displayed. The user specified a folder name from his or her desktop. Alternatively, a new folder may be created and specified. The folder complete path is returned in the variable `folder`, which may be later used in the program.

Likewise, when the `filename` input help is called, the relevant function module is called and the dialog box is displayed. The user selects the file of his or her choice. Only one file may be selected. After the function module call, the first row of `file_names_tab` is called and the `filename` input field is filled with the filename and path stored in the first row of `file_names_tab`.

There's more...

The function module's call for the files may be slightly altered in order to take input multiple filenames from the desktop of the user. Then the `multiselection` parameter of the function may be passed the value X in order to allow multiple files to be selected. In this case, additional coding is required to loop through the `file_names_tab` in order to read all the filenames specified.

As already mentioned, for the same requirement, the methods `directory_browse` and `file_open_dialog` of the class `cl_gui_frontend_services` may also be used.

The relevant coding is shown in the following screenshot:

```
at selection-screen on value-request for folder.
  data: temp_string type string .
  CALL METHOD cl_gui_frontend_services=>directory_browse
    EXPORTING
      window_title   = 'File Directory'
      initial_folder = 'C:'
    CHANGING
      selected_folder = temp_string.

  CALL METHOD cl_gui_cfw=>flush.
  folder = temp_string.


AT SELECTION-SCREEN ON VALUE-REQUEST FOR filename.
  data : number_of_files type i.
  data : file_names_tab type FILETABLE.
  data : wa_names_tab type line of filetable .

  clear file_names_tab.
  CALL METHOD cl_gui_frontend_services=>file_open_dialog
    EXPORTING
      window_title   = 'Enter the File Name'
      multiselection = ' '
    CHANGING
      file_table     = file_names_tab
      rc             = number_of_files.

  read table file_names_tab into wa_names_tab index 1.
  filename = wa_names_tab.
```

For the `directory_browse` method, a temporary variable having `string` type is declared. The call of the `cl_gui_cfw=>flush` method is necessary after the `directory_browse` method.

For the `file_open_dialog` method, necessary data objects are defined prior to the method call.

Coding search help exits for creating better F4 helps

In this recipe, we will see how search help (and help exits) will help you meet the user requirements when providing the input values of a particular selection screen's input field. We will create a search help in this recipe and will assign it to an input field.

The requirement is to provide a personnel number field with input help that shows all the employees whose birthdays fall in the current month. This means, if the program is run in March, all the employees whose birthdays are in March will be shown in the input help.

Getting ready

We will create a search help for personnel number. The name of the search help is `ZST9_SEARCH_HELP` and it uses the database table, `pa0002`. The fields **PERNR**, **NACHN**, **VORNA**, and **GBDAT** are selected and displayed in the hit list.

Attributes	Definition						
Data collection			**Dialog behavior**				
Selection method	PA0002		Dialog type	Display values immediately ▼			
Text table			Hot key				
Search help exit							

Search help parameter	IMP	E...	LPos	SPos	SDis	Data element
PERNR	☑	☑	1	1	☐	PERSNO
NACHN	☐	☐	2	2	☐	PAD_NACHN
VORNA	☐	☐	3	3	☐	PAD_VORNA
GBDAT	☐	☐	4	4	☐	GBDAT

Next, we will create a program in which we will declare a parameter `pernr`, based on **PERNR** of the table **PA0002**. We use the `matchcode object` addition to assign the search help `ZST9_SEARCH_HELP` to it.

```
REPORT   ZST9_SEARCH_HELP_DEMO.


parameters :  pernr type pa0002-pernr matchcode object ZST9_SEARCH_HELP   .
```

How to do it...

For defining search help exit function module, proceed as follows:

1. Copy `F4IF_SHLP_EXIT_EXAMPLE`. We will give it the name `ZST9_SEARCH_HELP_EXIT`.

2. Within the function module, we will add the following code under the step `DISP`. This is the part where the filtering of employee data for birthdays falling in the current month takes place. The function module is then activated.

```
*"------------------------------------------------------------
* STEP DISP      (Display values)
*"------------------------------------------------------------
* This step is called, before the selected data is displayed.
* You can e.g. modify or reduce the data in RECORD_TAB
* according to the users authority.

  if callcontrol-step = 'DISP'.
    delete record_tab where string+490(2) ne sy-datum+4(2).
    exit.
  endif.
```

3. We will now assign the newly created function module in the **Search help exit** field of the search help. The search help is then activated.

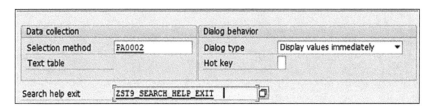

How it works...

The logic we used in this example is that we first fetched all records of the employees from **PA0002**, irrespective of their dates of birth, using the search help. Then, within the **Search help exit**, we removed all the employees whose dates of birth does not fall in the month the program is run.

When the user takes the *F4* help, the search help is called. The search help fetches the data from the table **PA0002** and the relevant fields—**PersNo**, **First name**, **Last name**, and **Birth date**. Next, the search help exit is called.

The table **RECORD_TAB** within the function module contains the content of the hit list. The **RECORD_TAB** table contains a large string field that is comprised of all the fields **PERNR**, **NACHN**, **VORNA**, and the **GBDAT** combined. (Prior to writing the code, we used the debugger to find out the exact positions of the date of birth **GBDAT** field).

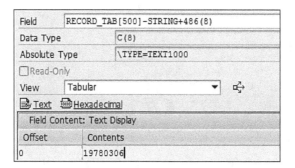

The step `DISP` is called just before the hit list is about to be displayed. We will use this to remove any records we do not want. The `delete` statement removes all the records where the month does not match the month of the system date (`sy-datum`). The ones that remain are the ones having birthdays in the current month. For example, when the report is run in March, the input help is shown as in the following screenshot:

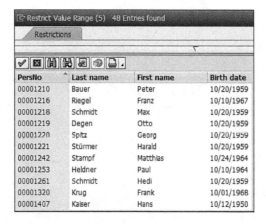

See also

- ABAP Keyword Documentation for AT SELECTION SCREEN OUTPUT statement
- http://www.sapdev.co.uk/dictionary/shelp/shelp_exit.htm

7
Smart Forms – Tips and Tricks

In this chapter, we will see recipes related to Smart Forms such as:

- ▸ Toggle on/off the Microsoft Word text editor
- ▸ Using background pictures and print preview
- ▸ Using folder options for page protection
- ▸ Printing several forms in one spool request
- ▸ Converting Smart Form to PDF output
- ▸ Applying sorting and subtotaling to table fields

Introduction

This chapter explores useful recipes related to Smart Forms. We will start with a simple recipe that will allow you to change the text editor of the Smart Form to Microsoft Word. Then we will see how page protection for a number of text lines may be applied using folders in order to ensure that certain lines are printed together on one page.

We will also see how to set an image as background of a form page for only preview and also for print. The procedure for generating multiple form outputs in a single spool request will be discussed in an upcoming recipe. We will also see how the preview and the print dialog may be suppressed, and the output directly converted to PDF. Finally we will see the recipe for calculating subtotals using sorting criterion at the Smart Form level.

We assume that the reader has basic Smart Forms knowledge. In addition, the familiarity with the structure of the form-calling program is needed.

Toggle on/off the Microsoft Word text editor

In this recipe, we will see how we can change the Smart Forms text editor to Microsoft Word.

How to do it...

Follow these steps:

1. Call transaction SE38 and enter RSCPSETEDITOR in the program field. Then execute the program. The selection screen of the program is shown as follows:

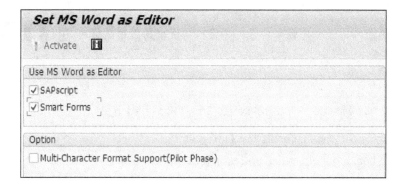

2. Make sure the **Smart Forms** checkbox is checked. Then, click the **Activate** button.
3. For switching off the Microsoft Word editor for Smart Forms, uncheck the **Smart Forms** indicator and then click the **Activate** button on the toolbar.

How it works...

Depending on the settings saved for Smart Form, the editor changes. If the **Smart Form** checkbox was on, the text editor appears as Microsoft Word. Otherwise, the normal Smart Form text editor appears.

See also

▶ http://wiki.sdn.sap.com/wiki/pages/viewpage.
  action?pageId=77987849

▶ http://forums.sdn.sap.com/thread.jspa?threadID=1679160

Using background pictures and print preview

In this recipe, we will see how a picture may be set as the background image of forms. We will see how we can set the graphic to appear both on the print preview and/or hard copy of the Smart Form.

Getting ready

We will first create a background image and upload the image on the SAP Document Server using the transaction SE78. The name of the image we upload is ZST9_BACKGROUND and is in color (the supported formats are .tiff and .bmp).

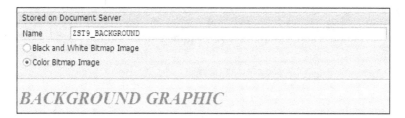

How to do it...

We will now set the graphic as the form background. Follow these steps:

1. Call the transaction SMARTFORMS. Double-click the relevant node in the left-hand pane of the page for which the background image is to be set.

2. In the right-hand pane, three tabs will appear for the page. The third is **Background Picture**. On this tab, enter the name of the uploaded graphic. Select the **Color Bitmap Image (BCOL)** radio button. Within the **Output Mode** list, select **Print Preview** from the listbox.

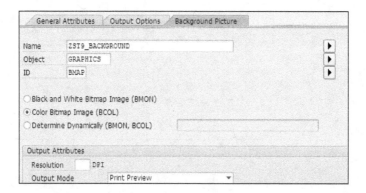

3. The main window is placed on top of the background graphic.

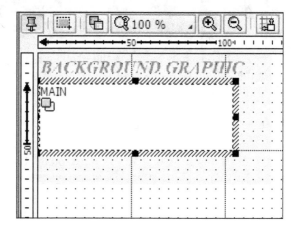

4. Next, we define a text within the **MAIN Main Window** on the page.

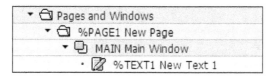

5. A suitable line TEST TEXT FOR BACKGROUND is created within the created text, as shown in the following screenshot:

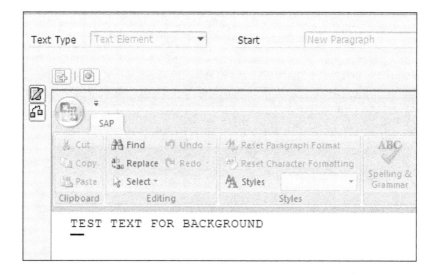

How it works...

When the Smart Form is called (using a calling program), the background graphic is displayed along with the line of text in the **Print Preview** mode. However, when the form is printed, no background image appears (only the line of text created appears). This setting is very useful when a pre-printed paper having the appropriate background graphic is used for printing, and should not be printed in the form output (since the paper already has the graphic in it). The user, however, needs to see the background graphic when the form preview is taken on the screen.

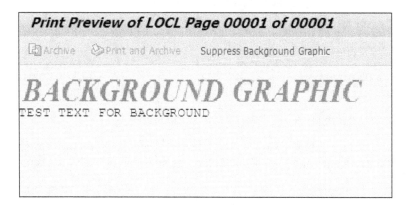

There's more...

If the background graphic appears blurred or the pixel artefacts are visible, we may need to use a high-resolution graphic. One option may be that we use a high quality (high-resolution graphic). Also, we may try to control this using the resolution setting through the **Resolution** field in the **Output Attributes** screen. Instead of keeping it blank, we may enter a value of 200. The higher the resolution, the clearer will be the graphic (however, the size of the graphic may decrease as the resolution increases).

We may also slightly change the image's output mode in order to make the image work as a watermark when printed on paper. Instead of the **Print preview and no print** option for the **Output Mode**, we can choose the **Print preview and print** option.

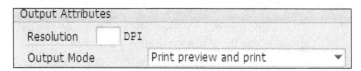

This will print the image on both the **Print** option (and the **Print Preview** option) and when printed on paper, it will make the image appear as a watermark on top of which text and data will appear.

See also

▶ `http://wiki.sdn.sap.com/wiki/display/ABAP/Background+pictures+in+Smart+Forms`

Using folder options for page protection

In this recipe, we will see how we can create a folder comprising a number of lines (block of text) so that they are all printed on the same page. If the space within a page is not enough for printing all the lines, the entire text block is printed on the subsequent page, that is, page protected.

How to do it...

For defining a folder with page protection, follow these steps:

1. Right-click on the **MAIN** window. Then, from the context menu that appears, choose the option **Create** and then select **Folder**, as shown in the following screenshot:

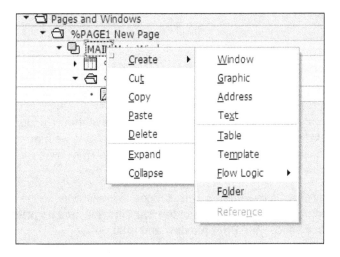

2. Next, enter a suitable folder name. In the right-hand pane, on the **Output Options** tab of the created folder, check the **Page Protection** indicator.

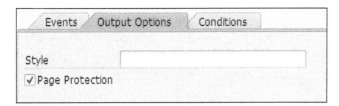

3. Then add a text under the given folder.

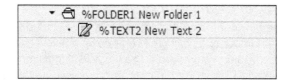

4. Add three lines to the text.

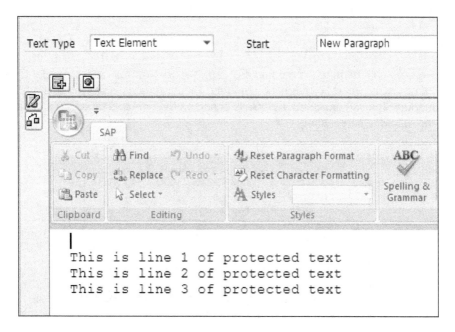

5. Save and activate your Smart Form.

How it works...

When the form output is generated, irrespective of the number of lines printed above our three-line text, a page protection is applied. If the space on the page is not enough so that all three lines may be printed, a page break is automatically triggered and the lines are printed on a fresh new page. Otherwise, the same page is utilized. In no case will the three lines be broken into two pages.

Printing several forms in one spool request

In this recipe, we will see how printed multiple forms may be included in a single spool request. We will create a number of form pages comprising employees data. Each page will contain one employee's salary information. The recipe will focus on the important parts of the program related to Smart Form processing. We assume that an internal table `EMPLOYEE_LIST` exists that contain the employee numbers of all personnel to be processed.

How to do it...

Follow these steps:

1. First, we call the function module `SSF_FUNCTION_MODULE_NAME` in order to get the name of the Smart Form function module. The form name is passed to the function module. The `myfunction` variable is based on the type `RS38L_FNAM` (not shown in the following screenshot):

```
call function 'SSF_FUNCTION_MODULE_NAME'
  exporting
    formname = 'ZST9_GRAPHICS_BACKGROUND'
  importing
    fm_name  = myfunction
  exceptions
    no_form  = 1
    others   = 2.
```

2. Then appropriate variables are defined for the Smart Form control structure and output options based on dictionary structures.

```
data : cont_parameters  type ssfctrlop,
       output_options   type ssfcompop.
```

3. The function module `SSF_OPEN` is then called.

```
call function 'SSF_OPEN'.
```

4. A loop is run on the internal table `employee_list` for all employees. For each employee, the form `get_employee_data` is called, which fetches the necessary information of the employee in question and fills the internal table `employee_data`. The `no_open` and `no_close` fields of the control parameters structure are assigned the value `'X'`. In addition, the `tdnewid` field of the output options structure is assigned `'X'`.

5. The function module of the Smart Form is then called and necessary data of the employee provided along with control parameters and output option structures.

```
loop at employee_list.
  perform get_employee_data.

  cont_parameters-no_open = 'X'.
  cont_parameters-no_close = 'X'.
  output_options-tdnewid = 'X'.

  call function myfunction
    exporting
      control_parameters = cont_parameters
      output_options     = output_options
    tables
      employee_table     = employee_data
    exceptions
      formatting_error   = 1
      internal_error     = 2
      send_error         = 3
      user_canceled      = 4
      others             = 5.

endloop.
```

6. Finally, the `SSF_CLOSE` function module is called.

```
call function 'SSF_CLOSE'.
```

How it works...

After executing the program, multiple pages of the forms are generated. For each employee, a separate page appears along with the necessary information.

Print Preview of LOCL Page 00001 of 00002

Archive   Print and Archive   Suppress Background Graphic

BACKGROUND GRAPHIC

Emp.No	Allowance	Amount
00000012	Basic Pay	11,000.00
00000012	HR Allowance	1,000.00
00000012	Transport	1,300.00

The call of the function module `SSF_OPEN` opens the spool job for form printing. The `tdnewid` assigned to `'X'` creates a new spool request. Within the loop, the `no_open` and `no_close` fields are set to `'X'`, which ensures the spool request is not opened or closed within the loop. The function module of the Smart Form is called in the loop and generates the necessary output of each employee. When all employees are processed, the `SSF_CLOSE` function module is called and the spool request is closed.

There's more...

We can also avoid the usage of the `SSF_OPEN` and `SSF_CLOSE` function modules. In this case, when we program that on the first employee, the spool job is opened and when we program that on the last employee, the spool job is closed.

See also

▸   http://help.sap.com/saphelp_nw70/helpdata/en/64/
   bf2f12ed1711d4b655006094192fe3/frameset.htm

Converting Smart Forms to PDF output

In this recipe, we will see how the form output may be suppressed and returned as internal table to our calling program and then how a PDF is generated within the program. We will set values to some fields in the control structure of the Smart Form and use it with the `CONVERT_OTF_2_PDF` function module.

How to do it...

For generating PDF output without showing the Smart Form on the screen, follow these steps:

1. First, we define two structures `cont_parameters` and `myoutput` based on the dictionary structures `ssfctrlop` and `ssfcrescl` respectively.

    ```
    data : cont_parameters  type ssfctrlop.
    data : myoutput type ssfcrescl  .
    ```

2. Then, we assign `'X'` to the `setotf` and `no_dialog` fields of the control structure.

    ```
    cont_parameters-getotf = 'X'.
    cont_parameters-no_dialog = 'X'.
    ```

3. The dynamic call of the Smart Form function module is then carried out.

```
call function myfunction
   exporting
     control_parameters = cont_parameters
   importing
     job_output_info    = myoutput
   tables
     employee_table     = employees
   exceptions
     formatting_error   = 1
     internal_error     = 2
     send_error         = 3
     user_canceled      = 4
     others             = 5.
```

4. Appropriate variables are then defined. The most important is the internal table pdf_content used for storing the converted PDF output of the form. The filesize and doc_archive tables are necessary for calling the function module CONVERT_OTF_2_PDF.

```
data : pdf_content type standard table of tline.
data : filesize type i.
data : doc_archive  type standard table of docs.
```

5. The function module CONVERT_OTF_2_PDF is then called. The OTF parameter passes the value of the field otfdata of the myoutput structure.

```
call function 'CONVERT_OTF_2_PDF'
   importing
     bin_filesize   = filesize
   tables
     otf            = myoutput-otfdata
     lines          = pdf_content
     doctab_archive = doc_archive.
```

How it works...

The control structure fields `no_dialog` and the `getotf` are assigned the value `'X'`. This ensures that the form output is suppressed but the form generated is returned to the program in `otf` format. The call to the `Smart Form` function module (stored in the variable `myfunction`) returns to the program the `otf` format in the `otfdata` field of the `myoutput` structure.

We then pass this `otfdata` to the function module `CONVERT_OTF_2_PDF`. The function module converts the smart form `otf` to a PDF and stores it in the internal table `pdf_content` passed to the function module for table `lines`. The PDF file may then be saved on the desktop using the method `CL_GUI_FRONTEND_SERVICES=>GUI_DOWNLOAD`, or e-mailed to another user.

See also

▶ http://help.sap.com/saphelp_nw70/helpdata/EN/27/67443cc0063415e
   10000000a11405a/frameset.htm

Applying sorting and subtotaling to table fields

In this recipe, we will see how we can sort a given table within the Smart Form and calculate totals based on a particular field as the sort criterion. In this recipe, we will use an example of employees and their allowances and amounts.

Getting ready

For this recipe, we define a structure in the database **ZST9_EMPLOYEES** comprising three fields **PERNR**, **ALLOWANCE**, and **AMOUNT**. We define a table type also based on this structure, as shown in the following screenshot:

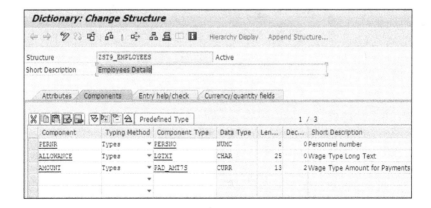

A table **EMPLOYEE_TABLE** (based on the defined dictionary table type) is included in the **TABLES** tab of the Smart Form interface, and a corresponding work area **WA_EMPLOYEE** in the global definition.

A table is then created on the Smart Form layout. The loop of the table is shown as follows:

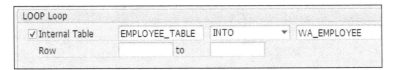

Appropriate texts are created within the cells in order to print the employee number, allowance, and amount values passed. A program is then created and the Smart Form is called. A tabular output is generated.

Emp.No	Allowance	Amount
00000012	Basic Pay	11,000.00
00000012	HR Allowance	1,000.00
00000012	Transport	1,300.00
00000017	Basic Pay	13,000.00

In this recipe, we will see how sorting along with totaling may be so that the total of each employee's allowance is printed at the end of each employee's details.

How to do it...

For subtotaling and sorting, proceed as follows:

1. Double-click the defined table node in the left-hand pane. In the right-hand pane, on the **Data** tab, within **Sort Criteria**, select the **Event on Sort End** checkbox. Also, enter PERNR as the field name.

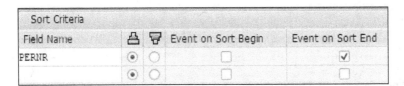

2. This will add a **PERNR Event on Sort End** node.

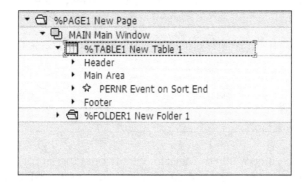

3. We define a subtotal variable in the global definition. This is a temporary storage variable for totals of each employee's allowances.

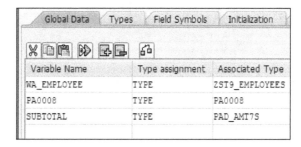

4. On the **Calculations** tab of the table, we enter the values shown in the following screenshot:

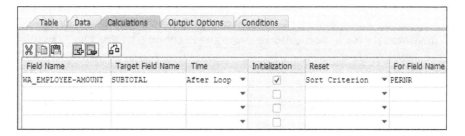

5. Right-click the **PERNR Event on Sort End** node to create a table line. Use the same line type used for the rows of the table (containing three cells).

6. For the second and third cell, we define texts outputting **SUBTOTAL** and **VARIABLE and SUBTOTAL** respectively.

7. Also, a line of code is added after the text that clears the **SUBTOTAL** variable.

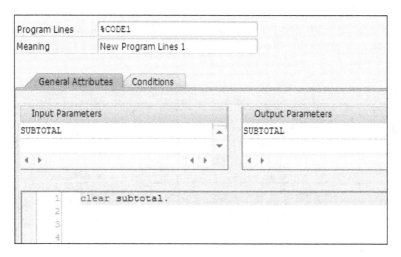

8. The final state will look like the one shown in following screenshot:

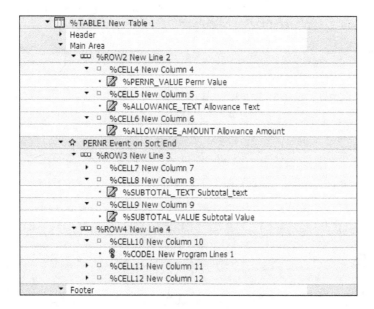

How it works...

The settings we did in the Smart Form will output the subtotal of the allowances of each employee as shown. At the end of each employee, the total allowances are calculated and printed.

Emp.No	Allowance	Amount
00000012	Basic Pay	11,000.00
00000012	HR Allowance	1,000.00
00000012	Transport	1,300.00
	Subtotal	13,300.00
00000017	Basic Pay	13,000.00
	Subtotal	13,000.00

The entries made on the **Calculation** tab of the table totals all the amounts of a particular **PERNR** field (the SORT criterion) and stores in the **SUBTOTAL** variable. The output will then be generated at the EVENT on SORT end. After that, we clear the old value of **SUBTOTAL** so that the value of the next employee may be calculated.

See also

▶ http://help.sap.com/saphelp_nw2004s/helpdata/en/8a/60da59394b11 d5b69b006094192fe3/frameset.htm

8

Working with SQL Trace

In this chapter, we will see recipes related to SQL trace such as:

- ▶ Carrying out SQL trace
- ▶ Generating and interpreting the trace result
- ▶ Carrying out restricted trace
- ▶ Filtering unwanted trace result entries
- ▶ Summarizing an SQL list and viewing table-related information
- ▶ Quickly finding the data source of a screen field
- ▶ Finding the data source of a field's hit list

Introduction

In *Chapter 5, Optimizing Programs*, we discussed the performance optimization and the tool Runtime Analyzer transaction SAT. This chapter explores useful recipes related to SQL trace. We will see in this chapter how the SQL trace may be used in order to optimize a program by pinpointing the exact "problem areas" in database-related code. Also, we will use the SQL trace to find out the underlying data source (table name and field name) of a particular screen field. We assume that the reader has basic selects and optimization knowledge.

We will start with a brief explanation of the steps required in carrying out an SQL trace. In the subsequent recipe, we will see how the performance trace results may be interpreted. Also, we will see how we can access the various menu and toolbar functions of the list display. Our other recipes will be tips and tricks for finding out quickly the data source of screen fields and their *F4* helps.

Carrying out SQL trace

In this recipe, we will see how we can carry out an SQL trace. We will run the trace on the program RIBELF00 (Display Document Flow).

How to do it...

We will now carry out the following steps:

1. In one SAP session, open the transaction that is to be traced. In our case, we have to trace the program RIBELF00. We enter on transaction SE38 the program name in the field provided, and execute the program in order to display the selection screen. We will not execute the program, yet we will enter the input values on the selection screen.

2. Then, open another session and call transaction ST05. The screen appears, as shown in the following screenshot:

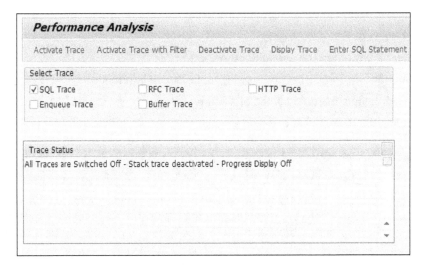

3. Make sure the SQL trace checkbox is on. Click the **Activate Trace** button on the toolbar. Make sure that before doing this, the message in the lower part of the screen reads, **All Traces are Switched Off...**.

4. Now return to the first SAP session and execute the report with the relevant input values, as shown in the following screenshot:

Order				
Order	200000	to	900000	⇨
Equipment		to		⇨
Functional Location		to		⇨
Customer		to		⇨
Created on		to		⇨
Entered by		to		⇨

5. Once the output is displayed, go back to the SQL trace session and click on the **Deactivate Trace** button.

6. Then, click on the **Display Trace** button to generate the results.

How it works...

The **Activate Trace** button switches on the database trace. Then, any database-related activity related to SELECT and UPDATE statements are recorded. This may be displayed using the **Display Trace** button.

For carrying out a trace, you may even stop a program in the debugger in one session and then switch on the trace in another session. In addition, you may enter data on a SAP entry screen and just before pressing the **Save** button, switch on the SQL trace, and then switch off the trace after **Save** is pressed and the success message appears. In this case, all database statements are executed between the time the **Save** button is pressed and the message display are recorded.

It is recommended that you run only the concerned program transaction and stop any other activity. Otherwise, many irrelevant entries will also be included in the trace result, making it very large and difficult to read.

The next recipe will cover how the trace results may be displayed.

Generating and interpreting the trace result

In this recipe, we will generate the results of the trace carried in the previous recipe, _Carrying out SQL trace_. The mentioned recipe should be completed in order to proceed with this one. We will then interpret the results in order to get a better idea of the various tables and their access times involved.

How to do it...

We will now carry out the following steps:

1. From the main screen of the transaction ST05, click on the **Display Trace** button. This will take you to the screen, as shown in the following screenshot:

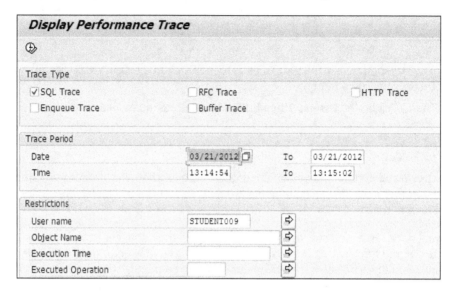

2. The **User name** field and the **Date** and **Time** fields appear by default. You may change the **Date** and **Time** fields, and also enter data in the other fields if desired.

3. Then press *F8*. This will display the **Performance Trace**.

How it works...

When the **Display Trace** option is chosen, the performance trace is displayed. All the database activities (database access and database update statements) that were recorded during the time between the trace on and off duration are displayed, as shown in the following screenshot:

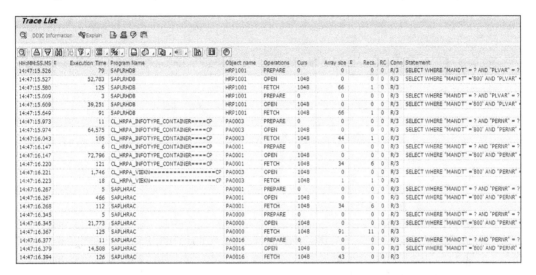

In this example, since we had a report that only reads data from the database, no database update statements are involved.

Each statement that is contained in the ABAP program is subdivided into various operations such as PREPARE, OPEN, and FETCH. There are various useful columns in the displayed performance trace. The trace results contain the table name (Object name) that refers to the table from which data is read. The duration of the statement/operation is also shown in milliseconds, along with the name of the program that contained the ABAP statement in question. Most importantly, the number of records fetched from the database as a result of the FETCH operation is also shown.

The various operations are as follows:

▸ **PREPARE**: After the PREPARE operation, the Open SQL statement is translated into native SQL of the underlying database. The statement is not assigned the parameter values for which the data is to be read (that is, the WHERE clause specification). Double-clicking the particular PREPARE operation line will show this detail. The data access method (execution plan) is determined at this point.

```
SELECT
  "MANDT" AS c ,"OTYPE" AS c ,"OBJID" AS c ,"PLVAR" AS c ,"RSIGN" AS c ,
  "RELAT" AS c ,"ISTAT" AS c ,"PRIOX" AS c ,"BEGDA" AS c ,"ENDDA" AS c ,
  "VARYF" AS c ,"SEQNR" AS c ,"INFTY" AS c ,"OTJID" AS c ,"SUBTY" AS c ,
  "AEDTM" AS c ,"UNAME" AS c ,"REASN" AS c ,"HISTO" AS c ,"ITXNR" AS c ,
  "SCLAS" AS c ,"SOBID" AS c ,"PROZT" AS c ,"ADATANR" AS c
FROM
  "HRP1001"
WHERE
  "MANDT" = ? AND "PLVAR" = ? AND "OTJID" = ? AND "SUBTY" = ? AND "ISTAT" = ?
  AND "BEGDA" <= ? AND "ENDDA" >= ?   /* R3:SAPLRHDB:2992 T:HRP1001 */
```

▸ **OPEN**: The OPEN operation opens a cursor declared earlier using the DECLARE operation, and assigns the relevant comparison values to the WHERE clause fields. The records fulfilling the selection criteria are read from the database table using the relevant execution plan (involving either a sequential or an index search). Until here, the records are at the database level.

```
SQL Statement

  SELECT
    "MANDT" AS c ,"OTYPE" AS c ,"OBJID" AS c ,"PLVAR" AS c ,"RSIGN" AS c ,
    "RELAT" AS c ,"ISTAT" AS c ,"PRIOX" AS c ,"BEGDA" AS c ,"ENDDA" AS c ,
    "VARYF" AS c ,"SEQNR" AS c ,"INFTY" AS c ,"OTJID" AS c ,"SUBTY" AS c ,
    "AEDTM" AS c ,"UNAME" AS c ,"REASN" AS c ,"HISTO" AS c ,"ITXNR" AS c ,
    "SCLAS" AS c ,"SOBID" AS c ,"PROZT" AS c ,"ADATANR" AS c
  FROM
    "HRP1001"
  WHERE
    "MANDT" = ? AND "PLVAR" = ? AND "OTJID" = ? AND "SUBTY" = ? AND "ISTAT" = ?
    AND "BEGDA" <= ? AND "ENDDA" >= ?   /* R3:SAPLRHDB:2992 T:HRP1001 */   /*unc.
    rd.*/

Variable

A0(CH,3)   = 800
A1(CH,2)   = 01
A2(CH,10)  = P 00000001
A3(CH,4)   = A209
A4(CH,1)   = 1
A5(NU,8)   = 99991231
A6(NU,8)   = 19000101
```

Note the difference between the SQL statement pertaining to the OPEN and the
PREPARE statement.

> ▸ **FETCH**: Finally, the FETCH operation transfers the record(s) matching the criteria
> specified to the application server. The various records read are shown in the
> **Records** column.

There's more...

If a FOR ALL ENTRIES construct is involved, the data records are not read by a single set of
operations. Rather, multiple sets of **PREPARE-OPEN-FETCH** operations are involved. You may
see them in the following screenshot:

COEP	OPEN	9233	0	0	0	R/3	SELECT WHERE T_00 ."MANDT" ='800' AND T_00 ."KOKRS" ='1000'
COEP	FETCH	9233	512	54	0	R/3	
COEP	PREPARE	0	0	0	0	R/3	SELECT WHERE T_00 ."MANDT" = ? AND T_00 ."KOKRS" = ? AND T_00 ."BELNR" ▪
COEP	OPEN	9233	0	0	0	R/3	SELECT WHERE T_00 ."MANDT" ='800' AND T_00 ."KOKRS" ='1000'
COEP	FETCH	9233	512	53	0	R/3	
COEP	PREPARE	0	0	0	0	R/3	SELECT WHERE T_00 ."MANDT" = ? AND T_00 ."KOKRS" = ? AND T_00 ."BELNR" ▪
COEP	OPEN	9233	0	0	0	R/3	SELECT WHERE T_00 ."MANDT" ='800' AND T_00 ."KOKRS" ='1000'
COEP	FETCH	9233	512	54	0	R/3	
COEP	PREPARE	0	0	0	0	R/3	SELECT WHERE T_00 ."MANDT" = ? AND T_00 ."KOKRS" = ? AND T_00 ."BELNR" ▪
COEP	OPEN	9234	0	0	0	R/3	SELECT WHERE T_00 ."MANDT" ='800' AND T_00 ."KOKRS" ='1000'
COEP	FETCH	9234	512	56	0	R/3	

If database update statements are involved, the EXEC operation appears in the Trace List.
In addition, in this case, the **Records** column will show the number of records updated in the
database table rather than the records read.

At the end of the list is the total of the number of fetched records and the total execution time.

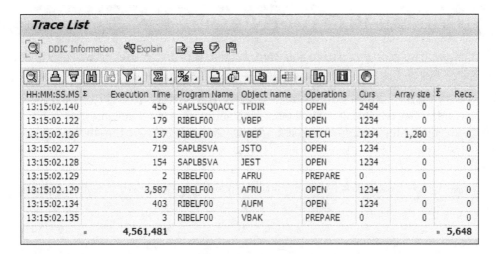

Also, we can go to the ABAP code and display the execution plan from the performance **Trace List**. For finding out the exact location, in the ABAP program, of the corresponding statement shown in the **Trace List**, keep the cursor on a line showing an OPEN operation, and then click the ( ) icon from the toolbar. This will take you to the exact line in the program that generated the entry in the trace list.

In addition, for viewing the execution plan of a particular statement, select the FETCH operation line and click the toolbar button **Explain**. The details about the index used (or whether the search within the table was sequential) are shown. After clicking the **Explain** button, the screen looks like the one shown in the following screenshot (for a MS SQL server database). Click on the **EXPLAIN TREE** tab to view whether an index has been used for the statement in question.

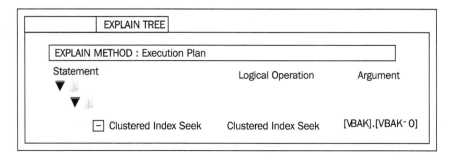

See also

▸ http://blogs.msdn.com/b/saponsqlserver/archive/2009/05/10/sql-
   execution-plans-part-3-how-to-get-the-plan.aspx?Redirected=true

Carrying out restricted trace

Until now, we have seen how we are able carry out the trace on our user, as well as without any restrictions. In this recipe, we will see how a trace may be carried out on other users along with additional imposed restrictions.

Problem areas may be difficult to find at first. One approach is to run an unrestricted trace in order to find out the problematic program/transaction or a user. We may then run a "restricted" trace focusing only on the particular program or user.

In addition, one more use of a restricted trace is when we run multiple programs/transactions in various sessions. We may run a time-consuming report of Finance (FI) module in one session, and at the same time, want to trace an HR transaction code, say PA30, in another session. We can then specify the transaction code of HR in the restriction criteria of a restricted trace. In this way, the trace records of the FI report that is running or any other activity in any session will not be included in our trace results.

How to do it...

1. For carrying out a trace that is restricted, call transaction ST05.

2. On the main screen, click the **Activate Trace with Filter** button. The **Set Restrictions for Writing Trace** dialog appears.

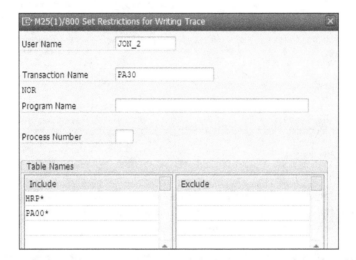

3. Enter the **User Name** in the field provided. We enter the value JON_2. In the **Transaction Name** field, we enter the transaction code PA30. In the **Include Table Names** area, we enter HRP* and PA00*. In addition, if we know the **Process Number** of the process, we can simply enter the three digit **Process Number** in the field provided. This will only trace the process number in question.

4. Press *Enter* when all entries are done. The trace is on. When we like to switch off the trace, the same **Deactivate Trace** button is used.

How it works...

In this recipe, we have switched on the trace for the user **JON_2** and focused only on the transaction PA30 and also the tables whose names start with either **HRP** or **PA**. The trace file will therefore look like the following screenshot:

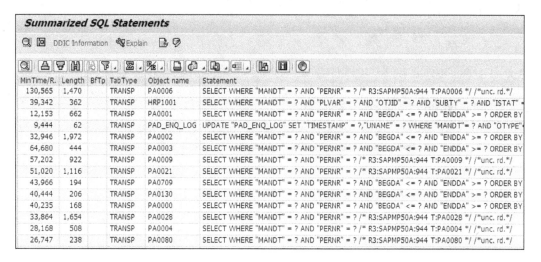

MinTime/R.	Length	BfTp	TabType	Object name	Statement
130,565	1,470		TRANSP	PA0006	SELECT WHERE "MANDT" = ? AND "PERNR" = ? /* R3:SAPMP50A:944 T:PA0006 */ /*unc. rd.*/
39,342	362		TRANSP	HRP1001	SELECT WHERE "MANDT" = ? AND "PLVAR" = ? AND "OTJID" = ? AND "SUBTY" = ? AND "ISTAT" =
12,153	662		TRANSP	PA0001	SELECT WHERE "MANDT" = ? AND "PERNR" = ? AND "BEGDA" <= ? AND "ENDDA" >= ? ORDER BY
9,444	62		TRANSP	PAD_ENQ_LOG	UPDATE "PAD_ENQ_LOG" SET "TIMESTAMP" = ?,"UNAME" = ? WHERE "MANDT"= ? AND "OTYPE"
32,946	1,972		TRANSP	PA0002	SELECT WHERE "MANDT" = ? AND "PERNR" = ? AND "BEGDA" <= ? AND "ENDDA" >= ? ORDER BY
64,680	444		TRANSP	PA0003	SELECT WHERE "MANDT" = ? AND "PERNR" = ? AND "BEGDA" <= ? AND "ENDDA" >= ? ORDER BY
57,202	922		TRANSP	PA0009	SELECT WHERE "MANDT" = ? AND "PERNR" = ? /* R3:SAPMP50A:944 T:PA0009 */ /*unc. rd.*/
51,020	1,116		TRANSP	PA0021	SELECT WHERE "MANDT" = ? AND "PERNR" = ? /* R3:SAPMP50A:944 T:PA0021 */ /*unc. rd.*/
43,966	194		TRANSP	PA0709	SELECT WHERE "MANDT" = ? AND "PERNR" = ? AND "BEGDA" <= ? AND "ENDDA" >= ? ORDER BY
40,444	206		TRANSP	PA0130	SELECT WHERE "MANDT" = ? AND "PERNR" = ? AND "BEGDA" <= ? AND "ENDDA" >= ? ORDER BY
40,235	168		TRANSP	PA0000	SELECT WHERE "MANDT" = ? AND "PERNR" = ? AND "BEGDA" <= ? AND "ENDDA" >= ? ORDER BY
33,864	1,654		TRANSP	PA0028	SELECT WHERE "MANDT" = ? AND "PERNR" = ? /* R3:SAPMP50A:944 T:PA0028 */ /*unc. rd.*/
28,168	508		TRANSP	PA0004	SELECT WHERE "MANDT" = ? AND "PERNR" = ? /* R3:SAPMP50A:944 T:PA0004 */ /*unc. rd.*/
26,747	238		TRANSP	PA0080	SELECT WHERE "MANDT" = ? AND "PERNR" = ? /* R3:SAPMP50A:944 T:PA0080 */ /*unc. rd.*/

There's more...

It is recommended that for performance optimization, we first run a trace without restrictions. We can then filter the results according to the various criteria of the selection fields or the **Display Trace** screen. We will see how this is done in the next recipe.

Filtering unwanted trace result entries

SQL performance trace files may be very huge and searching for tables may be a time-consuming task. In this recipe, we will see how we can filter irrelevant values from the SQL trace list. We assume that an unrestricted trace like the one shown in the first recipe, *Carrying out SQL Trace* has already been done.

How to do it...

1. After a trace has been carried out from the transaction ST05 screen, press the **Display Trace** button. The portion of the screen that appears is shown in the following screenshot:

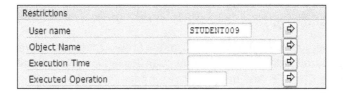

2. The **User name** appears as default. You may enter a particular table name in the **Object Name** field, or a set of letters followed by asterisk (*****), such as VB* or PA* may be entered.

3. You may enter one or more operations in the **Executed Operation** field.

4. Also, we can enter a value for execution time with a greater-than (GT) operator.

How it works...

Instead of the huge trace list, only the values that pertain to the values entered on the **Display Trace** screen are shown. For example, if we enter VB*, all tables with names beginning with VB such as VBAK, VBRP, and so on will be shown. Also, if we enter the EXEC operation, only this operation's entries will be displayed. Similarly, the **Execution Time** is taken into account. For finding the slowest statements, the **Execution Time** field is very important. We can enter a value greater than the particular time duration. This will list all costly statements that we need to optimize.

Summarizing a SQL list and viewing table-related information

For each SQL statement in the program, the trace list shows a number of lines corresponding to the various operations, thus making the list very huge in size. We can see a summarized (view), and also apply table-related functions on the list values. In this recipe, we will see how to apply these functions.

How to do it...

For displaying summarized information, carry out the following steps:

1. From the SQL list, choose the menu option **Trace List | Summarize Trace by SQL Statement**. Alternately, you may use the keys *Shift + F8*.

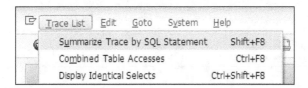

2. In order to see a list of all identical selects within the trace, choose the menu option **Display Identical Selects**.

3. For generating a combined view for various table accesses and without the details of the SQL statement, use the menu option **Trace List | Combined Table Accesses** or use keys *Ctrl + F8*. You may also see an Aggregate table view from the Combined Table Accesses list, by using the menu path **Table List | Aggregate**.

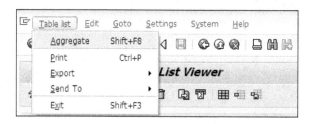

How it works...

The summarized table view generates a shorter list, as shown in the following screenshot. The details of the operations such as OPEN, FETCH, and so on are omitted, and only one line exists for each SELECT or UPDATE statement used in the program. In addition, no detail of the SQL statement or parameters passed from the program for the WHERE clause is shown. If there are multiple accesses to a particular table, each access is shown in the list along (in the following screenshot) with the time at which the access was made:

Combined Table Accesses

Work Proc. No.	PType	Client	HH:MM:SS.MS	Transaction	Table Name	Statement	Σ Records	Σ Access Time	DB Connection
4	DIA	800	14:47:15.527	PA30	HRP1001	SELECT	1	52,908	R/3
	DIA	800	14:47:15.609	PA30	HRP1001	SELECT	1	39,342	R/3
	DIA	800	14:47:15.974	PA30	PA0003	SELECT	1	64,680	R/3
	DIA	800	14:47:16.147	PA30	PA0001	SELECT	6	72,917	R/3
	DIA	800	14:47:16.221	PA30	PA0003	SELECT	1	1,764	R/3
	DIA	800	14:47:16.267	PA30	PA0001	SELECT	6	578	R/3
	DIA	800	14:47:16.345	PA30	PA0000	SELECT	11	21,898	R/3
	DIA	800	14:47:16.379	PA30	PA0016	SELECT	0	14,634	R/3
	DIA	800	14:47:16.405	PA30	PA0041	SELECT	2	17,810	R/3
	DIA	800	14:47:16.467	PA30	PA0000	SELECT	1	40,235	R/3
	DIA	800	14:47:16.627	PA30	PA0709	SELECT	1	43,966	R/3
	DIA	800	14:47:16.678	PA30	PA0105	SELECT	0	16,919	R/3
	DIA	800	14:47:16.804	PA30	PA0003	SELECT	1	2,447	R/3
	DIA	800	14:47:17.002	PA30	PA0322	SELECT	0	6,912	R/3
	DIA	800	14:47:17.058	PA30	PAD_ENQ_LOG	UPDATE	1	56,702	R/3
	DIA	800	14:47:17.114	PA30	PAD_ENQ_LOG	UPDATE	1	9,444	R/3
	DIA	800	14:47:17.160	PA30	PA0001	SELECT	6	833	R/3
	DIA	800	14:47:17.164	PA30	PA0003	SELECT	1	2,432	R/3
	DIA	800	14:47:17.250	PA30	PA0130	SELECT	0	40,444	R/3

If we further want to refine and want an **Aggregate Table Accesses** list showing the total time taken for accessing a particular table along with the number of records read and the number of times the respective table was accessed throughout the trace period, we will go for the **Aggregate Table Accesses** view. For each table accesses, there is a single line shown in this list, as shown in the following screenshot:

Aggregated Table Accesses

Transaction	Table Name	Σ Access to tables	Statement	Σ Records	Σ Access Time	Σ Percentage	DB Connection
PA30	HRP1001	4	SELECT	4	93,305	10.0	R/3
	PA0000	6	SELECT	36	68,192	7.3	R/3
	PA0001	7	SELECT	37	78,408	8.4	R/3
	PA0002	4	SELECT	5	68,789	7.3	R/3
	PA0003	6	SELECT	6	72,210	7.7	R/3
	PA0004	1	SELECT	0	28,168	3.0	R/3
	PA0006	1	SELECT	1	130,565	13.9	R/3
	PA0007	1	SELECT	2	20,108	2.2	R/3
	PA0009	1	SELECT	1	57,202	6.1	R/3
	PA0016	2	SELECT	0	15,073	1.6	R/3
	PA0021	1	SELECT	1	51,020	5.4	R/3
	PA0028	1	SELECT	0	33,864	3.6	R/3
	PA0041	2	SELECT	4	18,302	2.0	R/3
	PA0080	1	SELECT	0	26,747	2.9	R/3
	PA0105	2	SELECT	0	17,489	1.9	R/3
	PA0130	1	SELECT	0	40,444	4.3	R/3
	PA0322	1	SELECT	0	6,912	0.7	R/3
	PA0709	2	SELECT	2	44,412	4.7	R/3
	PAD_ENQ_LOG	2	UPDATE	2	66,146	7.1	R/3
		46		101	937,356	100.1	

We also have a percentage column that will show the table whose access takes the most percentage of the runtime.

If the appropriate path is chosen, a list of identical selects may also be generated.

List Identical Select Statements

DDIC Information   Explain

Σ Executions	Σ Durtn	Σ Records	Time/Exec	Rec/Exec	AvgTime/R.	MinTime/R.	Length	BfTp	TabType	Obj. name	Statement
3	27,554	3	9,185	1.0	9,185	427	148		TRANSP	REPOTEXT	SELECT WHERE "PROGNAME" ='RIBELF00' AND
2	17,489	0	8,745	0.0	8,745	570	704		TRANSP	PA0105	SELECT WHERE "MANDT" ='800' AND "USRTY"
2	1,231	12	616	6.0	103	96	662		TRANSP	PA0001	SELECT WHERE "MANDT" ='800' AND "PERNR"
2	1,144	2	572	1.0	572	531	42	FUL	TRANSP	EUOBJ	SELECT WHERE "ID" ='O'
2	1,065	2	533	1.0	533	522	3,052	CUST	TRANSP	VARI	SELECT WHERE "MANDT" ='000' AND "RELID"
4	984	0	246	0.0	246	170	0				COMMIT
15	49,467	19									

Here, the number of times the `SELECT` statement was executed is shown, along with the number of records read and the duration of the execution. Reducing/eliminating the number of identical selects (particularly the more expensive ones in terms of execution time) will greatly help in performance optimization. They are just repeated `SELECT` statements that only consume runtime and resources.

Quickly finding the data source of a screen field

In this recipe, we will see a quick method that will enable us to find the database table and field in which the data of a particular SAP screen field is stored. We will use the SQL trace and the EXEC operation for this purpose.

Getting ready

We will use `PA30` and its Infotype `0002` in this example transaction. We assume that we are not sure which table name and field stores the first name of an employee.

How to do it...

Proceed as follows:

1. Call transaction `PA30`. Enter an employee number in the field provided. Also enter `0002` (personal data)in the **Infotype** field, and then click on the **Change** button.

2. Once you are in the Change Screen, change the **First Name** of the employee in the relevant field. Do not press the **Save** button.

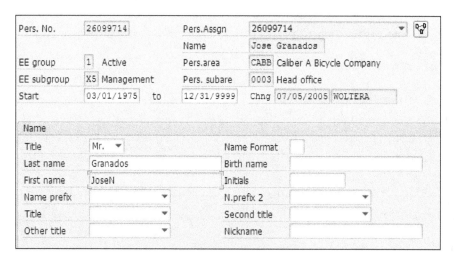

3. In another session, switch on the SQL trace.

4. Go back to the transaction PA30 and save the data.

5. Once the save message appears, go back to the SQL trace transaction and click the **Display Trace** button.

6. On the **Display Trace** selection screen, enter EXEC* in the Operation field and take the **Trace List**.

How it works...

We used a small trick to find out the data source of a screen field. In order to avoid searching through a lot of table names by using display of data, we only focused on the relevant field and used a change operation. Since we changed a record, the corresponding field must be updated in the database. Also the operation name must begin with EXEC. So, we generated a list and searched for only EXEC operations. From this, we found out the name of the table **PA0002** shown in the list. When we look at this closely, we see that the value we entered in the first name field was passed for update in the field **VORNA**.

Finding the data source of a field's hit list

In this recipe, we will use the SQL trace in order to find out the data source of the *F4* help of a screen field. The aim of this recipe is to devise a strategy that will make the procedure for finding the data source quicker and easier.

Getting ready

We will use the transaction SE24 as an example. We assume that we are not sure of the various tables in which the class names and descriptions reside. We may take the **Class Field** input help for names starting with any letter. For our example, we view a list of all classes with names starting from **y**.

How to do it...

Proceed as follows:

1. In one session, call transaction SE24. Enter y* in the **Object type** field.

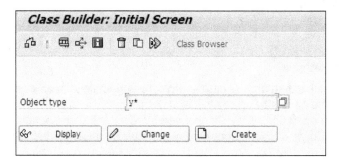

2. In another session, call transaction ST05 and switch on the trace using the **Activate Trace** button.

3. Now go back to the transaction SE24 and press *F4* while keeping the cursor on the **Object type** field. The list of values will appear.

4. Now go back to the ST05 screen, switch off the trace, and take the display of the trace.

How it works...

When we pressed *F4*, the classes whose names start with **Y** appear as shown in the following screenshot:

Object Type Name	Short description
YCHCL_B11A_EINKAUF	
YCHCL_B11A_LAGER	
YCHCL_B11A_MATERIAL	
YCHCL_B13A_AGENT	
YCHCL_B13A_SINGLETON	
YCHCL_B13B_AGENT	
YCHCL_B13B_SINGLETON	
YCHCL_B14B_2DIVISION	
YCHCL_B14B_2MULTIPLIKATION	
YCHCL_D10A_RECHNER	
YCHCLASS_FLUGAUSWERTUNG	
YCHCLASS_RECHNER	
YCHIF_B10A_BESTANDSBUCHUNG	
YCHIF_B10B_EINAUSZAEHLUNG	
YCHIF_B14B_1RECHNER	
YSVMA_TGT_DYNAMIC_VALUES	Disjunction ID CACS_TGT_DYNAMIC_VALUES
YTEL05_TGT_DYNAMIC_VALUES	Disjunction ID CACS_TGT_DYNAMIC_VALUES

M25(2)/800 Repository Info System: Class/Interface Find (36 Hits)

The number of entries fetched (number of the entries in the hit list) is also shown. In our system, we get 39 hits. This figure is very important and will be used later.

Then, we take the **Combined Table Accesses** to see which table access shows 39 records fetched. We find two tables **SEOCLASS** and **TADIR** from which 39 records are read. After looking at the two tables, we find that **SEOCLASS** contains the class names. For description we can go the class text table **SEOCLASSTX**.

Work Proc. No.	PType	Clie...	HH:MM:SS.MS	Transaction	Table Name	Stateme...	Σ Records Σ	Access Time
2	DIA	800	16:16:43.061	SE24	SEOCLASS	SELECT	39	1,462
2	DIA	800	16:16:43.082	SE24	TADIR	SELECT	39	80,101

Combined Table Accesses

Another method for arriving at the text table can be used. For the list shown in our system for classes beginning with **Y**, we have only four descriptions shown with the rest being blanks. If we further look at the trace list, we find that the table **SEOCLASSTX** is accessed and four records are shown as accessed (for blank texts, no corresponding records are fetched).

9
Code Inspector

In this chapter, we will see recipes related to the Code Inspector tool. We will look at:

- ▶ Carrying out quick code inspection
- ▶ Carrying out a full-fledged inspection
- ▶ Carrying out database-specific performance checks
- ▶ Suppressing messages using pseudo comments
- ▶ Searching for ABAP statement patterns and tokens within code
- ▶ Creating your own Code Inspector checks

Introduction

The Code Inspector allows you to check your program for consistency, performance, and quality. It also allows you to search for patterns of ABAP statements or tokens within a program. The variable-naming convention adherence may also be verified. Unlike SQL trace and SAT tool, the Code Inspector does not execute the program. It only checks the syntax, and some times, depending on the checks selected, refers to the dictionary attributes of the table(s) involved.

Some of the categories of checks are shown as follows:

- ▶ **Performance**
- ▶ **Security**
- ▶ **General**
- ▶ **Syntax**
- ▶ **Robust Programming**
- ▶ **Search Function**

For programs, the simplest way of running the Code Inspector is to use the **Menu** option and go to **Program | Check | Code Inspector**. However, you do not have control over the checks carried out through this **Menu** option. The default variant DEFAULT is executed and the set of checks contained within it are run. Moreover, only one program at a time may be inspected through the **Menu** option.

This chapter explores useful recipes related to the Code Inspector. We will start with the simplest method for running inspections on one program or a small number of programs. Then, a full-fledged inspection with further options such as inspection saving and background execution will be discussed. Next, we will focus on the performance checks and the various cases they generate messages in the inspection results. Search functions and the procedure for suppressing messages in exceptional cases will also be discussed. Finally, we will see how we can create our own checks and add it in the list of standard checks.

For simplicity sake, I will use the term programs throughout the chapter when inspection is involved. However, other repository objects may be included in the inspection for checking purpose.

Carrying out quick code inspection

In this recipe, we will see how we can do a quick code inspection on a single program or an object set. This is also termed as an Ad Hoc Inspection, since the inspection results are not saved and are not available for future.

How to do it...

We will now carry out these steps:

1. Call the SAP transaction SCII. Alternatively, you may go to transaction SCI and on the main screen, leave the **Inspection** field blank and press the **Create** button below the **Inspection Input** field. The screen appears as follows:

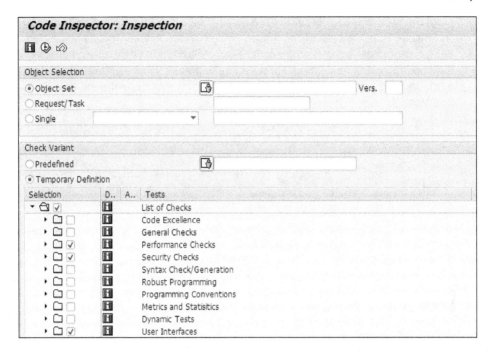

2. Select the **Single** radio-button option. From the list box, select the **Program** option and then enter the name of the program in the field provided. We enter the name of a previously created program ZST9_TEST_FOR_ALL_ENTRIES_2.

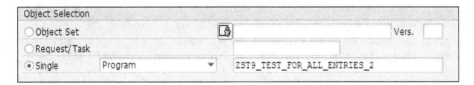

3. From the area in the lower part of the screen, we will select the option **Temporary Definition**. Then we select from the available checks that we want to be carried out. Selecting or deselecting a particular category will include or exclude all checks within the category in the inspection. For resetting to default values at any time, select the menu path by going to **Utilities | Set Initial**. Alternatively, use the toolbar button 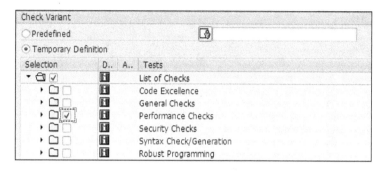 or press *F7*.

Check Variant			
○ Predefined			
● Temporary Definition			
Selection	D..	A..	Tests
▾ 🗀 ✓	ℹ		List of Checks
▸ 🗀 ☐	ℹ		Code Excellence
▸ 🗀 ☐	ℹ		General Checks
▸ 🗀 ✓	ℹ		Performance Checks
▸ 🗀 ☐	ℹ		Security Checks
▸ 🗀 ☐	ℹ		Syntax Check/Generation
▸ 🗀 ☐	ℹ		Robust Programming

4. Finally, press *F8* to carry out the inspection.

How it works...

The code of the program mentioned is scanned and checked based on the selected checks. The results are then displayed. The results comprise of tree structure (hierarchy) within nodes corresponding to the checkbox selected. There are three columns shown for messages within the different categories and then the checkboxes pertaining to the category in question. These are **Errors**, **Warnings**, and **Information** messages. You may open the various categories to see the detail of the messages found in each category. For example, we have two information messages found under **Use of Indexes in SELECT statement**.

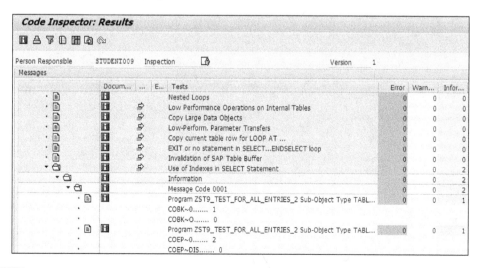

You may double-click on a particular message to reach the actual line of the code in the program that generated the message in question.

There's more...

While selecting the checks to be run from a particular category, a check may have further attributes. This is denoted by the ⇨ icon before it. You may click on the icon to view a list of the attributes and choose the ones relevant for your requirement. If you find an icon, it means that there is at least one value that must be set for the attributes contained within the check. Otherwise, selecting the check will produce an error and the inspection will not run.

▾ 🗀 ☑		⊞			Performance Checks
• 🖹 ☑		⊞	⇨		Analysis of WHERE Condition for SELECT
• 🖹 ☑		⊞	⇨		Analysis of WHERE Condition in UPDATE and DELETE
• 🖹 ☑		⊞			SELECT Statements That Bypass the Table Buffer
• 🖹 ☐		⊞			SELECT Statements with Subsequent CHECK
• 🖹 ☐		⊞			SELECTs in Loops

For running another inspection from the results screen, use the toolbar button ↩ .

For viewing the results in a compact display format, use the toolbar button ⊞ .

You have also the option of checking objects using object sets or the object contained within a request. However, the transaction has a limitation that you may not check over 50 objects and that the inspection may not be saved for reuse. In this case, the inspection is not stored and does not have a name (that is, it is anonymous). The next recipe will cover the ones that will overcome these limitations.

Carrying out a full-fledged inspection

For checking over 50 programs, you may use a reusable inspection. In this recipe, we will see how we can carry out such an inspection. Existing standard and custom variants may be used for this recipe. However, we will create variant and object sets from scratch. We will create a global inspection that will check all programs that begins with ZST9_*, and as well as create global variant and global object set.

As the name indicates, an object set is a collection of objects that may be comprising of ABAP programs, class, function groups, and classes. All repository objects may be assigned to an object set. An object set may also have a number of versions such as 001, 002, and so on.

How to do it...

Follow these steps:

1. Call the SAP transaction SCI. The screen appears as follows:

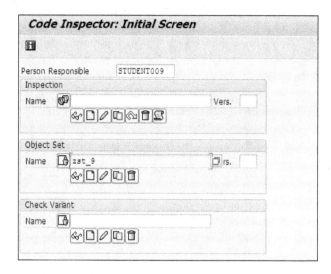

2. We will first create an object set (that is, the set of programs on which we need to run the inspection) of type global. For doing so, we will toggle the local icon 🖪 so that the global icon 🌐 appears. Then, enter a name (in our case, ZST9_OBJ_SET) in the field and then click the **Create** button.

3. The screen having the block appears as follows:

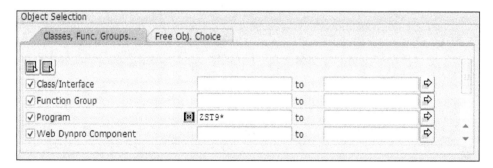

4. Enter `ZST9*` in the **Program** field within the **Object Selection** block. Then save your object set and come back to the initial screen of the transaction `SCI` (you will see **001** entered automatically in the **Version** field).

5. Next, we will define the variant. Enter a suitable name in the variant field. Then click the **Create** ⬚ button below the variant input field.

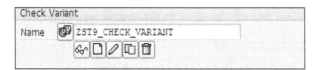

6. On the screen that appears, check the various checks that you need to include. You may include from various categories as discussed in the previous recipe.

7. We then create an inspection. Enter a suitable name in the **Name** field.

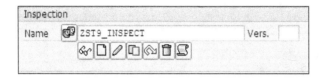

8. Finally, we run the inspection by pressing the **Execute** button.

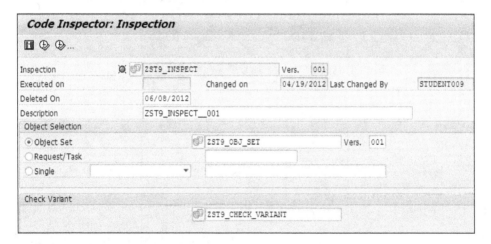

How it works...

Once the inspection is run, it takes some time for executing. The time taken depends on the number of programs included in the object set and the number of checks selected on the variant. Initially the inspection has the status **Not Yet Executed** ⬚.

This will carry out the inspection on programs having names that begin with ZST9_ based on the checks of the two categories that we selected, **Performance** and **Robust Programming**.

Once execution is completed, you may then click on the **Results** ⌸ icon to view the results. The new status will then be denoted by a green **Executed** icon.

After making corrections in the program(s) involved, rerun the inspection by generating a new version of the inspection. This may be done by the **Create New Version** ⟲ icon.

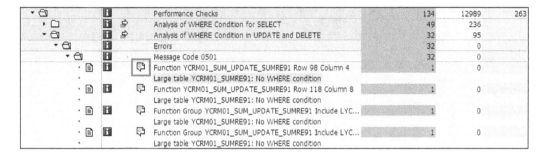

There's more...

You can also execute to schedule the inspection using as a background job. For this, click on the **Toolbar** button ⊕... in the inspection screen. The dialog box appears as follows:

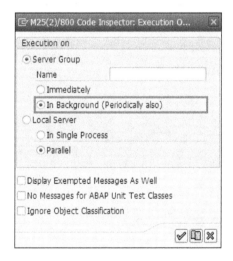

Enter a suitable name of the screen group and select the **In Background (Periodically also)** option. Then, you may then click ▥ (**Maintain Server group**) and enter further details.

You may schedule the inspection to be scheduled every week, or month, and so on.

▶ http://help.sap.com/saphelp_nw70ehp2/helpdata/en/82/
e6e8abfd59490e9e811940cc1027ef/frameset.htm

Carrying out database-specific performance checks

In this recipe, we will see a few examples of problems of the SELECT statements that the code inspector may highlight. This may help in improving performance of the program at the development stage. The performance checks are available in both the transactions SCI and SCII. We will emphasize on the selection of the database-specific performance checks during variant creation, and some of the typical statements/constructs that may be caught using code inspector.

How to do it...

1. Within the checks, expand the **Performance Checks** category.

2. From the list of checks that appear, select the checks shown in the following screenshot:

· 🖹 ☑	🗓	⮞	Analysis of WHERE Condition for SELECT
· 🖹 ☑	🗓	⮞	Analysis of WHERE Condition in UPDATE and DELETE
· 🖹 ☑	🗓		SELECT Statements That Bypass the Table Buffer
· 🖹 ☑	🗓		SELECT Statements with Subsequent CHECK
· 🖹 ☑	🗓		SELECTs in Loops
· 🖹 ☐	🗓		Changing Database Accesses in Loops
· 🖹 ☐	🗓		Nested Loops
· 🖹 ☐	🗓	⮞	Low Performance Operations on Internal Tables
· 🖹 ☐	🗓	⮞	Copy Large Data Objects
· 🖹 ☐	🗓	⮞	Low-Perform. Parameter Transfers
· 🖹 ☐	🗓	⮞	Copy current table row for LOOP AT ...
· 🖹 ☑	🗓	⮞	EXIT or no statement in SELECT...ENDSELECT loop
· 🖹 ☑	🗓	⮞	Invalidation of SAP Table Buffer
· 🖹 ☑	🗓	⮞	Use of Indexes in SELECT Statement
· 🖹 ☐	🗓	⮞	Instance Creation of BAdIs
· 🖹 ☑	🗓	⮞	Table Attributes Check

How it works...

The inspection checks the various program and highlights as warning statements that are performance statements. During this, the code inspector checks the syntax of the program and refers to the attributes and technical settings of the tables involved.

▶ CHECK or EXIT statements used within a SELECT statement instead of highlighting a WHERE clause.

- ▶ SELECT statements included in a loop such as a DO loop or within a loop at ITAB.

- ▶ Any SELECT statements that use the BYPASSING BUFFER addition.

- ▶ SELECT statements that are without a WHERE clause will be included in the warning. The following is one such example:

```
SELECT * FROM ZMYTAB INTO IT_TAB
```

- ▶ In addition to this, any table that is buffered but is included in a subquery will also result in a warning. This is because the buffering may not be used in this case, since the result of the subquery will be used at the database level in order to determine the selection set of the main SELECT statement.

```
SELECT FIELD1 INTO TABLE IT_FIELDS
FROM ZTAB1
WHERE FIELD2 EQ 'ABC' AND
        FIELD3 IN ( SELECT FIELD1 FROM ZTAB2
                    WHERE FIELD2 EQ 'Z1' AND FIELD3 EQ'A'.)
```

- ▶ If the ZTAB2 table is buffered, a warning message will appear in the result.

- ▶ Also, if the coding includes a SELECT statement on any table that is single-record buffered and a SELECT * ENDSELECT statement is used in the program, the corresponding statement will be highlighted in the results.

- ▶ Any query that may cause problems as far as the index selection is concerned will result in a message. In case, the WHERE clause of the query does not correspond to any index in the database for the table in question, a message appears in the inspection results. This hints that there is a possibility that a full sequential scan will be run for the query that could be very time-consuming.

- ▶ Also for indexes, if a particular field is not included in the WHERE clause—for example, if the index in the database comprise of fields A1, B1, and C1, and the WHERE clause of the query includes B1 and C1 but not A1, a warning is generated.

There's more...

Though the Code Inspector aid in writing better code, they have certain limitations. It is possible that a program generates no messages during the inspection, but may be slow when actually executed in QAS or production system.

The code is only analyzed and scanned along with the information pertaining to attributes of the dictionary tables used. The code is not executed (with actual data). The true performance test and analysis must be based on the actual execution tools such as transaction SAT and SQL trace. The checks of code inspector do not replace these tools.

► http://blogs.msdn.com/b/saponsqlserver/archive/2008/01/03/
using-sap-code-inspector-to-improve-quality-and-performance.
aspx

Suppressing messages using pseudo comments

In this recipe, we will see how we can suppress messages (generated from checks) of a particular category so that they do not appear in the results tree. It is not possible to hide all messages. However, there are some that may be hidden. These are known as exception.

In this recipe, we will see the different ways of finding out whether a particular message may be hidden and the code for hiding such messages using pseudo-comments.

How to do it...

Carry out these steps:

1. From the message results, navigate to the specific message that you like to suppress.

2. Expand the message to display its details.

3. Then, check if the icon 🗭 is displayed before the message as shown in the following screenshot:

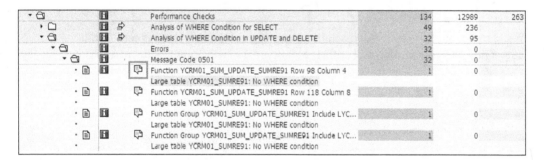

4. Click the 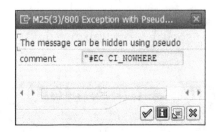 icon. This will display the dialog box, as shown in the following screenshot:

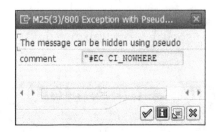

5. Note the comment. This may be included in the coding with the statement that generated the message as shown as follows:

```
SELECT * FROM ZTAB.                    "EC# CI_NOWHERE
```

How it works...

We used the results to find out whether the message may be suppressed or not. The presence o f the icon confirmed the possibility of hiding the NO_WHERE message. We then wrote the pseudo comment along with the SELECT statement. When we rerun the inspection, the SELECT statement with the pseudo comment will not be shown in the messages.

Suppose we need to suppress message for multiple SELECT statements, we need to write the corresponding pseudo comment correctly with each statement.

There's more...

We can also find out the pseudo comment of a check (if applicable) directly from the categories and checks display. For this, expand the relevant category folder in order to display the relevant check. Click the icon next to the check title. This will display the documentation of the check in a separate window. The pseudo comment will then be displayed at the end of the window as shown in the following screenshot:

Code Inspector

Analysis of the WHERE condition for UPDATE and DELETE

Table xyz: No WHERE condition

`UPDATE dbtab SET ...` or `DELETE FROM dbtab ...` without a WHERE condition
changes or deletes all the entries of the table. Check whether dataset to be changed or
deleted can be limited by a suitable WHERE condition.

Priority of the message is dependent on the size category of the table:
Size category   0, 1   => Warning
Size category   >= 2   => Error

Message can be suppressed using the pseudo comment "#EC CI_NOWHERE

Searching for ABAP statement patterns and tokens within code

In addition to the quality, performance checks, you may use the **Search Function** node
provided to formulate your own criteria in order to search for tokens and ABAP statement
patterns within the program(s) in question. In this recipe, we will see how this may be done.

How to do it...

Follow these steps:

1. In the variant specification, expand the **Search Function** node. This checks appear as
   shown in the following screenshot:

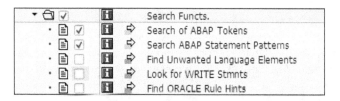

2. Click the 📝 icon to enter values for the **Search of ABAP Tokens** function.

3. Then, enter the search string in the **Search String** dialog box that appears.

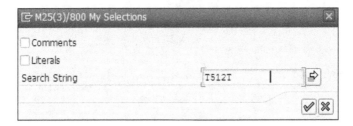

4. Enter one token in the field. For search of multiple tokens within the code, select the icon.

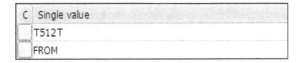

5. For searching for ABAP statement patterns, click the ⇨ icon for the check.

6. Then enter the single value in the field provided as shown in the following screenshot:

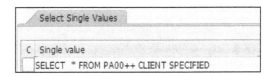

7. Finally run the inspection.

How it works...

The search for token function will search all the programs for the token FROM and T512T and will highlight when found in the results. Suppose the word FROM occurs twice and T512T appears once in the display, then total three messages will be displayed, that is, one for each found token.

For the pattern search, the programs are scanned for all SELECT statements that read data from tables having names beginning from PA00 followed by two characters such as PA0023, PA0008, and so on, followed by CLIENT SPECIFIED. The asterisk (*) after SELECT does not mean the code for fetching all fields of the database table but is a search function operator that means any set of tokens after the token SELECT such as *, PERNR INTO WA_PERNR, and so on.

Creating your own Code Inspector checks

In this recipe, we will see how we can create our own company specific checks and categories and display them with the standard check categories. For simplicity's sake, we will create a check by the name `My Check` under a new category **My Check** category. When this check will run, it will search for the token `T512T` in the program and will display the number of occurrences and the corresponding line numbers.

How to do it...

Follow these steps:

1. Call the SAP transaction `SE24`. Enter the class name `CL_CI_CATEGORY_TEMPLATE` in the class field and click the **Copy** button. The screenshot appears as follows:

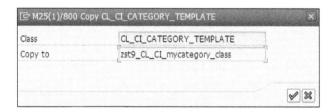

2. Open the new class in the **Change** mode and the `CONSTRUCTOR` method in the **Edit** mode. Add the code given in the following screenshot:

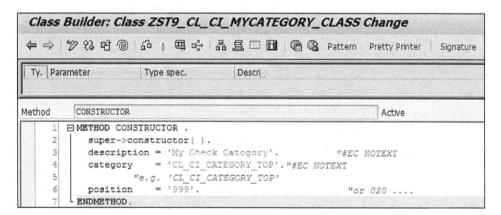

3. Next, we will create a copy of the `CL_CI_TEST_SCAN_TEMPLATE` class having the name `ZST9_CL_CI_CHECK`. In the `CONSTRUCTOR` method, add the code given in the following screenshot:

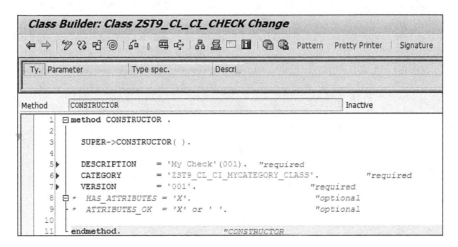

4. Add the code in the `run` method of the `Check` class, which is given in the following screenshot:

```
Method      RUN                                                      Active
    1  method run .
    2      if ref_scan is initial.
    3         check get( ) = 'X'.
    4      endif.
    5
    6      loop at ref_scan->tokens into token_wa  .
    7         if  token_wa-str eq 'T512T'.
    8            inform(
    9            p_kind          = c_note
   10            p_test          = 'ZST9_CL_CI_CHECK'
   11            p_line          = token_wa-row
   12            p_column        = token_wa-col
   13            p_param_1       = 'T512T found in program'
   14            p_code          = '0001' ).
   15         endif.
   16
   17      endloop.
   18
```

5. Add the code for the `GET_MESSAGE_TEXT` method of the class given in the following screenshot:

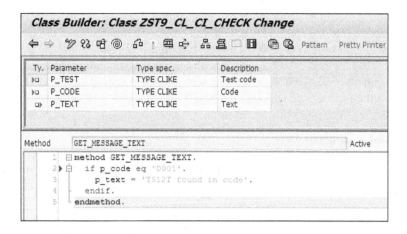

6. Activate the two classes. Make sure all components are also active.

7. Next we will do the necessary setting for displaying the newly created check and category along with standard checks in transactions SCI and SCII. Follow the menu path from the transaction SCI.

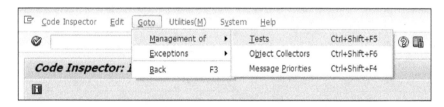

8. The two newly created classes will appear in the list that is displayed.

9. First, select the category class and click **Save**. A confirmation dialog box appears. Click **Yes**.

10. Repeat the last step for the check class.

How it works...

First we create the category class. We assign the necessary text (**My Check Category**) to be displayed in the CONSTRUCTOR method. The folder of the category will have this text displayed. Next the check class is defined and the text **My Check**. The linkage between the check class and the category class is done in the CONSTRUCTOR method of the check class.

The `run` method is executed when the check is executed. The `REF_SCAN` object supplied with the `TOKENS` table within the method is used for checking all the tokens of the program code that is to be included in the inspection. A loop is run on the `TOKENS` table and if the token `t512T` is found, the method `INFORM` is called with the necessary information supplied. We want the information message to be displayed along with the row and column of the token. The `P_CODE` value `0001` is also supplied, for which an appropriate text message is added in the `GET_MESSAGE_TEXT` method.

Then, both classes were activated.

Finally, the activation setting will display the new check and the category along with standard categories and checks for transactions `SCI` and `SCII`, as shown in the following screenshot:

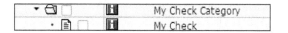

We ran the inspection for a program having two occurrences of the token `T512T`. The output of the results is shown in the following screenshot:

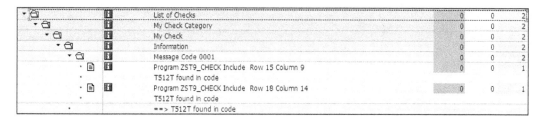

See also

- http://sapignite.com/enhancement-of-code-inspector/
- http://wiki.sdn.sap.com/wiki/display/Snippets/
  Code+Inspector+Check

10
Simple Transformations

In this chapter, we will see the following recipes for simple transformations:

- ▶ Creating simple transformations
- ▶ Creating transformations for structures and calling them in programs
- ▶ Creating transformations for internal tables
- ▶ Generating transformations for dictionary table types
- ▶ Downloading into Excel made easy using simple transformations

Introduction

This chapter explores useful recipes related to simple transformations. We will start with a brief overview of simple transformations and their structure. We will also discuss the process of the conversion of ABAP data into an XML stream (serialization) and the reverse process (deserialization).

We will start with a simple recipe in which we create a simple transformation that contains no root element but only XML literal elements and text. We will then see how to create transformations to interpret ABAP structures and internal tables. Next, we will see how we can quickly generate a transformation for a dictionary-defined table type using the transaction XSLT_TOOL.

There are two types of transformations possible via the transformation editor transaction XSLT_TOOL. They are the XSLT transformation the and simple transformation. XSLT transformations are defined using the XSLT programming language (and additional SAP-related statements). In addition to XSLT elements, ABAP calls are also allowed in XSLT transformations. They may be used, for example, to read data from the database. On the other hand, simple transformations are created using the simple transformation language.

Simple transformations allow XML-to-ABAP and ABAP-to-XML conversion, whereas for XSLT transformation, XML-to-XML and ABAP-to-ABAP transformations are also possible.

A recipe for calling transformations from ABAP programs will also be discussed. Finally, we will see a recipe that uses transformations to generate Excel output for internal table contents from within an ABAP program.

An entire discussion of Simple transformation commands is not possible in one chapter. However, we will see the most important and commonly used features. The primary emphasis will be on simple transformations for structure (simple and nested) as well internal tables.

Simple transformation is a meta language that allows the conversion of ABAP data into XML form and vice versa. The conversion of data into XML is known as **Serialization**. On the other hand, the processing of an XML stream in order to populate ABAP data objects is termed **Deserialization**. Simple transformations may be called from ABAP programs using the CALL TRANSFORMATION statement. Simple transformation programs are created using the transaction XSLT_TOOL.

A "simple" simple transformation is as follows:

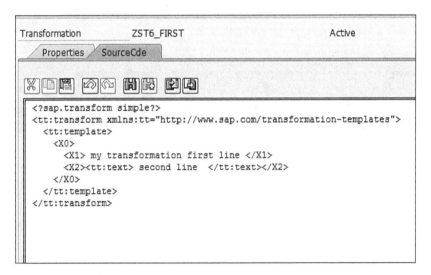

The first line signifies the type of the transformation. It is automatically inserted by the system while creating a new transformation.

All objects contained within < and > are termed XML elements. The XML elements may be divided into two categories, ST commands or literal elements.

ST commands serve a special purpose and have been defined in the namespace `http://www.sap.com/transformation-templates`. `tt:transform`, `tt:root`, and `tt:template` are XML elements that are ST commands (the prefix `tt` is used in the namespace for ST commands).

The literal XML elements are not contained in the namespace. `X0`, `X1`, and `X2` are the XML literal attributes. These are neither literal XML elements nor ST commands. `my transformation first line` in the figure is literal text. Within the literal XML element `X2`, there is the literal text `second line` defined with the identification using `<tt:text>`. The literal text between `<tt:text>` and `</tt:text>` is included in the serialization even if it comprises of only blank spaces. If the text is without identification (that is, if `<tt:text>` and `</tt:text>` are not used) the elements comprising of only blank spaces are ignored at the time of serialization.

Data roots are those that serve as the interfaces between the XML and the ABAP. Transformations that do not have a data root do not use any ABAP data during serialization and deserialization. At the minimum, one root element must be present for ABAP data to be used by the transformation.

The command `tt:value` is used for serialization of elementary data objects and fields of structures, whereas the command `tt:loop` is used for the serialization of internal tables. `tt:template` defines the block used to create the XML document from ABAP data during serialization (or the block used to extract ABAP data objects from an XML document when deserialization is carried out).

See also

- `http://help.sap.com/abapdocu_70/en/ABAPCALL_TRANSFORMATION.htm`
- `http://help.sap.com/saphelp_nw70ehp2/Helpdata/EN/7f/` `b7463c32a3fe13e10000000a114084/frameset.htmA`

Creating simple transformations

In this recipe, we will see how we can create a simple transformation comprising of literal texts and no data root. We will use the transaction `XSLT_TOOL`.

How to do it...

We will carry out the following steps:

1. Call the transaction `XSLT_TOOL`. Enter a suitable transformation name in the field provided (we give the name `zst6_first`). Then, press the **Create** button.

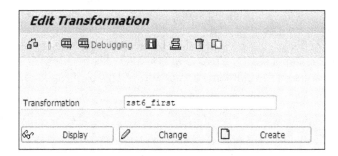

2. This will display a dialog box asking you for the description and the type of the transformation. Enter a short description in the field provided. From the **Transformation Type** list box, make sure to choose the option **Simple Transformation**. Then, press **Enter**.

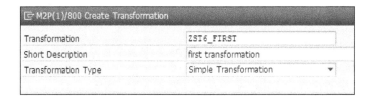

3. From the screen that appears, choose the **SourceCde** tab. You will find the source code editor filled with the basic code.

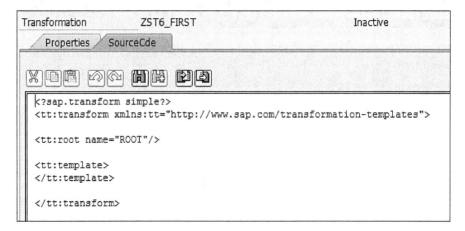

4. We will now write the code for our "simple" simple transformation. We will delete the root element. Within the template, we will add literal elements along with the necessary literal texts with and without identification. We create a literal element X0 that contains the literal elements X1 and X2. After the addition of the lines, the code appears as shown in following screenshot:

```
Transformation        ZST6_FIRST                    Active
   Properties   SourceCde

 [toolbar icons]

 <?sap.transform simple?>
 <tt:transform xmlns:tt="http://www.sap.com/transformation-templates">
   <tt:template>
     <X0>
       <X1> my transformation first line </X1>
       <X2><tt:text> second line  </tt:text></X2>
     </X0>
   </tt:template>
 </tt:transform>
```

How it works...

We created a simple transformation. It contains no root element, meaning that it can be passed any ABAP data object when called from an ABAP program.

When the transformation is serialized, the resulting XML code looks like the following code:

```
<X0>
    <X1>  my transformation first line </X1>
    <X2>  second line </X2>
</X0>
```

The literal element X1 contains literal text without identification, whereas X2 contains text with identification defined within <tt:text> and </tt:text>.

There's more...

To better understand the literal text with the identification feature, consider the following example:

```
Transformation Editor: Change Transformation ZST12_FIRST

←  →   ✎ ♔ ♣ │ ♠ │ ♞ ♝ Debugging   ♧ │ ♟ □ ♜ █ │ ♙  Tag Library   Pretty Printer

Transformation        ZST12_FIRST                        Active
   Properties  SourceCde

 1   <?sap.transform simple?>
 2   <tt:transform xmlns:tt="http://www.sap.com/transformation-templates">
 3
 4   <tt:root name="ROOT"/>
 5   <tt:template>
 6   <X0>
 7       <X1>  my transformation first line </X1>
 8       <X2>                    </X2>
 9       <X3> <tt:text>       </tt:text> </X3>
10   </X0>
11   </tt:template>
12   </tt:transform>
13 ▶
```

We create an element X2 without identification and an element X3 with identification. Both contain blank spaces. The resulting XML string (as seen in the debugger) will be as follows:

Variable	V.	Val.
XML_STRING+41(4)		<X0>
XML_STRING+45(40)		<X1> my transformation first line </X1>
XML_STRING+85(5)		<X2/>
XML_STRING+90(14)		<X3> </X3>
XML_STRING+104(5)		</X0>

For element X3, the white spaces are preserved, whereas for X2 they are not.

Creating transformations for structures and calling them in programs

In this recipe, we will see how we can create transformations that correspond to a nested structure defined within an ABAP program. We will create a transformation, then call the transformation from a program using the CALL TRANSFORMATION statement and pass it to a populated ABAP structure corresponding to the root element of the transformation. We will then see how serialization will generate the XML stream.

How to do it...

We will now see the steps needed to create a transformation corresponding to a structure:

1. Call the transaction XSLT_TOOL. Then, enter a suitable name for your transformation. We gave it the name ZST6_FOR_STRUCTURE.

2. Click on the **Create** button. Then, on the **Create Transformation** dialog box that appears, choose the option **Simple Transformation** and proceed further.

3. Enter the following code within the transformation editor:

```
<?sap.transform simple?>
<tt:transform xmlns:tt="http://www.sap.com/transformation-templates">
  <tt:root name="STRUC"/>
  <tt:template>
    <X0>
      <X1>
        <tt:value ref="STRUC.FIELD1"/>
      </X1>

      <X2>
        <X3>
          <tt:value ref="STRUC.NEST1.FIELD1"/>
        </X3>

        <X4>
          <tt:value ref="STRUC.NEST1.FIELD2"/>
        </X4>
      </X2>
    </X0>
  </tt:template>
</tt:transform>
```

4. When done, click on the **Activate** (🛈) button.

5. Next, we will create the program that will call the transformation and pass it to an ABAP structure.

6. In the program, we will first define the nested structure, as shown in the following screenshot. The name of the structure is struc. It has a field field1 and contains another structure nest1, comprising of the fields field1 and field2.

```
DATA : BEGIN OF struc,
         field1 TYPE c LENGTH 10,
         BEGIN OF nest1,
           field1 TYPE c LENGTH 10,
           field2 TYPE c LENGTH 10,
         END OF nest1,
       END OF struc.
```

7. Then, populate the structure fields with suitable values.

```
struc-field1 = '123'.
struc-nest1-field1 = '678900'.
struc-nest1-field2 = '7665678'.
```

8. Finally, in the ABAP program we will define a string named `xml_string` and call the transformation using the `CALL TRANSFORMATION` statement. The result of the `CALL TRANSFORMATION` statement corresponding to the passed structure is returned in `xml_string`.

```
DATA: xml_string TYPE string.

CALL TRANSFORMATION zst6_for_structure
    SOURCE struc = struc
    RESULT XML xml_string .
```

How it works...

The transformation created is comprised of a structure that will be passed during serialization via the root variable `struc`. Within the XML literal elements X1, X3, and X4, the current node is set using the reference of the data root `struc`. For X1, we include the field `field1` of `struc`. For X3, we address the `field1` field of the `nest1` structure contained within `struc`.

The ABAP program calls the transformation using the `CALL TRANSFORMATION` statement. Since it is serialization, we passed a populated ABAP structure `struc` as the `SOURCE` structure. The result is read into `xml_string`. The contents of the string `xml_string` may be viewed in the ABAP debugger, as shown in the following screenshot:

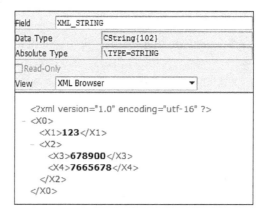

Creating transformations for internal tables

In this recipe, we will see how we can create transformations for internal tables. We will use the transformation editor to define the transformation for the internal table, ITAB, comprising of two fields, FIELD1 and FIELD2.

How to do it...

We will now see the steps for creating a transformation corresponding to internal tables:

1. Create a simple transformation using the steps shown in the previous recipe. We will give it the name zst6_internal_table.

2. Enter the following code in the transformation editor:

```
<?sap.transform simple?>
<tt:transform xmlns:tt="http://www.sap.com/transformation-templates">

  <tt:root name="ITAB"/>

  <tt:template>
    <itab>
      <tt:loop ref=".ITAB">
      <line>
        <field1>
          <tt:value ref="FIELD1"/>
        </field1>
        <field2>
          <tt:value ref="FIELD2"/>
        </field2>
      </line>
      </tt:loop>
    </itab>
  </tt:template>

</tt:transform>
```

3. Next, we will write the code of the ABAP program that calls the transformation and supplies it with an ABAP internal table.

4. We create an internal table with the name `itab` with fields `field1` and `field2` and fill it with the necessary data.

```
data : begin of itab occurs 0,
         field1 type c length 10,
         field2 type c length 10,
       end of itab.

       itab-field1 = 'ABC'.
       itab-field2 = 'ABC text'.
       append itab.

       itab-field1 = 'XYZ'.
       itab-field2 = 'XYZ text'.
       append itab.

       itab-field1 = 'ATC'.
       itab-field2 = 'ATC text'.
       append itab.
```

5. Finally, the `CALL TRANSFORMATION` statement is called, the internal table is passed, and the result is stored in `xml_string`.

```
DATA : xml_string TYPE string.

CALL TRANSFORMATION zst6_internal_table
  SOURCE itab = itab[]
  RESULT XML xml_string.
```

How it works...

The transformation contains a root element representing the internal table by the name of `ITAB`. Within the template, the XML literal element, `itab`, is defined to show the contents of the internal table. The `tt:loop` command is included. This command addresses each line of the table `itab` (since `ref=".ITAB"` is used as the current node). For each record of the table, the content of the XML element `line` is included in the XML file. Within the XML elements `FIELD1` and `FIELD2`, the contents of the `FIELD1` and `FIELD2` fields of the relevant line of the table `itab` is written. Since the current node is the row of the internal table in question, including `FIELD1` and `FIELD2` it will print the right contents.

We create the program and pass the necessary data for `itab`. After the serialization, the resulting XML file appears as shown in the following screenshot:

```
<?xml version="1.0" encoding="utf-16" ?>
- <itab>
  - <line>
      <field1>ABC</field1>
      <field2>ABC text</field2>
    </line>
  - <line>
      <field1>XYZ</field1>
      <field2>XYZ text</field2>
    </line>
  - <line>
      <field1>ATC</field1>
      <field2>ATC text</field2>
    </line>
  </itab>
```

Generating transformations for dictionary table types

In this recipe, we will see how we can create transformations for dictionary table types. We will first create a table type using `SE11` and then generate its transformation using the graphical tool editor of the transaction `XSLT_TOOL`.

We will create a table type, `ZST6_TT_PER`, that will comprise of employee number, **PERNR**, employee name, **NAME**, and grade field, **GRADE**.

How to do it...

We will now carry out the following steps:

1. Call transaction `SE11`. We will first create a line type by the name of **ZST6_ST_PER**. Enter the name in the **Data Type** field. Then, click on the **Create** button and choose the **Structure** option in the dialog box that appears.

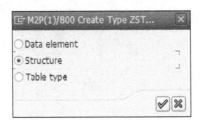

2. Next, we specify the fields of the line type. These are: **PERNR**, **GRADE**, and **NAME**. These are based upon the component types, **PERSNO**, **TRFGR**, and **EMNAM**, respectively.

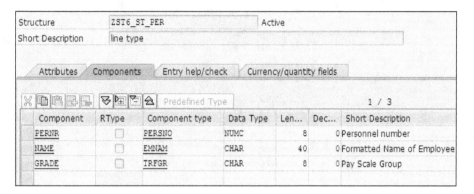

Structure	ZST6_ST_PER		Active			
Short Description	line type					

Attributes | Components | Entry help/check | Currency/quantity fields

1 / 3

Component	RType	Component type	Data Type	Len...	Dec...	Short Description
PERNR	☐	PERSNO	NUMC	8	0	Personnel number
NAME	☐	EMNAM	CHAR	40	0	Formatted Name of Employee
GRADE	☐	TRFGR	CHAR	8	0	Pay Scale Group

3. We then create a table type using the transaction SE11. We give it the name ZST_TT_PER. We make sure that the line type defined earlier is used as the line type for the table type.

4. Then, call the transaction XSLT_TOOL. Create a simple transformation.

5. From the transformation change screen, click the **Edit Transformation Graphically** (🖉) button from the toolbar. This will take you to the screen shown as Transformation Editor.

6. On the left-hand side, select the **ROOT** node and choose the context menu option **Insert new root**.

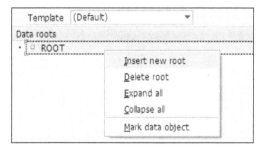

Template	(Default)	▼

Data roots
• ☐ ROOT

Insert new root
Delete root
Expand all
Collapse all
Mark data object

7. In the dialog box that appears, enter MYTAB and ZST_TT_PER in the **Root-Name** and **Type-Name** fields respectively. (Alternatively, we may enter the line type created earlier, that is, ZST6_ST_PER, in the **Type-Name** field and check the **Line Type?** indicator). Then, press **Enter**.

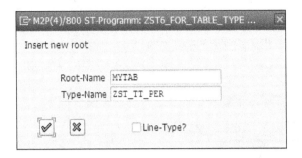

8. This will add the **MYTAB** table node to the **Data roots** section. Drag-and-drop the **MYTAB** node to the right-hand side (the **Simple Transformation** pane). This will create **MYTAB** and its components within the **Simple transformation** pane.

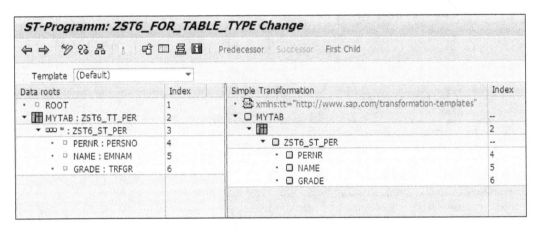

9. We need to make adjustments in the nodes. We will delete the **ROOT** node on the left-hand side so that only one **ROOT** element (that is, **MYTAB**) remains.

How it works...

We first declared a line type and then created a table type. We then created a new simple transformation. We then inserted a root element named `MYTAB` based on the dictionary type `ZST6_TT_PER` defined earlier. Drag-and-drop added the table `MYTAB` to `Transformation` and also included all the components, `PERNR`, `NAME`, and `GRADE`. The generated code of the transformation is shown in the following screenshot:

```
Transformation          ZST6_FOR_TABLE_TYPE                    Active
    Properties    SourceCde

<?sap.transform simple?>
<tt:transform xmlns:tt="http://www.sap.com/transformation-templates"
   xmlns:ddic="http://www.sap.com/abapxml/types/dictionary"
   xmlns:def="http://www.sap.com/abapxml/types/defined">
<tt:root name="MYTAB" type="ddic:ZST6_TT_PER"/>
<tt:template>
   <MYTAB>
     <tt:loop ref=".MYTAB">
       <ZST6_ST_PER>
         <PERNR tt:value-ref="PERNR"/>
         <NAME tt:value-ref="NAME"/>
         <GRADE tt:value-ref="GRADE"/>
       </ZST6_ST_PER>
     </tt:loop>
   </MYTAB>
</tt:template>
</tt:transform>
```

In the template, a loop is run on each line of the table **MYTAB**. The contents of the fields **PERNR**, **NAME**, and **GRADE** are written within the XML text element **ZT6_ST_PER** (based on the name of the line type). The completed graphical form of the transformation is shown in the following screenshot:

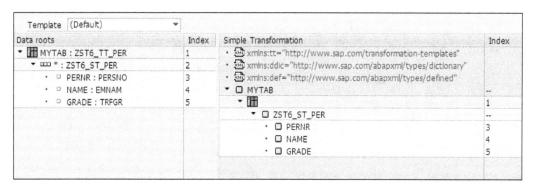

The transformation may then be called in programs using the statement
`CALL TRANSFORMATION.`

Downloading into Excel made easy using simple transformations

In this recipe, we will see how we can use simple transformations in order to download the contents of an internal table into Excel format. The advantage of this method is that the Excel file will contain the desired font size and colors without any programming effort required.

We will first create a sample Excel file in XML format. Then, we will upload it via the transformation editor `XSLT_TOOL` and generate a transformation accordingly. (The Excel XML and the transformation language may be mixed, thus the Excel XML is converted into a transformation.) The generated transformation will serve as a template representing our Excel file format. We will make slight changes in it and call it in our ABAP program in order to generate the Excel file.

The primary emphasis of this recipe is to generate an XML string containing the content of the Excel data in XML format. The download part of the XML will not be shown.

How to do it...

We will now see in detail the required steps:

1. We first create an Excel file with the appropriate required column headings and some sample data. We will consider an example of employee number, name, and grade.

	A	B	C	D
1				
2				
3				
4	**Emp. No**	**Name**	**Grade**	
5	190	John Reed	16	
6	200	Amy Jones	17	
7				
8				
9				
10				
11				

2. Next, we will save the Excel file in the **XML Spreadsheet 2003** format.

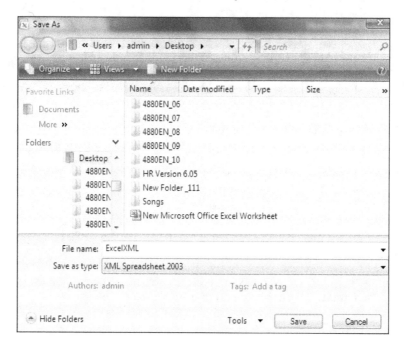

3. Next, we will create a new simple transformation using transaction XSLT_TOOL.

4. Then, from the **Source Code** tab, click on the **Import** (📥) button. On the **File** dialog box that appears, select the **ExcelXML** file created earlier. This will create a transformation program within the editor.

5. Next, we need to make some minor changes within the transformation. First, we will remove ss:ExpandedRowCount="6" from the Table element. The data rows pertaining to the sample data uploaded must be removed as well. These are contained within Row and Cell elements. (Our uploaded Excel XML file generated a transformation for our sample data. We need to delete the hard-coded lines pertaining to the sample data within the Row and Cell elements. We then make the necessary changes so that the transformation may be used for dynamic data passed in an internal table from our program.)

```
<Worksheet ss:Name="Sheet1">

 <Table ss:ExpandedColumnCount="3" ss:ExpandedRowCount="6" x:FullColumns="1"

  x:FullRows="1" ss:DefaultRowHeight="15">
  <Column ss:Width="62.25"/>
  <Column ss:Width="54.75"/>
  <Column ss:Width="45.75"/>
  <Row ss:Index="4" ss:Height="21">
   <Cell ss:StyleID="s65"><Data ss:Type="String">Emp. No</Data></Cell>
   <Cell ss:StyleID="s65"><Data ss:Type="String">Name</Data></Cell>
   <Cell ss:StyleID="s65"><Data ss:Type="String">Grade</Data></Cell>
  </Row>

  <Row>
   <Cell><Data ss:Type="Number">190</Data></Cell>
   <Cell><Data ss:Type="String">John Reed</Data></Cell>
   <Cell><Data ss:Type="Number">16</Data></Cell>
  </Row>
  <Row>
   <Cell><Data ss:Type="Number">200</Data></Cell>
   <Cell><Data ss:Type="String">Amy Jones</Data></Cell>
   <Cell><Data ss:Type="Number">17</Data></Cell>
  </Row>

 </Table>
```

6. We will now add a root element table at the beginning of the transformation, before the `tt:template` command.

```
<?mso-application progid="Excel.Sheet"?>
<?sap.transform simple?>
<tt:transform xmlns:tt="http://www.sap.com/transformation-templates">
  <tt:root name="table"/>

  <tt:template>
    <Workbook xmlns="urn:schemas-microsoft-com:office:spreadsheet"
```

7. `tt:loop` is then added in place of the removed employee data. The loop addresses each line of the internal table `"table"`. We print the contents of the fields PERNR, NAME, and GRADE as texts within the element Cell for every Row.

```
<tt:loop ref=".table">
        <Row>
            <Cell>
                <Data ss:Type="Number"> <tt:value ref="PERNR"/></Data>
            </Cell>
            <Cell>
                <Data ss:Type="String"><tt:value ref="NAME"/></Data>
            </Cell>
            <Cell>
                <Data ss:Type="Number"><tt:value ref="GRADE"/></Data>
            </Cell>
        </Row>
</tt:loop>
```

8. We will save and activate the transformation.

9. We will then make a simple program to populate an internal table based on the root element table. We define an internal table, `itab`, and work area, `wa`, based on the table type `zst6_tt_per` and line type `zst6_st_per`, respectively. We then populate the table with suitable values.

```
DATA : itab TYPE zst6_tt_per    .
DATA : wa TYPE zst6_st_per    .

wa-pernr = '13'.
wa-name = 'John Mann'.
wa-grade = '15'.
APPEND wa TO itab.

wa-pernr = '14'.
wa-name = 'Elizabeth Jones'.
wa-grade = '17'.
APPEND wa TO itab.

wa-pernr = '15'.
wa-name = 'Harold Mann'.
wa-grade = '16'.
APPEND wa TO itab.
```

10. Then, the `CALL TRANSFORMATION` statement is called and the internal table `itab` is passed. The resulting `xml_string` string contains the Excel data in XML format.

```
DATA: xml_string TYPE string.

CALL TRANSFORMATION zst6_excel_download2
   SOURCE table = itab
   RESULT XML xml_string .
```

How it works...

We uploaded the transformation using the `XSLT_TOOL` transaction's **Import** button. This transformation is based on the file that we uploaded. If we call the same transformation, the result will be the same file that was uploaded. Since we want the Excel output to be based on the content of the internal table of the ABAP program, we made the necessary changes to the transformation in order to incorporate a loop on a root element table. During serialization, the internal table `itab` was passed in place of the root element table defined within the transformation. The loop was run and the content of the table was included in the XML string. The `xml_string` may then be written as saved on the desktop or emailed to another user. When opened in Excel, it will show the user the data in Excel format along with the column heading colors and the fonts of the original sample file.

See also

- ► `help.sap.com`
- ► `http://sapblog.rmtiwari.com/2009/04/generate-simple-transformation-for-xml.html`

11
Sending E-mail Using BCS Classes

In this chapter, we will see recipes of e-mail programming using the **Business communication services** (**BCS**). We will look at:

- ▸ Creating a simple e-mail message
- ▸ Sending e-mail to Internet e-mail addresses
- ▸ Adding attachments to your message
- ▸ Creating HTML e-mail
- ▸ Running a program and sending its output as an e-mail

Introduction

This chapter explores useful recipes related to the programming of e-mail sending. We will start with a brief overview of BCS and the various classes available. Then we will see a simple recipe that will generate an e-mail to an SAP user in his or her inbox. Then, we will show how the same program may be changed in order to send the e-mail to Internet e-mail addresses.

We will then add attachments such as an Excel (XML file) to the e-mail. Creating HTML documents will also be discussed. Finally, we will create a program that will execute another ABAP program, convert its output into PDF, and attach the PDF to an e-mail message.

We will see the most important and commonly used classes (and their methods) used for e-mail creation. In addition to e-mail programming classes such as CL_BCS and CL_BCS_DOCUMENT, we will also see classes such as CL_CONVERT_BCS that are used for converting files into appropriate formats suitable for attaching to e-mail documents.

Throughout the chapter, the terms e-mail and SAP Office Document will be used interchangeably.

The BCS classes provide a newer object-oriented means of generating e-mails programmatically. The function modules should no longer be used for sending e-mails. The BCS classes are much simpler to program, particularly when we have attachments involved.

The classes relevant to e-mail programming are discussed as follows:

Class name	Use
CL_BCS	This class is for creating sent requests. The document (e-mail body and attachments) is assigned to it and recipients are specified. Finally, the request is sent.
CL_DOCUMENT_BCS	This is the document class for specifying the content of the e-mail and attachments (if any).
CL_CAM_ADDRESS_BCS	This class provides a number of useful methods. The notable one uses an Internet e-mail address such as abc@yahoo.com and returns a recipient user object.
CL_SAPUSER_BCS	This class creates a recipient object based on an SAP user ID to be used.
CL_BCS_CONVERT	This class converts data from one format to another, such as conversion of text string to binary table or from a hexadecimal string to a binary table, and so on.

Creating a simple e-mail message

In this recipe, we will see how we can create a simple program that will send an e-mail (SAP Office Mail) to an SAP user AJON1. There are no attachments involved in this recipe. However, we will want the SAP user AJON1 to see a pop-up express message when the e-mail document is received in his or her inbox.

How to do it...

We will now perform the steps shown as follows:

1. Declare two reference variables sendrequest and myrecpient to the classes cl_bcs and cl_sapuser_bcs.

```
DATA : sendrequest TYPE REF TO cl_bcs.
DATA : myrecipient TYPE REF TO cl_sapuser_bcs.
```

2. We will then declare a variable for specifying the content of the e-mail `email_text`. This is based on the type `bcsy_text`. We also declare an object reference to the class `cl_document_bcs` with the name `document`.

```
DATA : email_text TYPE bcsy_text.
DATA : document TYPE REF TO cl_document_bcs.
```

3. We call the static factory method `create_persistent` of the class `cl_bcs`.

4. The returned reference is stored in the `sendrequest` reference variable declared earlier.

```
sendrequest = cl_bcs=>create_persistent( ).
```

5. An SAP user object is then created using the CREATE method. This will be used later for specifying the e-mail recipient. The returned object is stored in `myrecipient` variable. The corresponding object for the user AJON1 is created.

```
myrecipient = cl_sapuser_bcs=>create( 'AJON1' ) .
```

6. Next, we call the `add_recipient` method of the `cl_bcs` class for the object reference `sendrequest`. We supply the recipient through the `myrecipient` object and we pass the value `'X'` for the `i_express` parameter.

```
CALL METHOD sendrequest->add_recipient
  EXPORTING
    i_recipient = myrecipient
    i_express   = 'X'.
```

7. Next, we create the e-mail text. A simple one-line text `My first email content` is added to the internal table `email_text`. In addition, the factory method `create_document` is called for class `cl_document_bcs`. The type RAW is specified through the parameter `i_type`.

```
APPEND 'My first email content' TO email_text.

document = cl_document_bcs=>create_document(
                  i_type    = 'RAW'
                  i_text    = email_text
                  i_subject = 'my email subject' ).
```

8. We then call the SET_DOCUMENT method and pass the document object as the parameter. The send method of the class cl_bcs for the object reference sendrequest is also called.

```
CALL METHOD sendrequest->set_document( document ).
sendrequest->send( ).
```

9. Finally, we call the COMMIT WORK statement.

```
COMMIT WORK.
```

10. The entire code block is placed within a TRY .. ENDTRY statement and the cx_bcs exception class will be used for catching exceptions.

How it works...

We created object references for the send request and the e-mail document as well for the recipient user object. The static factory method create_persistent of the cl_bcs class is called in order to create a send request.

Then, we define appropriate text for the content of the e-mail body and add it to the created send request along with the subject of the e-mail.

A recipient object (based upon the class cl_sapuser_bcs) is created for the SAP user AJON1. This recipient is then added to the send request using the method add_recipient of the cl_bcs class. For the i_express parameter of the add_recipient method, the value 'X' is passed so that the user receives an express message when the e-mail is received in his or her inbox. A new document is created using the static create_document method of the cl_document_bcs class. The document is having type RAW and relevant subject and content. The add_document method is then called in order to add the document to the send request. Finally, the COMMIT WORK statement is called and the e-mail is sent.

An express message is generated as shown in the following screenshot:

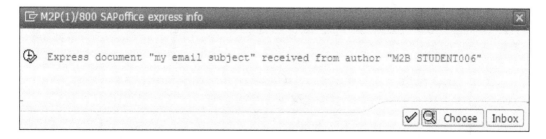

The message appears in the document (`Unread Documents`) of the SAP Business Workplace (transaction `SBWP`). The message header for the corresponding message appears as shown in the following screenshot:

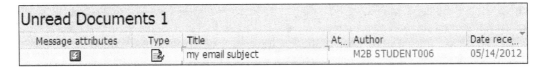

It contains the red icon that denotes an express message has been generated. The title (**Title**), author name (**Author**), and the date received (**Date received**) are shown as well. The preview of the document body is shown in the following screenshot:

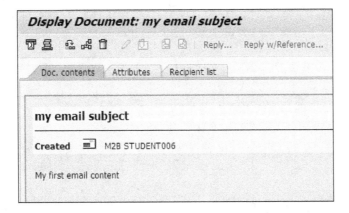

The **My first email content** text is the e-mail text, whereas as the **my email subject** text is the subject as coded in the program.

There's more...

In case the e-mail is to be sent immediately, the `SET_SEND_IMMEDIATELY` method of the `cl_bcs` class must be called before the `SEND` method (and the `COMMIT WORK` statement), as shown as follows:

```
SENDREQUEST->SET_SEND_IMMEDIATELY( 'X' ).
```

Sending e-mail to Internet e-mail addresses

In this recipe, we will see how we can modify the existing program so that, instead of the SAP user, we can send the same e-mail to an Internet address. We will make a copy of the same program and add additional code. The class that is to be used, in this case, is `cl_bcs_cam_address` (instead of the `cl_sapuser_bcs` class). The method `create_internet_address` will be used for creating Internet user addresses.

How to do it...

We will now see the changes we need to make to the given program:

1. Instead of the `myrecipient` object reference being based upon the class `cl_sapuser_bcs`, we will use the class `cl_cam_address_bcs`.

   ```
   DATA : myrecipient TYPE REF TO cl_cam_address_bcs.
   ```

2. Next, we will call the method `create_internet_address` of the `cl_cam_addess_bcs` class for creating an e-mail address.

   ```
   myrecipient = cl_cam_address_bcs=>create_internet_address( 'myemail@yahoo.com' ) .
   ```

3. We may remove the `i_express` parameter assignment from the `add_recipient` method call of the `cl_bcs` class (since the e-mail is going to an e-mail address outside the SAP system, pop-up express messages are irrelevant).

   ```
   CALL METHOD sendrequest->add_recipient
       EXPORTING
          i_recipient = myrecipient
          .
   ```

4. Next we define a reference to the interface `if_sender_bcs` for our e-mail address (that is, sender e-mail address).

   ```
   DATA : myemailaddress TYPE REF TO if_sender_bcs .
   ```

5. An Internet address is created for our e-mail address using the same `create_internet_address` method of the `cl_cam_address_bcs` class. The created object is stored in the variable `myemailaddress` defined earlier.

```
myemailaddress =
cl_cam_address_bcs=>create_internet_address( 'myuser@packtpub.com').
```

6. Finally, the e-mail address is added as the sender of the send request using the `set_sender` method of the `cl_bcs` class.

```
sendrequest->set_sender( myemailaddress ).
```

7. The rest of the coding remains the same as in the previous recipe.

How it works...

We made a copy of the program in the previous recipe. The class `cl_cam_bcs_address` is used for defining the recipient user. Since we have the e-mail address of the recipient, we used the static method `create_internet_address` of the `cl_cam_address_BCS` class. The necessary recipient is returned because of the method call. This is later added to the send request, thus specifying the Internet address.

Once the `COMMIT WORK` statement is executed, the e-mail is sent to the Internet user address. In the receiver's inbox, we will see our e-mail address as the sender (since the `set_sender` method has been used).

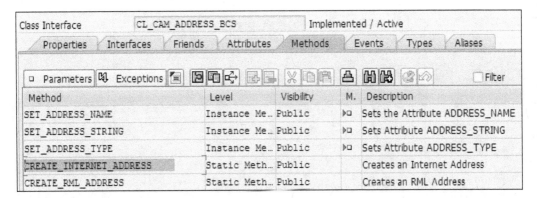

E-mail transfers are complicated. It may be possible that the programming done is correct but the e-mails are not sent. From experience, many times the problems arising when testing programmatic e-mail sending are e-mail server configuration/routing problems.

Adding attachments to your message

In this recipe, we will see how we can add attachments to our e-mail message (we will use the program created in the previous recipe). We will also use the code fragment from the XML String (for Excel data) generated in the *Downloading into Excel made easy using simple transformations* recipe of *Chapter 10, Simple Transformations* chapter.

We will copy the program of the last recipe and add the transformation code for the conversion into binary file of the XML string. We will then write the code for attaching the XML file to the e-mail message. The recipe shows the additional code required to attach a file to the e-mail.

The necessary steps for defining the send request and the subsequent steps are the same. This recipe code will be inserted after the `create_document` method call of the `cl_document_bcs` class and before the `set_document` method call of the `cl_bcs` class.

How to do it...

We will now perform the steps shown as follows:

1. After the `CALL TRANSFORMATION` statement, we will declare internal table `attached_xml` based on the table type `solix_tab`. We then call the static method `string_to_solix` of the `cl_bcs_convert` class for creating binary content out of the XML string. The `solix_tab` type is an internal table in binary format. The code page for `Unicode UTF-16LE` is passed `4103`. The result is then stored in converted form in the `attached_xml` file.

```
DATA: xml_string TYPE string.

CALL TRANSFORMATION zst6_excel_download2
  SOURCE table = itab
  RESULT XML xml_string .

DATA : attached_xml TYPE solix_tab   .

CALL METHOD cl_bcs_convert=>string_to_solix
  EXPORTING
    iv_string    = xml_string
    iv_codepage  = '4103'
  IMPORTING
    et_solix     = attached_xml.
```

2. Next, we call the method `add_attachment` of the class `cl_bcs_document`. For the parameter attachment type `I_ATTACHMENT_TYPE`, we pass the value `BIN`. For the name of the file (`i_attachment_subject`), we specify the name `XML Excel Data.XLS`. The parameter `i_att_content_hex` is for passing the internal table containing the file to be attached.

```
CALL METHOD document->add_attachment
    EXPORTING
        i_attachment_type    = 'BIN'
        i_attachment_subject = 'XML Excel Data.XLS'
        i_att_content_hex    = attached_xml.
```

How it works...

After the `CALL TRANSFORMATION` statement, we have the file content in the form of a large XML string. This string needs to be converted to an Excel format. We convert this into a binary format (an internal table based on dictionary structure **SOLIX**) using the static method `string_to_solix` of the class `cl_bcs_convert`. The structure of **SOLIX** is as follows:

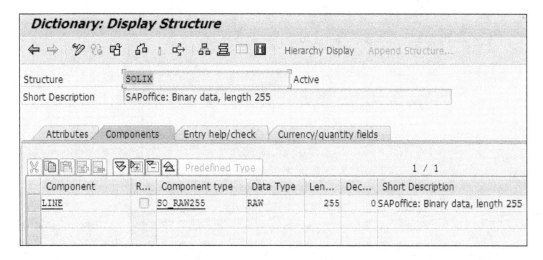

For converting the XML string into binary data, we use the code page `4103`. Excel files expect the data to be in the `UTF-16 LE` format, that is, `4103`.

The code is then added to insert the attachment to the created document using the `add_attachment` method of the `cl_bcs_document` class.

The attachment subject is the name of the file (in our case `XML Excel Data.XLS`) as it should appear in the receiver's inbox, the type is `BIN` meaning binary. For the content of the file, the `i_att_content_hex` parameter is supplied with the converted Excel file data. The attachment appears as shown in the following screenshot:

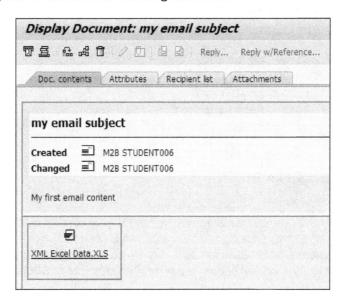

The file when opened in Excel looks like following screenshot:

	A	B	C
1			
2			
3			
4	**Emp. No**	**Name**	**Grade**
5	13	John Mann	15
6	14	Elizabeth Jones	17
7	15	Harold Mann	16
8			
9			
10			

There's more...

Similarly, other types of attachments such as PDF or HTML may be added to your documents.

If we need to know the code page of the underlying application server, we go to transaction SNL1. For our server, the code page `4103` is used for the `UTF-16 LE` encoding.

Adj. DB according to country		Not completely installed
System language (database)		
Database codepage		Unicode
Current Codepage of Appl. Server	4103	
Codepage of Front End	4110	UTF-8 GUI

New Interface

See also

▶ http://scn.sap.com/thread/1842532

▶ http://ceronio.net/2012/02/unicode-in-abap/

Creating HTML e-mail

In this recipe, we will see how we can display the body of our e-mail in HTML to our messages body. We will see how text may be displayed in bold, in various colors, for example, red and how to set the background color of the e-mail body. We will copy the program shown in the first recipe and make few changes in it. The detail of HTML coding is beyond the scope of this book. The focus of the recipe will be on how basic HTML code is shown in the e-mail body.

How to do it...

We will now carry out the steps shown as follows;

1. For the `email_text` internal table, we will append a number of rows. Each row appended will correspond to the lines of the HTML code. We will specify a background color for the e-mail body. Then on the first line, we will write a text Dear Sir in font size = 2. On the next line, we will write text in red color. Finally, on the last line we write text in bold format, as shown in the following screenshot:

```
APPEND '<html> <body style="background-color:#FFAABB;"> ' TO email_text.

APPEND '<p> <font size = 2> Dear Sir </p> </HTML>' TO email_text.

APPEND '<p> <font size = 2 color = Red > This is an important mail. </p> </HTML>'
TO email_text.

APPEND '<p> <b> Packt Team </b>  </p> </HTML>' TO email_text.
```

2. The e-mail text will then be used to create the document that will later be attached to the send request. While calling the `create_document` method, the type of document specified will be HTML, rather than RAW in the previous recipes.

```
document = cl_document_bcs=>create_document(
                    i_type    = 'HTM'
                    i_text    = email_text
                    i_subject = 'my html email' ).
```

How it works...

We made a few changes in the program. First, we entered the entire HTML code in the form of an internal table. It should be made sure that the entire code is enclosed within <HTML> and </HTML> tags.

In the next step, the appropriate type (HTML) of the document that is to be created is specified for the method `create_document` and the internal table containing the HTML coding is passed. The rest of the coding remains the same. The e-mail generated from the program appears as shown in the following screenshot:

We have used only one font size. However, within the HTML body we may have different font sizes.

Running a program and sending its output as an e-mail

In this recipe, we will see how we can create a small program that will run another ABAP program and will send the second program's output as an e-mail attachment in PDF form. The basic steps for creating the send request and defining the recipient will remain the same as mentioned in the previous recipes. This recipe will emphasize on the additional portion required in order to run the program, capture its output, and convert the output into PDF form. The second program (program to be called) is created first and we have named it `ZST_6_CALLED_PROGRAM`.

How to do it...

We will now list the steps needed:

1. We will call the `SUBMIT` statement that will call another program `zst_6_called_program` (which simply prints `Hello World`). The `EXPORTING LIST TO MEMORY AND RETURN` addition is used along with the `SUBMIT` statement.

   ```
   SUBMIT zst6_program_to_be_called
   EXPORTING LIST TO MEMORY AND RETURN.
   ```

2. Next, we define an internal table based on the dictionary type `abaplist`. We then call the `LIST_FROM_MEMORY` function module and use the `prog_output` object for storing the list fetched from the memory.

   ```
   DATA : prog_output TYPE STANDARD TABLE OF abaplist.

   CALL FUNCTION 'LIST_FROM_MEMORY'
     TABLES
       listobject = prog_output.
   ```

3. We then define an internal table `binary_tab` of dictionary type `solix`. The function module `TABLE_COMPRESS` is then called that converts the program output into a table of binary format `solix`.

```
DATA : binary_tab TYPE STANDARD TABLE OF solix.

CALL FUNCTION 'TABLE_COMPRESS'
  TABLES
    in  = prog_output
    out = binary_tab.
```

4. We then call the function module `SX_OBJECT_CONVERT_ALI_PDF`. Before the call of the function module, we define necessary variables and internal tables necessary for the function module call. The various parameters should be provided with appropriate values. The `format_src` parameter should be assigned value `ALI(` meaning ABAP list), the `format_dst` parameter is assigned `PDF`, whereas the `funcpara` parameter is assigned the value `DELETE`. The address type `addr_type` is passed `PRT`, whereas `devtype` is passed `PDF1`.

```
DATA : w_transfer_bin TYPE  sx_boolean VALUE 'X'.
DATA : it_content_txt TYPE soli_tab.
DATA : objhead TYPE  soli_tab.
DATA : w_len TYPE so_obj_len.

CALL FUNCTION 'SX_OBJECT_CONVERT_ALI_PRT'
  EXPORTING
    format_src            = 'ALI'
    format_dst            = 'PDF'
    addr_type             = 'PRT'
    devtype               = 'PDF1'
    funcpara              = 'DELETE'
  CHANGING
    transfer_bin          = w_transfer_bin
    content_txt           = it_content_txt
    content_bin           = binary_tab
    objhead               = objhead
    len                   = w_len.
```

5. We then call the `add attachment` method of the class `cl_bcs_document` for the document object. The type is specified as PDF and the `binary_tab` value is passed as the content of the file to be attached.

```
CALL METHOD document->add attachment
    EXPORTING
        i_attachment_type    = 'PDF'
        i_attachment_subject = 'Program Output'
        i_att_content_hex    = binary_tab .
```

How it works...

We have used the SUBMIT statement in order to run the other program. The output of the program is generated and sent to the memory using the SUBMIT statement. The function module `list_from_memory` then fetches the program's output from the memory and stores it in the internal table `prog_output`. We then use the function module `table_compress` in order to convert the ABAP list into an internal table of binary data format based on the dictionary structure `solix`.

The function module `sx_object_convert_ali_pdf` is then called. We supply it with the necessary parameters and the necessary variables and internal table. The ALI corresponds to the ABAP list format (for the source format) whereas the target format is specified as PDF. The function module converts the ABAP list stored in the binary format into PDF. After the function module execution is complete, the PDF generated is stored in the internal table named `binary_tab`. For the parameters of the function module `addr_type` and device type `devtype`, the values PRT (meaning printer name) and PDF1 are passed, respectively. The `funcpara` parameter is supplied with DELETE. This is to delete the spool request created by this function module created during the PDF conversion process.

This PDF content stored in the internal table `binary_tab` is then attached to the e-mail document using the `add attachment` method. We specify the type as PDF and pass the `binary_tab` for the method's importing parameter `i_att_content_hex`.

The PDF output generated will be attached to the e-mail document.

There's more...

This is one of the ways of capturing the output of a program. We may also use the `SEND TO SAP-SPOOL` addition for the `SUBMIT` statement. This allows the generated list to be sent to the SAP spool, which can then be turned into a PDF.

Also, we covered a scenario where a simple program is called. The called program may contain a number of selection screen input fields. You may supply appropriate values for these selection screen parameters while calling the program using the `SUBMIT` statement. This may be done, for example, using the `WITH SEL1 EQ VAL1` addition of the `SUBMIT` statement.

See also

- `http://help.sap.com/abapdocu_70/en/ABAPSUBMIT_SHORTREF.htm`
- `http://help.sap.com/erp2005_ehp_04/helpdata/en/2d/1c5d3aebba4c3 8e10000000a114084/frameset.htm`

12
Creating and Consuming Web Services

In this chapter, we will look at the following recipes related to Web services:

- ▸ Creating a Web service from a function module
- ▸ Configuring the created Web service
- ▸ Consuming a Web service
- ▸ Creating a consumer proxy's logical port
- ▸ Calling a Web service from an ABAP program

Introduction

The **Service-Oriented Architecture** (SOA) is the current paradigm in which one type of software communicates with another software written in a different language and exchanges information. In a service-oriented design, we have a service provider that provides a particular service. Web service technology is not specific to SAP.

For a Web service, a Web Service Definition Language (WSDL) file exists that contains the necessary information required in calling the Web service in question, such as the input and the output parameters (that is, the interface). The information about the necessary input and output parameters for Web service call is specified using the WSDL. The WSDL and the SOAP and HTTP are universal concepts and therefore allow SAP integration with the outside world.

There is a registry called UDDI (acronym for *Universal Description, Discovery, and Integration*) where the service provider may be registered and the necessary information about the service is stored. The caller or potential consumer may refer to the registry for information about the service. We may also have a direct binding between the service provider and the service caller using SOAP and HTTP. The necessary input is sent to the provider, which then returns the relevant results after the Web service execution back to the consumer.

In a service-oriented architecture (SOA) world, the service consumer and the service provider may use different technologies, and both of them do not need to worry about the technology used by the other. They communicate using SOAP over HTTP. A SAP system can call a Web service provided by a non-SAP system and vice versa. A Web service encapsulates a particular process and accepts input as well as provides output to the caller. The consumer may call the service to send input data into the specified format and receive the results. The technology used inside the service is not to be of concern to the consumer.

SAP allows you to both create, as well as consume Web services from the outside world. This chapter will take an approach from the SAP side—the creation and consumption of services. The wizard that quickly and easily creates Web service providers and consumers will also be discussed. We will start with the creation of a Web service using the Web service creation wizard and then cover the configuration of the Web service in question using the SOAMANAGER transaction. While defining a Web service, an *endpoint* is specified, which is the ABAP object used as the basis for the creation of the Web service. This could be a function module, a BAPI, an entire function group, or an XI message interface. We will use the existing objects (in our case, a function module) to generate or create a Web service. This approach is known as an **Inside-Out** approach in the chapter. The primary emphasis of this chapter will be on the Inside-Out approach.

In order to create a consumer program for calling a Web service, a consumer proxy has to be generated. It creates a link to the Web service that is to be consumed. During the generation of the proxy, a class is generated that encapsulates the process of communicating with the Web service provider and the formation of SOAP messages that are to be sent to the provider. Once you have generated a proxy (and then a logical port is created), the ABAP code may be written for calling the Web service and getting the desired results. We will cover recipes related to consumer proxy generation, creation of a logical port, and the coding related to service call.

For the sake of illustration, in this chapter we will create a Web service in our system and will generate a proxy for calling the same service from within the system (though practically the service consumer and provider will not be in the same system). All the recipes in this chapter are based on this service provider and consumer scenario.

A diagram showing the client service relationship of Web service consumer and provider is as follows:

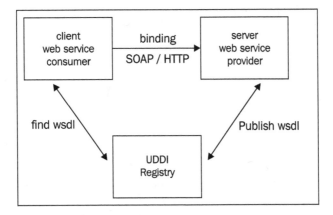

See also

- http://www.adfahrer.com/workplace/Sem/2006-11-28-ADSIG-SBN-WalldorfABAP/SRothaug-ProvidingWebServinABAPNordicABAP.pdf

- http://www.w3schools.com/webservices/ws_intro.asp

- http://www.xmethods.net/ve2/index.po

Creating a Web service from a function module

In this recipe, we will see how we can create a Web service using a Web service creation wizard from a remote-enabled function module. The function module simply takes as input an amount (in figures, for example, 1000) and currency such as USD, and then outputs the corresponding amount in words such as One Thousand US Dollars (similar to the function module **SPELL_AMOUNT**).

Getting ready

Since the **SPELL_AMOUNT** function module is not remote-enabled, it cannot be used for generating a Web service. One such attempt will result in the following error during creation of the service.

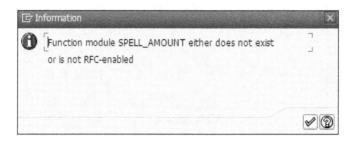

So, we will copy the function module **SPELL_AMOUNT** and rename it as **ZST8_MY_SPELL_AMOUNT** and make the copy remote-enabled after making necessary changes in the interface. In this recipe, we will use our remote-enabled function module as the basis for creation of a Web service. The function group containing this function module was created by the name **ZST8_SPELL**.

How to do it...

We will now follow the steps as shown:

1. Call transaction SE80. From the list of the local objects of your user ID, we select the root node and right-click to access the context menu. We then navigate to **Create | Enterprise Service**.

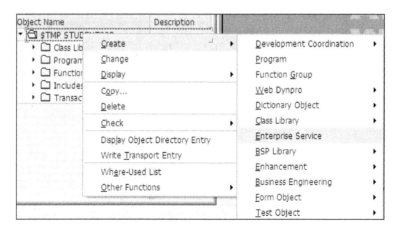

2. This will start the wizard for Web service creation. On the first screen of the wizard, a number of radio buttons are presented.

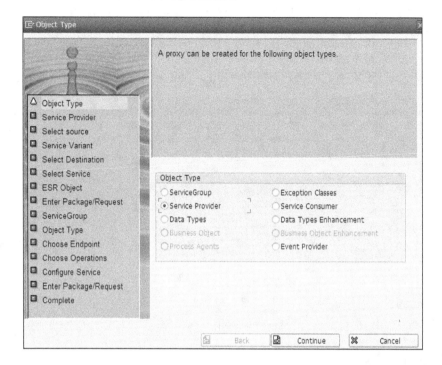

3. Since we are creating a Web service, (we will choose the option **Service Provider**). The same wizard may be used for creating proxies for a number of object types such as a **Service Consumer**, or a **Service Group**. Then click on the **Continue** button.

4. Next, a number of options are again presented. You may either create a **Service Provider** using the **ESR Service Interface**, a **Service Variant**, or an **Existing ABAP Object (Inside Out)** option. We will choose the third option **Existing ABAP Object (Inside Out)** approach. (A **Service Variant** uses certain parameters of a service that are relevant to a particular business scenario. The **ESR object** option allows us to create a proxy based on the Outside-In approach. In this case, the service interface exists in the enterprise service repository.) Then, click on the **Continue** button.

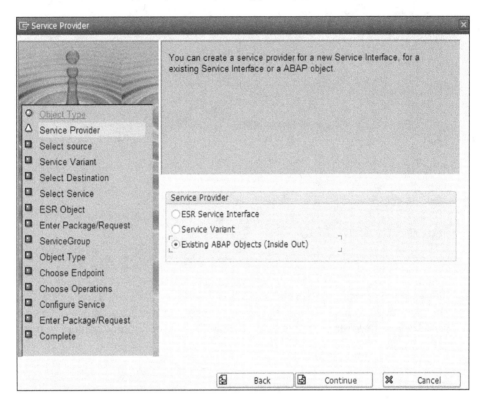

5. On the next screen (step of the wizard), we need to enter the **Service Definition** name, its description, and the **Endpoint type** (meaning whether a BAPI, function group, or a function module) is used as the basis for creating the service. Appropriate entries are made and the function module option is selected as the **Endpoint type**. Then, click on the **Continue** button.

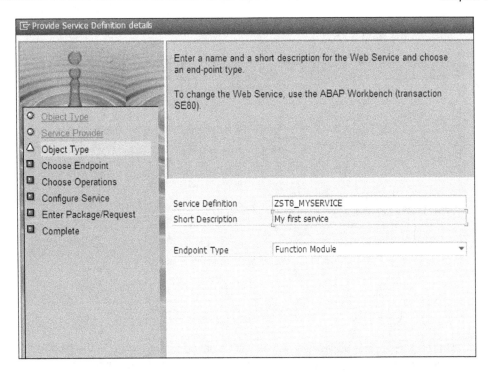

6. This will take you to the next screen where you are able to enter the name of the function module, based on which the Web service is to be created. Enter the function module name in the field provided.

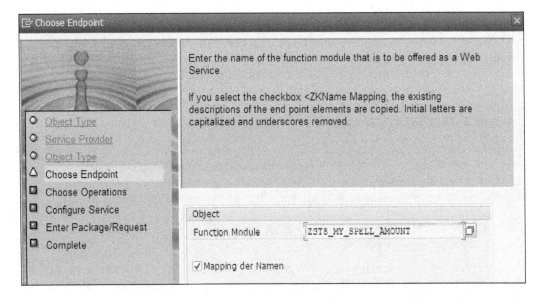

7. On the next screen, enter the profile PRF_DT_IF_SEC_NO in the **Profile** field. Then click on the **Next** button.

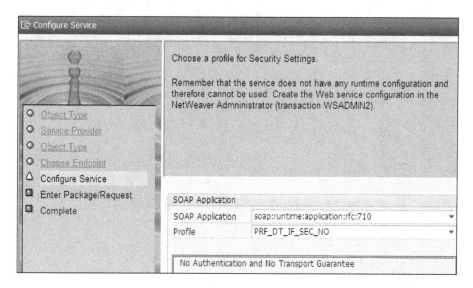

8. On the screen that appears now, you will be asked to enter data in the **Request number** and the **Package** fields. We will choose the checkbox **Local Object**. Then click on the **Next** button.

9. Finally, you will be asked to complete your action. Click on the **Complete** button.

How it works...

We first created a remote-enabled function module that was used for creation of the Web service. The essential steps that we need to carry out for creation of a Web service are done using the wizard. The approach we follow is the Inside-Out approach. We used a function module as the basis of our Web service—the endpoint. The wizard guides us through the various steps and essentials for creating a service provider. The Web service is created by the name **ZST8_MYSERVICE**, as specified. We did not keep any authentication for the Web service.

This web service has been created but cannot be called yet. Now we need to make this configuration of the Web service created. The runtime configuration needs to be undertaken via transaction SOAMANAGER. We will do this in the next recipe.

There's more...

Instead of the path shown in the recipe, we may use transaction SE37, which directly creates creating a Web service. From inside the **Function Builder**, navigate to **Utilities | More Utilities | Create Web Service**.

An alternate path is to go to transaction SE80 and then navigate to **Edit | Other Object**. Then choose the tab **Enterprise Services**. Now, enter a name in the **Service Definition** field and click on the **Create** button.

On the **Security Settings** profile screen, we choose **PRF_DT_IF_SEC_NO** (meaning without authentication and no transport guarantee). There are three other possibilities:

▸ PRF_DT_IF_SEC_LOW: Authentication with user ID and password but no transport guarantee

▸ PRF_DT_IF_SEC_MEDIUM: Authentication with user ID and password as well as transport guarantee

▸ PRF_DT_IF_SEC_HIGH: Authentication with certificates as well as transport guarantee

Configuring the created Web service

In this recipe, we will see how we can create the runtime configuration of our Web service.

How to do it...

We will now follow the steps as shown:

1. Call transaction SOAMANAGER. This opens a new browser session. Choose the **Single Service Configuration** link on the **Service Administration** tab.

SOA Management (R3_800;M25;800)

| Technical Administration | Service Administration | Logs and Traces | Monitoring | Tools |

Single Service Configuration
Administer and configure web services and service consumers

Simplified Service Configuration
Configure web service providers intended for simple web service consumers

Business Scenario Configuration
SOA configuration of multiple service providers and service groups

Logical Receiver Determination
Define rules for routing a service call to a provider system

Publication Rules
Create publication rules for service providers and service groups

User Account Management
Manage user accounts and their assignment to provider systems, individual service providers, and service groups

2. We now need to locate our newly created service. Make sure the **Search by** listbox has the value **Service** selected. Enter `zst8*` in the **Search Pattern** field, and click on the **Go** button.

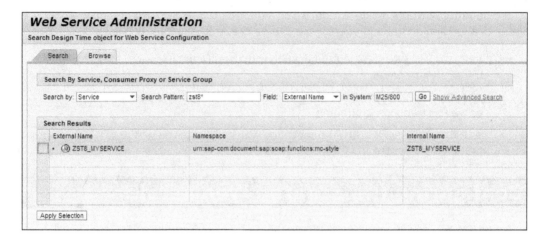

3. This will bring up your service in the results area. Select the service name and click on the **Apply Selection** button.

4. The lower part of the screen will show additional settings related to the service in question. On the **Configurations** tab, you click on the button **Create Endpoint**. The dialog box will appear as shown in the following screenshot:

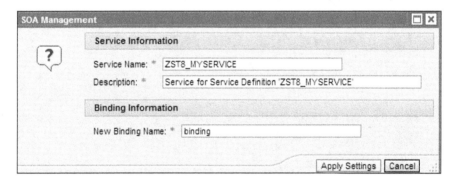

5. Enter a suitable name for the binding. Then click on the **Apply Settings** button.

6. This will add a new row to the table in the **Configurations** tab.

7. Click on the **Save** button.

How it works...

We created the runtime configuration of the Web service. The service may now be called by a consumer. You may open the WSDL generated for the given service by clicking on the **Open WSDL document for selected binding or service**.

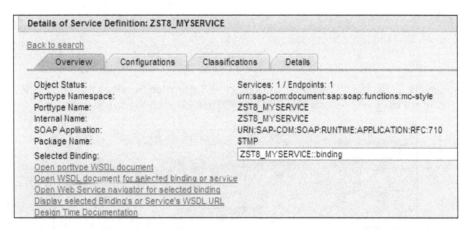

In this recipe, we have a created the configuration for our newly created service. Now any consumer can call the given service using the binding.

If you go to transaction `SICF`, you can see your service running, as shown in the following screenshot:

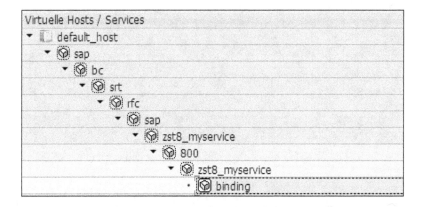

Consuming a Web service

In this recipe, we will see how we can create a client proxy based on a given Web service (using its WSDL document). As an example, we will use the Web service that we created earlier in this chapter. We will use the Web service wizard from the transaction `SE80`. This will generate the class and other necessary objects that are needed to call the Web service.

How to do it...

We will now follow the steps as shown:

1. Go to transaction `SE80`, and select the menu option **Edit Other Object**.

2. On the dialog box that appears, choose the **Enterprise Services** tab and in the **Client Proxy** field enter a suitable name. Then click on the **Create** button.

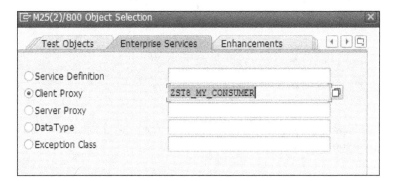

3. The wizard will then start. The first step will ask for the **Source** of the Web service. Choose the option **URL/HTTP Destination** and click on **Continue**.

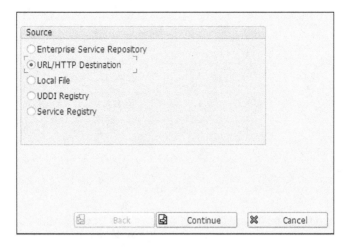

4. For the next step of the wizard, enter the WSDL URL of our Web service binding. This is the same URL as shown in the **Service Definition Overview** tab in the SOAMANAGER transaction.

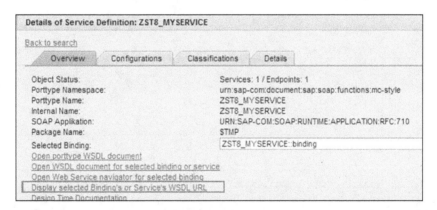

5. Enter the URL in the **URL** field and then click on **Continue**.

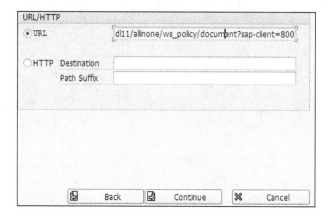

6. You will then be asked to specify the **Package** and **Request** number. Choose the **Local Object** checkbox and enter a suitable **Prefix** of the class to be generated. We will use the prefix ZST8_. Then click on **Continue**.

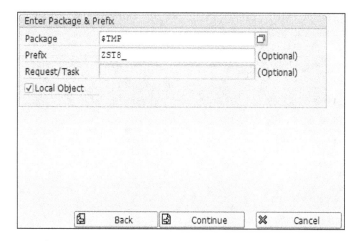

7. Finally, the screen appears where it is specified that clicking the complete button will generate the proxy class. Press the **Confirm** button to complete the action.

How it works...

This will create the service consumer proxy as shown in the following screenshot. The proxy by the name **ZST8_CO_ZST8_MYSERVICE** is created. The relevant class corresponding to the proxy is also generated and activated along with the necessary methods.

Service Consumer (external definition)		ZST8_MYSERVICE		Active
Properties	External View	Internal View	Used Objects	Configuration	Warnings

External Key

Type	Service Interface	Source	External WSDL
Name	ZST8_MYSERVICE		
Namespace	urn:sap-com:document:sap:soap:functions:mc-style		
Description			
Direction	Outbound		

Proxy

Proxy Name	ZST8_CO_ZST8_MYSERVICE	Prefix	ZST8_
Description	Proxy Class (generated)		

Interface

Communication Type	Point to Point enabled

The method contains the necessary logic for converting the amount based on the function module used while defining. The input structure corresponds to the importing parameters, whereas the output structure corresponds to the exporting parameters of the function module used for generating the Web service. All the necessary objects are generated. In addition, the relevant structures needed for the Web service call (consumer proxy method call) are also generated.

In the next recipe, we will see how to create a logical port for the Web service consumer. After this, the service may be called from a program using the proxy class methods.

There's more...

Apart from WSDL URL, you may use other options as the source of your web service. You may use a local file that contains the WSDL document pertaining to the service or the enterprise service repository of a PI instance. In addition, a UDDI registry (maintained on the SAP server that provides access to information about published Web services) may also be specified.

Alternatively, a more sophisticated Service Registry may be used as the source. The service registry is a UDDI v3 complaint registry within an SOA landscape. It may have services published from activated service interfaces from ESR, or from sender agreements from Integration Directory. Also, it may be used on ABAP or Java services definitions from AS, ABAP, or Java, respectively. They provide important information about services along with the reference to WSDL data. After entering the name of the UDDI registry or service registry the name of the relevant service may then be specified on the next screen.

See also

- ► http://help.sap.com/saphelp_nwpi711/helpdata/en/fa/82f552b49249 5d8961df56c0fa2dde/content.htm

- ► http://help.sap.com/saphelp_nw70ehp2/helpdata/en/69/8a1e9553dc4 baba6026a3db510cadb/frameset.htm

- ► http://help.sap.com/saphelp_nwpi71/helpdata/en/47/0ae6a14ddb0e8 ae10000000a155369/frameset.htm

- ► http://www.netweavercentral.com/index.php/2011/consume-a-web- service-in-abap/old link

- ► http://sapignite.com/consuming-a-web-service-in-abap/

- ► http://help.sap.com/saphelp_nw04/helpdata/en/81/845f3c31727d59e 10000000a114084/frameset.htm

- ► http://help.sap.com/saphelp_nwpi71/helpdata/en/e6/6d0f3fb35c48f a9fdf5f4e70d9f37d/frameset.htm

Creating a consumer proxy's logical port

In this recipe, we will see how we can create a logical port for the consumer proxy created in the last recipe.

How to do it...

We will now perform the following steps:

1. Call transaction SOAMANAGER. Follow the the same single service administration link we used for creation of the Web service in the previous recipe. On the **Search** tab, make sure that, instead of **Service**, the **Search by** listbox contains **Consumer Proxy**. In the **Search Pattern**, we will enter the prefix of our service, zst8*, and click on the **Go** button. This will search and show the consumer proxy **ZST8_CO_ZST8_MYSERVICE** that we created for our service **ZST8_MYSERVICE**. Select this and click on the **Apply Selection** button.

2. Select the **Consumer Proxy** and click on the **Apply Selection** button. Note that the **Internal Name** will be the same as the proxy generated in the previous recipe.

3. The lower part of the screen will open the details of the proxy definition. On the **Configuration** tab, click on the button **Create Logical Port**. A dialog box will appear. Enter the relevant details pertaining to your service. Use the same WSDL URL for the binding shown in the SOAMANAGER transaction for your Web service definition. Enter any user ID and password that you need to set. You may set the logical port as default if you like. Then press *Enter*.

4. This will add a new logical port to your proxy definition.

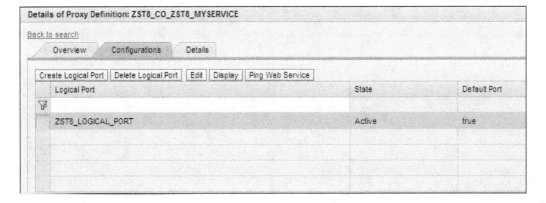

How it works...

In this recipe, we created the logical port for our consumer proxy. We created one logical port. However, a given proxy can have multiple logical ports, only one of which may be the default port. In the next recipe, we will see how we can call the Web service using the logical port we have created.

Calling a Web service from an ABAP program

In this recipe, we will see how we can programmatically call a web service using the proxy class generated in the previous recipes. We will see the main steps required in coding the program.

Getting ready

For quickly creating the template code within a program, first create a new program in the ABAP editor using SE80 and open the code of the program in the right-hand side pane. Then, in the left-hand side pane navigate to the customer proxy generated under the **Service Consumer** node. Select the name of our consumer proxy and simply drag-and-drop from the left-hand side to the right-hand side pane (within the ABAP editor). The template code will be generated and added to your program. You may modify the code according to your requirements.

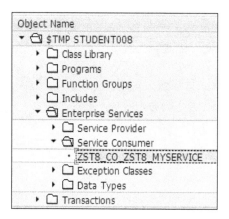

How to do it...

We will now dive into the details of the program:

1. We first declare an object reference to the ZST8_CO_ZST8_MYSERVICE proxy class that is generated. We will name the reference MYPROXY. We then instantiate the object using the CREATE OBJECT statement. We also specify the logical port name, ZST8_LOGICAL_PORT, created in the previous recipe. This is written within a TRY and ENDTRY statement.

```
DATA: MYPROXY TYPE REF TO ZST8_CO_ZST8_MYSERVICE .

TRY.
     CREATE OBJECT MYPROXY
        EXPORTING
           LOGICAL_PORT_NAME = 'ZST8_LOGICAL_PORT'.
   CATCH CX_AI_SYSTEM_FAULT .
 ENDTRY.
```

2. Then we declare our input and output structures based on the structures generated during the proxy class generation. The INPUT structure contains three fields (amount, currency, and language) corresponding to the importing parameters of our function module. Appropriate values are assigned to them.

```
data: OUTPUT type ZST8_ZST8MY_SPELL_AMOUNT_RESPO .
data: INPUT type ZST8_ZST8MY_SPELL_AMOUNT .

input-amount = '1200'.
input-currency = 'USD'.
input-language = 'EN'.
```

3. Finally, we call the method ZST8_MY_SPELL_AMOUNT and pass the input values via the INPUT structure. The result of the execution is the Web service execution and is in the OUTPUT structure. For printing the words, we can print the OUTPUT-IN_WORDS-WORD.

```
TRY.
     CALL METHOD myproxy->ZST8MY_SPELL_AMOUNT
        EXPORTING
           INPUT   = input
        IMPORTING
           OUTPUT = output.
   CATCH CX_AI_SYSTEM_FAULT .
   CATCH ZST8_CX_ZST8MY_SPELL_AMOUNT_EX .
   CATCH CX_AI_APPLICATION_FAULT .
 ENDTRY.
```

How it works...

We first declare an object based on our proxy class. Before calling the method for converting the amount into words we fill the INPUT structure with appropriate values. The two structures INPUT and OUTPUT correspond to the importing and exporting parameters of the function module, respectively. The ZST8MY_SPELL_AMOUNT method corresponds to the function module we initially used for creating the Web service. We call the method and pass the INPUT structure containing the relevant input values. The Web service is called and returns the result (amount in words) in the OUTPUT structure.

13
SAP Interactive Forms by Adobe

In this chapter, we will see recipes involving Adobe forms. We will look at:

- Creating nested tables
- Enabling duplex printing in forms
- Using form elements and scripting to create interactive forms
- Working with Adobe offline infrastructure
- Parallel printing of form
- Adding error messages for interactive forms
- PDF object API

Introduction

This chapter explores useful recipes related to SAP interactive forms by Adobe. For an introduction to forms, see `http://wiki.sdn.sap.com/wiki/display/ABAP/Adobe+Forms+from+Scratch`.

They involve two scenarios, print scenario and interactive scenario. In print scenarios, the user is not allowed to enter data on the form (PDF output) and this type of form has no buttons or interactive elements. This is not true, however, for the interactive scenarios. The interactive scenarios are of two types, namely, online and offline. The online scenario requires a connection with the SAP system while the user makes entries in the form. On the other hand, the offline scenarios, where user may download the blank form to his or her PC or the form may be sent through e-mail. The user may then fill the form and send through e-mail and then the data is extracted and updated in SAP system. There are some special settings needed for interactive forms while creating them in the **Adobe LiveCycle Designer**. Validation messages (or errors) are an important part of the interactive scenarios.

Scripting may also be used in Adobe forms. These are used for validation and generation of messages, or adding colors to elements on the form, as well as hiding form elements. They may be written in FormCalc or Javascript.

A typical program that calls the form in question (and generate its output) for one or multiple objects in question uses a number of function modules such as FP_JOB_OPEN, FP_FUNCTION_MODULE_NAME, the actual function module generating form output (determined at runtime and stored in a variable) and the function module FP_JOB_CLOSE.

The rendering of forms is done in the **Adobe Document Services** (**ADS**) that runs on the Java Stack. You may make the rendering and printing of the forms sequential or in parallel by the ADS. The form function module does the communication with the ADS in order to generate the PDF output. However, PDF Object APIs are also available that allows communication with the ADS. For example, if we have a form received that contains data entered by the user, we can use the PDF Object APIs to create PDF object instance for the given form and then extract the entered data from it.

Some new features are only available if you are using the NetWeaver Release 7.02. These will be covered in this chapter. Throughout the chapter, the terms Adobe forms and forms will be used interchangeably.

Creating nested tables

In this recipe, we will see how we can create a nested table. A nested table involves two internal tables, an inner and an outer table.

Before we dive into the details of creating our nested table, we will create two tables types in the ABAP dictionary. The first type ZST8_T_PERNR_ADDRESS is based on the line type shown as follows:

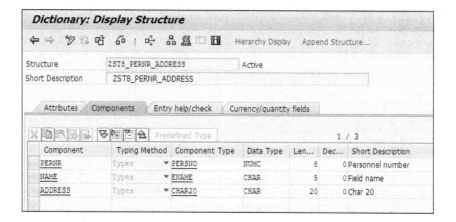

The table type `ZST8_T_PERNR_GRADES` is based on the on the line type shown as follows:

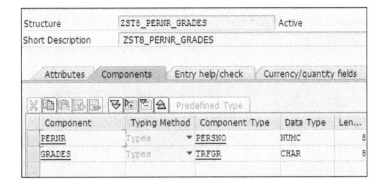

There has to be a connecting field or fields between the two. We keep the **PERNR** employee number as the connecting field between the two tables. We then create the interface based on ABAP dictionary type using transaction `SFP`.

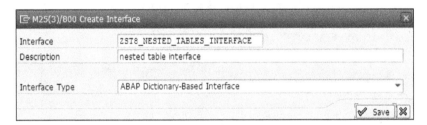

We define two variables in the data definition, the interface `EMPLOYEE_GRADES` and `EMPLOYEE_ADDRESS`, as shown in the following screenshot:

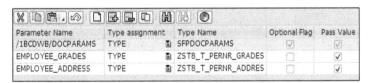

How to do it...

We will now carry out the following steps:

1. We create a new form using the transaction `SFP`. The name of the form is `ZST8_NESTED_TABLES_EXAMPLE` based on the interface defined earlier.

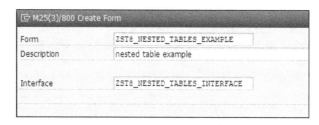

2. Within the context definition of the form, we include the `EMPLOYEE_ADDRESS` interface from the interface to the context through drag-and-drop. We then drag-and-drop the **EMPLOYEE_GRADES** node from the interface to the **EMPLOYEE_ADDRESS** node. This will include the **EMPLOYEE_GRADES** node under the **EMPLOYEE_ADDRESS** node.

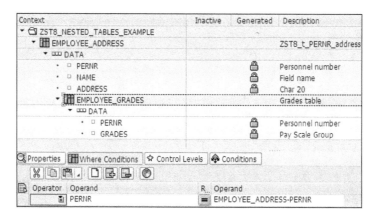

3. We will now link the two tables through the **PERNR** fields. For this, we need to click the **WHERE Conditions** tab after selecting the **EMPLOYEE_GRADES** node. Then we will enter the **PERNR** field as **Operand 1** and the **EMPLOYEE_ADDRESS-PERNR** node.

4. Now click on the **Layout** tab within the Adobe LiveCycle designer. Drag-and-drop the **EMPLOYEE_ADDRESS** table shown under the **Data View** panel to the **Form Layout** panel. Initially the nested table is created as shown in following screenshot:

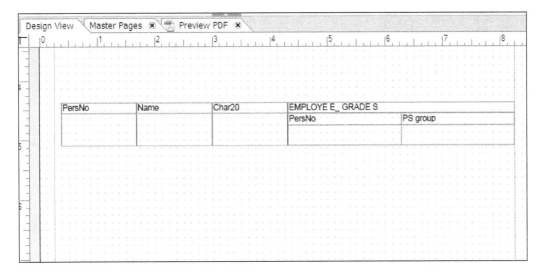

PersNo	Name	Char20	EMPLOYE E_ GRADE S	
			PersNo	PS group

5. We adjust the header of the table. We will delete the header line of the inner table **EMPLOYEE_GRADES** and adjust the text.

Employee number	Name	City	Employee Grades Since Joining

How it works...

We created two table types. Then we used them in the interface that is later used in our form. Within the context definition of the form, we included the **EMPLOYEE_ADDRESS** table from the interface to the context through drag-and-drop. Then we included the **EMPLOYEE_GRADES** table within the **EMPLOYEE_ADDRESS** table. After creating the **EMPLOYEE_ADDRESS** table on the form layout and making necessary changes, testing the form on sample data gave the output as shown in the following screenshot:

Employee number	Name	City	Employee Grades
00000001	JOHN	BRUSSELS	GRADE 11
			GRADE 14

There's more...

We can modify the header of the table in order to include a one-cell heading. For this we select the top header row and right-click in order to choose the context menu as shown in following screenshot:

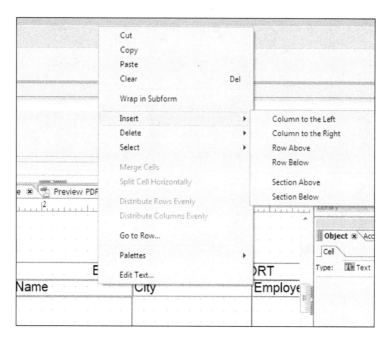

We then choose the option **Row Above**. This will include a new row. Then select the newly created row and right-click. From the context menu that appears, choose the option **Merge Cells**. This will combine the four cells and make a single cell. We then right-click and choose option **Edit Text** and then write the title of the form as EMPLOYEE DETAILS REPORT. The output of the report is shown as follows:

EMPLOYEE DETAILS REPORT			
Employee number	Name	City	Employee Grades Since Joining
00000001	JOHN	BRUSSELS	16
			15

If the table is to run on multiple pages, you may set the **Page Break Within Content** property for the table to make the table go on multiple pages.

Also, for performance reasons, while definition of the interface, we may also uncheck the checkbox **Pass Value** for the tables **EMPLOYEE_GRADES** and **EMPLOYEE_ADDRESS**.

See also

▶   http://blogs.adobe.com/blink/2007/10/best_practices_with_adobe_
inte.html

Enabling duplex printing in forms

In this recipe, we will see how we carry out the settings for enabling duplex (double-sided) form printing for your Adobe form. This will work on printers that have the capability of printing duplex forms.

We assume that we have two master pages, page 1 and page 2, and we need them to be printed in duplex form.

How to do it...

Follow these steps:

1. From the Adobe LiveCycle Designer's left-hand pane, select the **Master Page** root node. Also, select the root node **Page Set** under hierarchy tree.

2. Then on the **Object** palette, go to the **Page Set** tab.

3. Then, choose the **Print on Both Sides** option from the list box for the printing field.

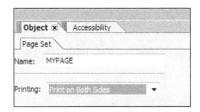

4. Click the **Yes** button to continue. The dialog box appears as shown in following screenshot:

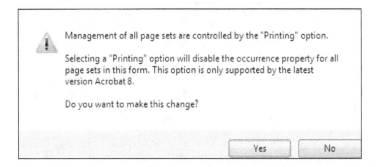

How it works...

The necessary settings have been made in order to enable duplex printing. However, as mentioned earlier, we need a duplex printer for the correct printing to take place. When the form is printed on such a printer, based on the settings, the printing will be done on two-sided format (that is, duplex).

Using form elements and scripting to create interactive forms

In this recipe, we will see how we can create a simple interactive form with form elements and some script written in FormCalc language. We will create an example where we create three fields on the screen and a button that will calculate the total of the value of the first two fields and display within the third field.

Getting ready

From the Adobe LiveCycle Designer, choose the menu option **Edit** and then select **Form Properties**. On the **Defaults** tab, within the **Preview** block, select **Interactive Form** within the **Preview Type** drop-down list and **Acrobat 8 (Dynamic) XML Form** for the **XDP Preview Format** drop-down list.

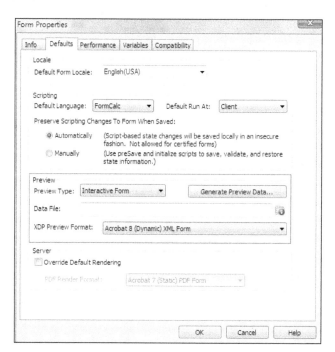

How to do it...

Follow these steps:

1. We create a new interface. We add three amount fields in the global definition of the interface.

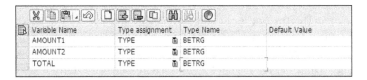

2. We create a new form using the interface and include the three variables defined in the interface. On the layout editor, add three fields for each of the three variables created earlier in the context. This will create three decimal fields on the layout.

3. Then add a button and give it the caption `Total`.

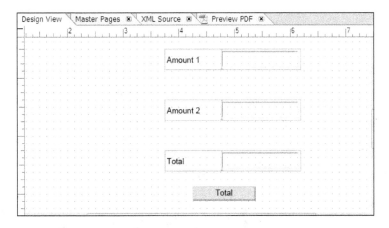

4. For the **Amount 1** and **Amount 2** fields, we set the **Display Pattern** drop-down list as **$9,999.99** using the **Field** tab on the **Object** palette.

5. For the two fields, we will set the **Type** drop-down list as **User Entered – Required** on the **Value** tab.

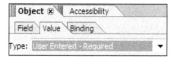

6. While being in the **Design View** window, click on the button that was created in the previous steps. Make sure the **Scripting** palette is visible. Then, from the list box of **Scripts**, choose the **Click** event. The script editor appears as shown in the following screenshot. Write the following code in the script editor and then activate.

How it works...

We can see the **PDF Preview** window by clicking on the **Preview PDF** tab in the layout editor. We can only enter a maximum of two decimal places. Any amount entered in the first two fields is shown in the format specified. For example, if we enter 1200.78, it will be changed to **$1,200.78**. When the **Total** button is pressed, the two values are totaled and shown in the **Total** field. Upon clicking the **Total** button, the script for the button-click event of the button is executed. The totaling is done and then displayed.

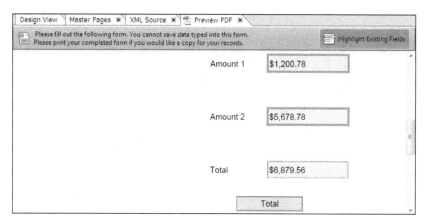

There's more...

We may also test the form through the **Test** button of transaction SFP. In this case, the SFP transaction will take us to the function module test screen. For testing the interactive scenario, the **FILLABLE** field for the **/1BCDWB/DOCPARAMS** structure must be passed the value 'X'. This will open the PDF form in the interactive mode, as shown in the following screenshot:

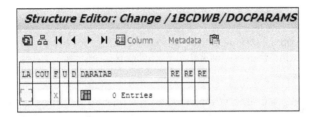

See also

▶ http://www.adobepress.com/articles/article.
   asp?p=1021020&seqNum=4

Working with Adobe offline infrastructure

In this recipe, we will see the usage of the Adobe offline infrastructure. The Adobe offline infrastructure allows you to process user-filled PDF forms (received by e-mail), and then extract data from it and update in the SAP database. It allows you to implement offline interactive scenario when you have the user to fill the PDF form offline and then send back to you at a given e-mail address.

The inbound processing of the form sent via e-mail requires a configuration setting in transaction SO50 (Exit Rules for Inbound Processing). In our context, it lets us specify how the received PDF form attachment at a given e-mail address is to be handled. The generic main inbound handler class CL_FP_INBOUND_HANDLER should be entered in the **Exit Name** field for the receiving e-mail address.

Once an e-mail is received, the PDF attachment is forwarded for processing to the generic inbound handler, which retrieves the entered data and then calls the application inbound handler relevant to the form in question.

In addition, an (application) inbound class handler based on the interface IF_FP_OFFLINE must be created and necessary code written in its methods. This class is used for processing the received form data in XML format (received from the generic handler) and extract the data entered by the user in it by converting them to ABAP variables.

The advantages are that with minimal configuration and coding, the desired requirement may be achieved. This recipe will cover the configuration of transaction SO50 and the inbound handler class (and its method coding).

The standard SAP examples were referred to while creating this recipe. This includes the inbound handler class CL_FP_OFFLINE_FP_TEST_IA_01 and the Adobe form FP_TEST_IA_01.

Getting ready

As a prerequisite, the basis consultant must do the settings for the activation of the SMTP plug-in in the SAP system. This ensures that e-mail communication takes place and is received without problems.

An ABAP program must be created that will send the PDF form to the respective user. This will then be filled by the user and then sent to the specified e-mail address in SO50 (and our inbound processing will take on from there). The program will use the **Business Communication Service**. An important thing to make sure is that when the function module for the Adobe form is called, the **FILLABLE** field of parameter structure /1BCDWB/DOCPARAMS must be assigned the value F (and not X).

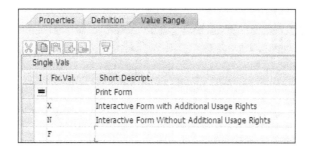

In addition to the earlier, the value **F** means **Activates Special handling for Offline Interactive Scenarios**.

For the sake of this recipe, we assume that we have created two fields FIELD1 and FIELD2 in the interface and the context respectively. The user has entered the values of the FIELD1 and FIELD2 fields in the form and these values are to be extracted.

How to do it...

We will now carry out the following steps:

1. The appropriate setting must be done in the transaction SO50. Call the transaction SO50. The screen appear as shown in the following screenshot:

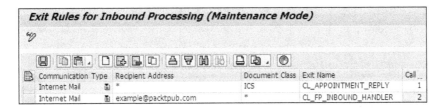

2. Click the ▫ button. A new row appears as shown. Enter the class name CL_FP_INBOUND_HANDLER in the **Exit Name** field. Select the **Communication Type** as **Internet Mail**. Enter the recipient address at which the user will send the filled form. For example, example@packtpub.com.

3. Next, we will create the inbound handler class.

4. Call transaction SE24 and enter the name of the inbound class that you like to create (in our case ZST8_OFF_HANDLER).

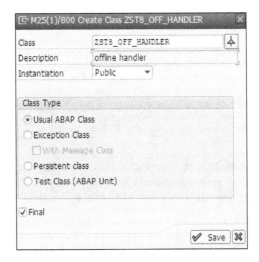

5. We will include the interface IF_FP_OFFLINE. This will include two methods in our class (namely, GET_INSTANCE and HANDLE_PDF).

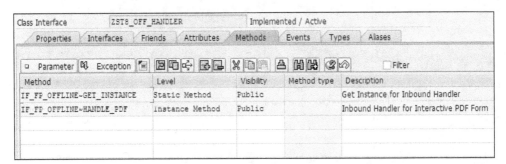

6. A simple one line code needs to be added to the `GET_INSTANCE` method as shown below:

Method	IF_FP_OFFLINE~GET_INSTANCE

```
1  ⊟ METHOD IF_FP_OFFLINE~GET_INSTANCE.
2       CREATE OBJECT RO_INSTANCE TYPE ZST8_OFF_HANDLER.
3    └ ENDMETHOD.
```

7. The method `HANDLE_PDF` code is then written. Within the `HANDLE_PDF` method, we first call the function module `FP_FUNCTION_MODULE_NAME`. The form name parameter of the function module is supplied with the form name stored in the method parameter `IV_FORM_NAME`. The inbound function module name is then imported in the variable `INBOUND_FM`. The code is shown in the following screenshot:

```
DATA :  INBOUND_FM TYPE  FUNCNAME.
TRY.
    CALL FUNCTION 'FP_FUNCTION_MODULE_NAME'
        EXPORTING
          I_NAME                = IV_FORM_NAME
        IMPORTING
          EV_FUNCNAME_INBOUND = INBOUND_FM.

  CATCH CX_FP_API_REPOSITORY CX_FP_API_USAGE
        CX_FP_API_INTERNAL.

ENDTRY.
```

8. We then declare variables corresponding to the two data fields defined in the context. The inbound function module is then called that transforms the XML data of the form into the variables `MYFIELD1` and `MYFIELD2` of our class.

```
DATA : MYFIELD1 TYPE char10.
DATA : MYFIELD2 TYPE char10.

CALL FUNCTION INBOUND_FM
  EXPORTING
    IV_XML_DATA      = IV_XML
  IMPORTING
    FIELD1           = MYFIELD1
    FIELD2           = MYFIELD2
  EXCEPTIONS
    USAGE_ERROR      = 1
    SYSTEM_ERROR     = 2
    INTERNAL_ERROR  = 3
    OTHERS           = 4.
```

9. The values of the two fields may then be saved into the database (for testing purpose, we save it in a cluster in a table `ZST_TAB` under cluster ID `ZA` under key with value in `MYFIELD1`).

```
export myfield1 from myfield1 myfield2 from myfield2
to database  zst_tab(ZA)  id myfield1.
```

10. Next, we need to connect the inbound class created with the form in question. For this we will go to transaction `SFP` and enter the name of the class created in the previous steps in the **Properties** tab of the form under consideration.

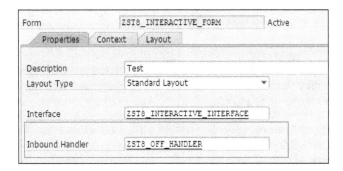

How it works...

Within the mail-sending program, the assignment of **F** for the **FILLABLE** field adds necessary information to the attached PDF relevant to the offline scenario. Once the form is filled and sent back by the user to the e-mail address specified in transaction SO50, it is handled by the Adobe Infrastructure offline, that passes it and the XML data contained in it to the inbound handler class.

The main method `HANDLE_PDF` is used for transforming the XML data entered in the form into data variables. The form name and the data in XML form are passed to the method through the parameters `IV_FORM` and `IV_XML` respectively. We first get the function module corresponding to our form that allows the transformations of the XML data into ABAP variables corresponding to context data. The `FP_FUNCTION_MODULE` function is passed the name of the form name contained in importing parameter `IV_FORM` and then the function module corresponding to `EV_FUNCNAME_INBOUND` parameter is imported and stored in `INBOUND_FM`. The function module whose name is stored in variable `INBOUND_FM` is then called and supplied with the XML Data (contained in `IV_XML`). The function module transforms the XML and the returned ABAP data is stored in `FIELD1` and `FIELD2` variables.

See also

- ▶ http://help.sap.com/saphelp_nw73/helpdata/en/4a/
  a193d2acd5007fe10000000a42189c/frameset.htm

- ▶ http://www.sdn.sap.com/irj/scn/go/portal/prtroot/docs/library/
  uuid/f091d8bb-7bce-2b10-c192-9d91090c6be9?QuickLink=index&overr
  idelayout=true&37804302173927

Parallel printing of form

In normal circumstances, we will have a sequential rendering and printing of PDF forms by the Adobe Document Services. In this recipe, we will see how we can enable parallel printing through a small change in the code.

In the newer release, a special parameter has been added to the function module parameter FP_OPEN. It is recommended to set the PARALLEL parameter value to 'X' when there are more than thousand forms to be printed.

For having print request to be processed in parallel, the Adobe Document Services must be running on a Java Stack 7.2 or higher.

How to do it...

Follow these steps:

1. First, we define a structure that is based on the dictionary structure SFPOUTPUTPARAMS.

2. The PARALLEL field of the structure must be assigned the value of 'X'.

3. Finally, the function module FP_JOB_OPEN is called. For simplicity sake, we have only shown the PARALLEL field assignment. For the changing parameter of the function module FP_JOB_OPEN, the structure MYOUTPUTPARAMS is passed.

```
data :
  myoutputparams     TYPE sfpoutputparams.
  myoutputparams-parallel  = 'X'.

* Opening print job
  CALL FUNCTION 'FP_JOB_OPEN'
    CHANGING
      ie_outputparams = myoutputparams
    EXCEPTIONS
      OTHERS          = 1.
```

How it works...

When values `'X'` is passed for the field `PARALLEL`, the ADS performs parallel printing of adobe forms. This involves usage of multiple processors for the rendering and printing of the generated forms. This parallel rendering significantly increase the performance particularly when the total number of forms to be processed are greater than 1000.

See also

▸ `http://help.sap.com/saphelp_nw73/helpdata/en/48/5849326b6a41379`
`c4d5511abfc2525/content.htm`

Adding error messages for interactive forms

In this recipe, we will see how we can add error messages to interactive forms. We will see how a **Date** input field may be set to produce error messages when a wrong date is passed.

How to do it...

Follow these steps:

1. On the **Object** palette of the **Date** panel, select the **Value** tab.

2. Select a validation pattern from the list box provided.

3. Select the **Error** checkbox and in the **Validation Pattern Message** area and enter the message that you like to be displayed.

4. Activate your form.

How it works...

When the user enters in the required format, no error is displayed. When a wrong date is entered, the error is shown as shown in the following screenshot:

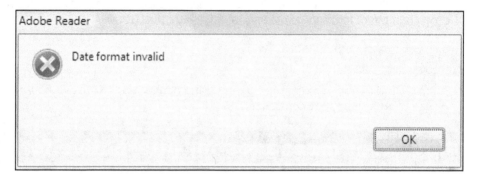

The error that you defined in the **Validation Pattern Message** area is displayed, and it is an error since we have checked the **Error** indicator.

See also

▸ http://help.adobe.com/en_US/LiveCycle/9.0/designerHelp/index.htm?content=000412.html

PDF object API

The PDF object API allows communicating with the ADS and carrying out necessary functions from an ABAP program. These include creation of forms and extraction of data, and so on. In this recipe, we will see the code that will allow you to communicate with the ADS in order to generate a PDF form object for a filled PDF form and then extract necessary data from it. We assume that we are not using the Adobe offline infrastructure.

There are a few classes and interfaces involved. The factory class CL_FP is used for creating the PDF document object instance that is based on the class CL_FP_PDF_OBJECT (using interface IF_FP_PDF_OBJECT). The main implementation class for the PDF object is CL_FP_PDF_OBJECT.

In this recipe, we will see how a filled form may be programmatically processed using the ADS functions and then the entered data within the form may be extracted. We assume that the form to be processed is stored in the variable MYFORM having type XSTRING. The recipe takes on from there. Only the part that is relevant to the instantiation of the PDF object and extraction is shown in the recipe.

How to do it...

Follow these steps:

1. We first need to declare variables for the factory class interface IF_FP and the interface IF_FP_PDF_OBJECT.

```
DATA: MY_FP TYPE REF TO IF_FP VALUE IS INITIAL.
DATA: MYPDFOBJECT TYPE REF TO IF_FP_PDF_OBJECT VALUE IS INITIAL,
      EXCEPTION TYPE REF TO CX_ROOT.
```

2. The static method GET_REFERENCE of the CL_FP interface is then called and the object returned is stored in MY_FP.

```
MY_FP = CL_FP=>GET_REFERENCE( ).
```

3. Next, the PDF object is then created using the CREATE_PDF_OBJECT method of the CL_FP class. The value ADS is passed for the CONNECTION parameter. Then the SET_DOCUMENT method is called and the PDF data contained in the xstring MYFORM is assigned to it.

```
MYPDFOBJECT = MY_FP->CREATE_PDF_OBJECT( CONNECTION = 'ADS' ).
MYPDFOBJECT->SET_DOCUMENT( PDFDATA = MYFORM ).
```

4. The SET_EXTRACTDATA method of the class CL_FP_PDF_OBJECT is then called followed by the EXECUTE method.

```
MYPDFOBJECT->SET_EXTRACTDATA( ).

MYPDFOBJECT->EXECUTE( ).
```

5. The GET_DATA method is then called.

```
DATA: MYXMLDATA TYPE XSTRING.
MYPDFOBJECT->GET_DATA( IMPORTING FORMDATA = MYXMLDATA ).
```

6. The entire block of code may be placed within the TRY and ENDTRY statements and the Exception class CX_FP_RUNTIME_SYSTEM may be used.

```
CATCH CX_FP_RUNTIME_SYSTEM INTO EXCEPTION.
```

How it works...

We initially declare references to the factory class `CL_FP` and the main implementation class `CL_IF_PDF_OBJECT` (using appropriate interface names). The static `GET_REFERENCE` method the `CL_FP` class is then called and an object is instantiated belonging to class `CL_FP`. This is pointed to by the reference variable `MY_FP`.

The `CREATE_PDF_OBJECT` method of the factory class `CL_FP` is then called to create the PDF object instance, the reference to which is stored in the variable `MYPDFOBJECT`.

The `SET_DOCUMENT` method is called for the variable `MYPDFOBJECT` in order to link the PDF data stored in the `MYFORM` xstring. The `SET_EXTRACTDATA` method is then called in order to specify the extraction of the entered data in the form. The `Execute` method allows the PDF form to be passed to the ADS and the extraction of data to takes place.

It is only at the `EXECUTE` method that the ADS comes into action (the `Execute` method triggers execution of all method beginning with `SET_`). The data entered in the form is extracted and is made available in XML format. Once the extraction has been done, the `GET_DATA` method may be called in order to read the form data into the xstring `XMLDATA`. We can use transformations to place the data in ABAP variables.

See also

- *SAP Interactive Forms by Adobe, Andreas Deutesfeld, Stephan Rehmann, Thomas Szücs, Philipp Thun, Jürgen Hauser, SAP press*
- `http://wiki.sdn.sap.com/wiki/display/ABAP/Reading+PDF+attachmen t+from+sap+inbox+through+ABAP`
- `http://help.sap.com/SAPhelp_nw70/helpdata/en/46/25ed5cb2bc00c3e 10000000a11466f/frameset.htm`
- `http://www.sdn.sap.com/irj/scn/go/portal/prtroot/docs/library/ uuid/4006d93c-3eed-2c10-ad9b-d11c4618c4e9?QuickLink=index&overr idelayout=true`

14
Web Dynpro for ABAP

In this chapter, we will see recipes involving Web Dynpro for ABAP. We will look at:

- ▸ Creating trees
- ▸ Creating navigation lists
- ▸ Creating tabstrips
- ▸ Displaying error messages
- ▸ Calling dialog boxes of the same component
- ▸ Displaying Adobe forms in Web Dynpros

Introduction

This chapter explores useful recipes related to Web Dynpro for ABAP. The Web Dynpro Development framework may be accessed using the transaction code SE80. Then, from the listbox on the left pane, select **Web Dynpro**. We will start with a discussion of the interfaces generated in Web Dynpro components.

Within a Web Dynpro component, a number of controllers exist, such as the component controller, the window controller, and the view controller. We may add our own attributes and methods to the various controllers. Each controller has a private interface (local interface) generated during design time. From the transaction code SE80 and Web Dynpro selected, you may use the menu path **Goto** | **Controller Interface** to see the details of this interface.

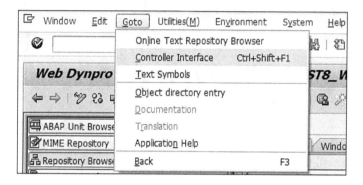

For the component controller the name of the interface is **IF_COMPONENTCONTROLLER**. For the view controller, the name of this interface is of the format **IF_<VIEWNAME>**, and for the window controller it is **IF_<WINDOWNAME>**.

The attribute **WD_THIS** contained within the controller is a reference to the local interface in question. A wd_get_api () method is defined within the interface and provides a set of APIs (controller-specific functions) related to the controller in question.

The type of interface reference returned by the WD_GET_API method depends on the controller for which it is used. For the component controller, the interface is IF_WD_COMPONENT. In case of the view and window controllers, the IF_WD_VIEW_CONTROLLER interface is returned.

Both the interfaces, **IF_WD_VIEW_CONTROLLER** and **IF_WD_COMPONENT** include the interface **IF_WD_CONTROLLER**.

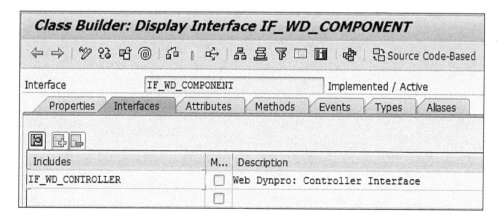

The API provides useful methods for Web Dynpro programming. The interfaces provided contain a number of useful methods including generation of messages and creation of dialog boxes possible through providing access to the Message Manager and Window Manager (this will be discussed in the recipes in this chapter). The IF_WD_CONTROLLER method provides the GET_MESSAGE_MANAGER method required for generating messages, such as error messages that appear on the user screen where an incorrect input is provided. The GET_WINDOW_MANAGER method is the method provided by the **IF_WD_COMPONENT** interface for generating dialog boxes.

Though the window and view controllers use the interface, some methods such as GET_CURRENT_ACTION can only be called from a view controller (from the WDDOBEFOREACTION method).

Creating trees

In this recipe, we will see how we can display a tree in our Web Dynpro application. We will create a tree that will display the employee department-wise data, that is, nodes showing department names, each of which when opened will display a list of employees within the department along with the employee names.

For the sake of this recipe, we assume that we have an internal table DATA_TAB comprising of three fields, department, pernr, and sname containing the department name, employee number, and the employee names respectively sorted according to the department name.

```
types : begin of ty_tab,
          department type char35,
          pernr type persno,
          sname type sname,
        end of ty_tab.

data: wa_tab type ty_tab.
data: data_tab type standard table of ty_tab.
```

How to do it...

We will now follow the steps as shown:

1. We first define a context node TREE_NODE. The TREE_NODE context node has a cardinality of 0..N and the Singleton property should be Off. An IS_OPENED attribute will be based on the type WDY_BOOLEAN.

2. Within the `TREE_NODE` context node there is another node, `TREE_NODE_ITEM`, which is also a non-singleton node having cardinality `0..N`. An attribute `ITEM_TEXT` is created within the `TREE_NODE_ITEM` node. The `ITEM_TEXT` attribute has a type `STRING`.

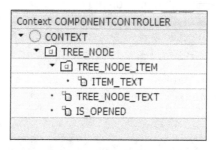

3. We will then define a `TREE` UI element in our view layout. We create a `TREE` UI element along with two subelements. These are based on `TreeNodetype` and `TreeItemtype`, having the names `MY_NODES` and `MY_ITEMS`, respectively.

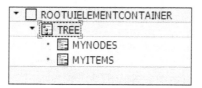

4. We bind the `TREE` UI element `datasource` property with the `TREE_NODE` context node. For `MYNODES`, the text property is bound with the `TREE_NODE.TREE_NODE_TEXT` attribute. Likewise, for `MYITEMS`, the text property is bound with the `TREE_NODE.TREE_NODE_ITEM.TREE_ITEM_TEXT` attribute. The `IS_OPENED` attribute of the context node is assigned to the expanded property of the `MYNODES` subelement.

5. Next, we will write the code into the `WDDOINIT` method of the view created. We define reference variables for the context nodes `root_node`, `TREE_NODE`, and `ITEM_NODE`. We also define data variables pertaining to the `ELEMENT_TREE_NODE` element and the `ELEMENT_TREE_NODE_ITEM` element.

```
DATA root_node TYPE REF TO IF_WD_CONTEXT_NODE.
DATA TREE_NODE TYPE REF TO IF_WD_CONTEXT_ELEMENT.
DATA ITEM_NODE TYPE REF TO IF_WD_CONTEXT_NODE.


DATA NODE TYPE WD_THIS->ELEMENT_TREE_NODE.
DATA ITEM TYPE WD_THIS->ELEMENT_TREE_NODE_ITEM.
```

6. We then get the reference to the TREE_NODE context node by calling the GET_CHILD_NODE method. The reference is stored in root_node.

```
root_node = WD_CONTEXT->GET_CHILD_NODE(
        NAME = WD_THIS->WDCTX_TREE_NODE ).
```

7. Next, we populate the context nodes with appropriate data that may be displayed in the tree.

8. We run a loop at the DATA_TAB, the table that contains the department name with employee name and numbers. We place a AT NEW DEPARTMENT statement within which we assign the department name to the NODE structure corresponding to our TREE_NODE context node. We then call the BIND_STRUCTURE method of the root_node context node and supply the data to be added to the node's element collection. We then get the reference to the TREE_NODE_ITEM child context node and store it in the ITEM_NODE variable (to be used later within the loop).

9. Outside the AT .. ENDAT block, we use the CONCATENATE statement in order to combine the personnel number and name and store it in the ITEM-ITEM_TEXT variable. This is then added to the ITEM_NODE context node's collection using the BIND_STRUCTURE method.

```
LOOP AT DATA_TAB INTO WA_DATA.
  AT NEW DEPARTMENT.
    NODE-TREE_NODE_TEXT =  WA_DATA-DEPARTMENT.
    TREE_NODE = root_node->BIND_STRUCTURE(
                    NEW_ITEM = NODE
                    SET_INITIAL_ELEMENTS = ABAP_FALSE ).
    ITEM_NODE = TREE_NODE->GET_CHILD_NODE(
    NAME = WD_THIS->WDCTX_TREE_NODE_ITEM )  .
  ENDAT.

  CONCATENATE WA_DATA-PERNR WA_DATA-SNAME INTO
  ITEM-ITEM_TEXT SEPARATED BY '-'.

  ITEM_NODE->BIND_STRUCTURE(
    NEW_ITEM = ITEM
    SET_INITIAL_ELEMENTS = ABAP_FALSE ).

ENDLOOP.
```

How it works...

We create a TREE UI element on the view layout. We create two subelements for the TREE element; one is the TreeNodetype type and the other TreeItemtype type. The MYNODES subelement (of type TreeNodetype) and MYITEMS subelement (of type TreeItemtype) correspond to the department names, and the employee names and number respectively in the final display. Appropriate bindings are defined for MYNODE and MYITEMS with relevant context data node attributes.

A loop is used to populate the data for the TREE_NODE context node. We kept the IS_OPENED attribute as a space while populating the data for the TREE_NODE context node and its child node TREE_NODE_ITEM. When displayed, the department nodes are not expanded. When the application is run, within the browser, we see a list of departments as shown in the following screenshot:

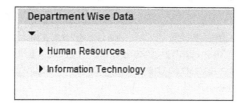

When the relevant nodes are expanded, the employees within the departments are displayed along with their number and name, as shown in the following screenshot:

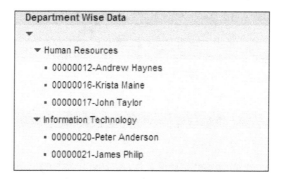

Creating navigation lists

In this recipe, we will see how we can display data in the form of a navigation list. The navigation list is similar to a tree. However, the nodes appear in expanded form when displayed and may not be compressed. The entire navigation list may be expanded and compressed (however, not the data nodes within it).

We assume that we have an internal DATA_TAB table comprising of three fields, department, pernr, and sname, containing the department name, employee number, and the employee names respectively in sorted order according to the department name.

```
types : begin of ty_tab,
          department type char35,
          pernr type persno,
          sname type sname,
        end of ty_tab.

data: wa_tab type ty_tab.
data: data_tab type standard table of ty_tab.
```

How to do it...

We will now see the steps required to create a navigation list:

1. We will first create the context node related to the navigation list in the component controller. We create a context node by the name NAVLIST.

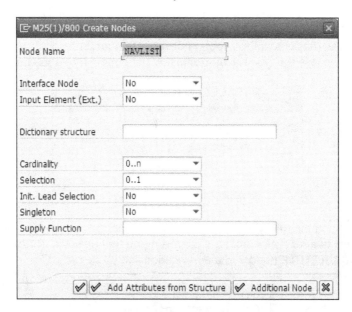

2. The **Init Lead Selection** field must be set to No (since, in this case, we do not require lead selection and its initialization). The **Singleton** property of the node must be set as No. The **Cardinality** field is set as 0..n.

3. We then add three attributes to the context node NAVLIST, namely DISPLAYED_ TEXT, PERNR, and IF_SELECTED based on the type STRING, PERSNO, and WDY_BOOLEAN, respectively.

4. We then add a recursive node to the NAVLIST context node and name it NAVLISTREC. Right-click on the NAVLIST context node and from the context menu that appears, navigate to **Create | Recursive Node**.

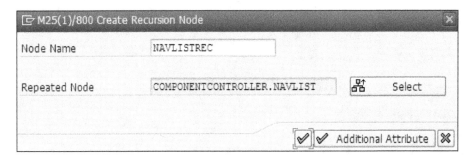

5. We then drag-and-drop the context node NAVLIST from the component controller to the relevant view controller (define the mapping).

6. Next, we will create the navigation list UI element on the Web Dynpro view. Right-click on the **ROOTUIELEMENTCONTAINER** option from the right pane of the layout editor and choose the context menu option **Create Element**. Enter Navigation in the **ID** field and choose the type **NavigationList** in the pop up that appears.

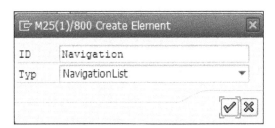

7. Right-click on the **NAVIGATION** node in the right pane of the layout editor and choose the **insert header** option from the context menu that appears. This will add the **EXPANDABLETITLE** header to the navigation list.

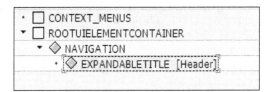

8. Enter the text `Department Wise List` in the **title** property.

Properties (ExpandableTitle)	
ID	EXPANDABLETITLE
expandable	☐
expanded	✓
title	Department Wise List
Events	
onToggle	

9. For the defined navigation list, we will set the **itemSource** property as the `MAIN.NAVLIST` context node defined earlier. For the **itemText** property, we set the value as the `DISPLAYEDTEXT` attribute of the context node.

Property	Value		Binding
Properties (NavigationList)			
ID	NAVIGATION		
contentHeight	0		
contextMenuBehaviour	Inherit	🔳	
contextMenuId			
enabled	✓		
itemSelectable	✓		
itemSource	MAIN.NAVLIST		👆
itemText	MAIN.NAVLIST.DISPLAYEDTEXT	🔲	👆
tooltip			
visible	Visible	🔳	
Events			
onSelect			☐
Layout Data (FlowData)			
cellDesign	padless	🔳	
vGutter	None	🔳	

10. Once this is done, we will see the navigation list added in our layout editor, as shown in the following screenshot:

```
Department Wise List

MAIN.NAVLIST.DISPLAYEDTEXT
    MAIN.NAVLIST.DISPLAYEDTEXT
    MAIN.NAVLIST.DISPLAYEDTEXT
    MAIN.NAVLIST.DISPLAYEDTEXT
MAIN.NAVLIST.DISPLAYEDTEXT
    MAIN.NAVLIST.DISPLAYEDTEXT
    MAIN.NAVLIST.DISPLAYEDTEXT
    MAIN.NAVLIST.DISPLAYEDTEXT
MAIN.NAVLIST.DISPLAYEDTEXT
    MAIN.NAVLIST.DISPLAYEDTEXT
    MAIN.NAVLIST.DISPLAYEDTEXT
    MAIN.NAVLIST.DISPLAYEDTEXT
```

11. The next step is to write the code for populating the context node with the appropriate department data that is to be shown in the navigation list.

12. Appropriate variables are first defined for the navigation list node (NODE_NAVLIST) and the navigation list recursive context node (RECNODE).

13. Also ELEMENT_NAVLIST is defined as a reference to a context element using interface IF_WD_CONTEXT_ELEMENT.

```
DATA NAVLIST TYPE WD_THIS->ELEMENT_NAVLIST.
DATA NODE_NAVLIST TYPE REF TO IF_WD_CONTEXT_NODE.
DATA ELEMENT_NAVLIST TYPE REF TO IF_WD_CONTEXT_ELEMENT.
DATA RECNODE TYPE REF TO IF_WD_CONTEXT_NODE.
```

14. The next step is to write the code for populating the data within the navigation list. We run a loop at the DATA_TAB internal table that contains data of the department and the personnel number and names.

15. At the beginning of a new department, we use the AT NEW DEPARTMENT statement to add data to the context node NAVLIST.

16. The GET_CHILD_NODE method is called to get a reference to the NAVLIST context node; the reference is stored in the NODE_NAVLIST navigation list node. The NAVLIST structure is assigned the department name. The IS_SELECTABLE property is kept as false.

17. The BIND_STRUCTURE node is then used to add the department name to the NAVLIST context node element collection. The reference to the added element is returned and stored in ELEMENT_NAVLIST. The GET_CHILD_NODE method is then called to get the reference to the NAVLISTREC recursion node for the element referred to by the ELEMENT_NAVLIST variable (this reference is stored in RECNODE) to be used later.

18. Outside the `AT .. ENDAT` block is the area that is executed for all rows in the data internal table `DATA_TAB`. This area pertains to the employee data (employee name and employee). We use the `NAVLIST` structure in this block.

19. We assigned the value `ABAP_TRUE` and the name and employee number to the `IS_SELECTABLE` property to be displayed in the `DISPLAYED_TEXT` field. The `BIND_STRUCTURE` node is then used for adding the employee data to the `NAVLISTREC` recursive node using the `RECNODE` reference variable.

```
LOOP AT DATA_TAB INTO WA_DATA.
  AT NEW DEPARTMENT.
    NODE_NAVLIST = WD_CONTEXT->GET_CHILD_NODE(
                NAME = WD_THIS->WDCTX_NAVLIST ).
    CLEAR NAVLIST.
    NAVLIST-DISPLAYEDTEXT = WA_DATA-DEPARTMENT.
    NAVLIST-IS_SELECTABLE = ABAP_FALSE.

    ELEMENT_NAVLIST = NODE_NAVLIST->BIND_STRUCTURE(
                        NEW_ITEM = NAVLIST
                        SET_INITIAL_ELEMENTS = ABAP_FALSE ).
    RECNODE = ELEMENT_NAVLIST->GET_CHILD_NODE(
                        NAME = 'NAVLISTREC' ).
  ENDAT.

  NAVLIST-IS_SELECTABLE = ABAP_TRUE.
  NAVLIST-PERNR = WA_DATA-PERNR.
  CONCATENATE WA_DATA-PERNR WA_DATA-SNAME
  INTO NAVLIST-DISPLAYEDTEXT SEPARATED BY '-'.
  RECNODE->BIND_STRUCTURE( NEW_ITEM = NAVLIST
                        SET_INITIAL_ELEMENTS = ABAP_FALSE ).

ENDLOOP.
```

How it works...

We first created a `NAVLIST` context node containing a `NAVLISTREC` recursion node. We then inserted a navigation list UI element on the view layout. Appropriate binding between the navigation list UI element and the context nodes was defined. In the code, we formed the higher nodes in the navigation list displaying departments (at the beginning of a new department within the data table `DATA_TAB`). We then added child nodes (to the department nodes) displaying the employee names and number contained within the department.

The employee names within the department are selectable but may not be compressed (the IS_SELECTABLE property is set to TRUE in the code). This navigation list is displayed as shown in the following screenshot:

```
Department Wise List

Human Resources
    00000012-Andrew Haynes
    00000016-Krista Maine
    00000017-John Taylor
Information Technology
    00000020-Peter Anderson
    00000021-James Philip
```

There's more...

We can further enhance the application by activating the selection feature of the selectable nodes, that is, displaying the details of an employee selected on the user's screen. For this, we first need to enter a suitable name in the Onselect property of the navigation list in the layout editor. Then double-click in order to write the code. The GET_CHILD_NODE method will be called when a particular selectable row is clicked by the user. The handler method will be called when the SELECT event is raised.

This handler method contains one parameter, WDEVENT. In order to determine which employee number and name has been selected, we will add a new parameter, SEL_NODE, having type IF_WD_CONTEXT_ELEMENT. We then need to call the GET_STATIC_ATTRIBUTES method for the SEL_NODE parameter in order to retrieve the details of the selected node (including the employee number pernr).

See also

> http://help.sap.com/saphelp_nw04s/helpdata/en/79/555e3f71e41e26 e10000000a114084/content.htm

Creating tabstrips

In this recipe, we will see how we can add tabstrips to an existing view containing various layout elements.

How to do it...

We will now follow the steps as shown:

1. We first go to the layout editor and in the right pane, right-click on the **ROOTUIELEMENTCONTAINER** element in order to access the context menu. We then select the **Insert Element** option. Now, we enter the name `Tabstrip` in the **ID** field and select the type `TabStrip`.

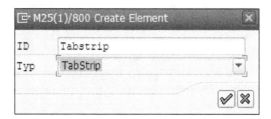

2. This will create a `TABSTRIP` in our layout. We select the tabstrip and then add two tabs by choosing the **Insert tab** option from the context menu.

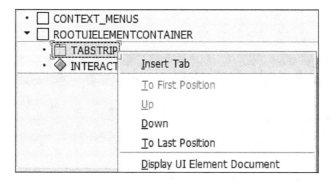

3. Next we assign appropriate text in the `text` property of the added caption headers for each of the two tabs.

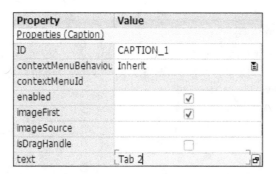

4. Then we will simply drag-and-drop any UI element already contained in our layout editor to the tab of our choice. Any width and height adjustments are made if required. We save and activate the component and run the relevant application.

How it works...

Suppose we had an interactive UI element that was transferred to the first tab. Running the application will show the relevant Adobe form in the first tab, as shown in the following screenshot. Selecting the other tab will show the elements contained in it.

	EMPLOYEE DETAILS REPORT		
Employee number	Name	City	Employee Grades
00000010	John	Mall Road, Brussels	15
			17

Tab 1 Tab 2

Displaying error messages

In this recipe, we will see how we can display messages, such as error messages when a user input is found to be incorrect. We will create a view that will have a button that displays a message when the input is correct (for simplicity's sake, we will focus on the error generation coding in this recipe).

In addition, it is recommended that you use assistance class for storing language-dependent text that is to be displayed in the form of messages. For simplicity's sake, the assistance class has not been shown in this recipe.

How to do it...

1. In the first step, we will create a `Button` element on our view and give it the caption `Check Data`. Within the events, we will select **BUTTON** (as the **onAction** property) from the listbox.

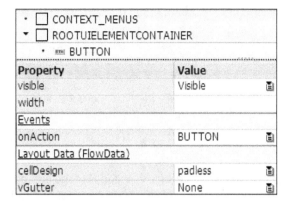

2. A public attribute MYMESSMANAGER is defined at the component controller level, the associated type of which is the IF_WD_MESSAGE_MANAGER interface.

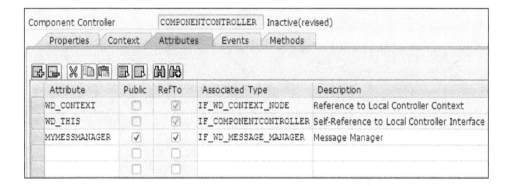

3. Next, we write the relevant code within the WDDOINIT method of the component controller. We define an interface reference for the IF_WD_CONTOLLER interface.

4. The WD_GET_API method is then used to get a reference to the interface containing appropriate APIs. We will then call the GET_MESSAGE_MANAGER method in order to get the handle to the message manager. This is assigned to the WD_THIS->MYMESSMANAGER interface we defined in the previous section.

```
METHOD WDDOINIT .

  DATA: THIS_CONTROLLER TYPE REF TO IF_WD_CONTROLLER.
  THIS_CONTROLLER ?= WD_THIS->WD_GET_API( ).
  WD_THIS->MYMESSMANAGER = THIS_CONTROLLER->GET_MESSAGE_MANAGER( ).

ENDMETHOD.
```

5. In the `WDDOBEFOREREACTION` method of the appropriate view, we will write the coding for generating an error message. First, a reference to the `IF_WD_VIEW_CONTROLLER` interface is defined. The `WD_GET_API` method is then called to get the relevant set of APIs for the view controller. This is then returned to the `LO_API_CONTROLLER` variable.

6. We use the `GET_CURRENT_ACTION` method in order to find out which of the events have been triggered by the user. The name of the event triggered is returned in the `LO_ACTION->NAME` attribute. We check if the name is equal to the `BUTTON` element, that is, the button we define. We then carry out the necessary checks, and if the data entered is invalid, the `REPORT_ERROR_MESSAGE` method of the `IF_WD_MESSAGE_MANAGER` interface is called with the appropriate error text. In this case, the public attribute, `MYMESSMANAGER`, defined in the component controller, is used.

```
DATA LO_API_CONTROLLER TYPE REF TO IF_WD_VIEW_CONTROLLER.
DATA LO_ACTION          TYPE REF TO IF_WD_ACTION.
LO_API_CONTROLLER = WD_THIS->WD_GET_API( ).
LO_ACTION = LO_API_CONTROLLER->GET_CURRENT_ACTION( ).

IF LO_ACTION IS BOUND.
  CASE LO_ACTION->NAME.
    WHEN 'BUTTON'.
      ...... " if error found in entered data
      WD_COMP_CONTROLLER->MYMESSMANAGER->REPORT_ERROR_MESSAGE(
      MESSAGE_TEXT = 'Error in Entry' ).
  ENDCASE.
ENDIF.
```

How it works...

In this case, the interface used for generating messages is the `IF_WD_MESSAGE_MANAGER` interface. The interface has a number of methods used for generating warning error messages on the screen.

First, we defined a public attribute `MYMESSAGEMANAGER` at the component controller level. Appropriate code is written in order to get the handle to the message manager that can be later used from any of the views in order to generate messages.

When the user clicks the button we defined, the `WDDOBEFOREREACTION` method of the relevant view is called. Within the method, we wrote code to gain access to the API of the view controller, the reference to which is used to call the `GET_CURRENT_ACTION` method. The `GET_CURRENT_ACTION` method is used for determining the event that has been raised as a result of the user interaction. We checked the `LO_ACTION->NAME` attribute in order to see whether our button has been clicked. In case our button is clicked, we carry out the necessary checks for checking the validity of the data that is entered (the code is not shown). Then the `REPORT_ERROR_MESSAGE` method is called in order to display an error message.

Calling dialog boxes of same component

In this recipe, we will see how we can display a dialog box based on a view of the same component. We will create a MAIN view in the MAIN window and another view by the name POP_UP in a new window, WIND_POP_UP. We will then create a button on the MAIN view, which when clicked will display the POP_UP view as a dialog box.

How to do it...

We will now carry out the following steps:

1. We will define a public attribute by the name MY_WINDOW to the IF_WD_WINDOW interface.

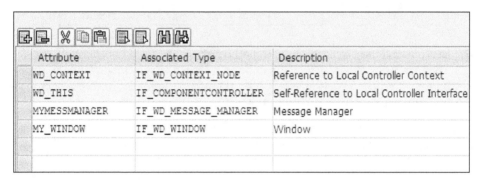

Attribute	Associated Type	Description
WD_CONTEXT	IF_WD_CONTEXT_NODE	Reference to Local Controller Context
WD_THIS	IF_COMPONENTCONTROLLER	Self-Reference to Local Controller Interface
MYMESSMANAGER	IF_WD_MESSAGE_MANAGER	Message Manager
MY_WINDOW	IF_WD_WINDOW	Window

2. We will have a main view embedded within the MAIN window.

3. In addition, we will create a POP_UP view embedded within a WIND_POP_UP window.

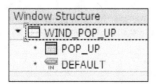

4. On the MAIN view, we will create a button.

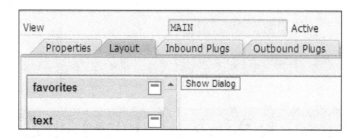

5. On action button event handler method, we will write the appropriate code for calling the POP_UP view as a pop-up dialog box. We use the WD_GET_API method of the component controller to get access to the relevant APIs. The GET_WINDOW_MANAGER function is then called in order to get reference to the IF_WD_WINDOW_MANAGER interface, which is stored in the public attribute MY_WINDOW_MANAGER, as defined in the previous section.

```
DATA: MY_WINDOW_MANAGER TYPE REF TO IF_WD_WINDOW_MANAGER,
      MY_CMP_API TYPE REF TO IF_WD_COMPONENT.

MY_CMP_API = WD_COMP_CONTROLLER->WD_GET_API( ).
MY_WINDOW_MANAGER = MY_CMP_API->GET_WINDOW_MANAGER( ).
```

6. Next, we call the CREATE_WINDOW method of the IF_WD_WINDOW_MANAGER interface. The necessary title, the desired message display mode, and the default button information is also passed. Also, the window name in which the pop-up view was created is mentioned (WIND_POP_UP).

```
WD_COMP_CONTROLLER->MY_WINDOW
  = MY_WINDOW_MANAGER->CREATE_WINDOW(
    WINDOW_NAME = 'WIND_POP_UP'
    TITLE = 'My Pop Up'
    MESSAGE_DISPLAY_MODE = IF_WD_WINDOW=>CO_MSG_DISPLAY_MODE_SELECTED
    BUTTON_KIND = IF_WD_WINDOW=>CO_BUTTONS_OK
    MESSAGE_TYPE = IF_WD_WINDOW=>CO_MSG_TYPE_NONE
    DEFAULT_BUTTON = IF_WD_WINDOW=>CO_BUTTON_OK ).
```

7. Finally, the OPEN method is called for the MY_WINDOW interface that is created.

```
WD_COMP_CONTROLLER->MY_WINDOW->OPEN( ).
```

How it works...

We carried out the necessary steps for displaying the pop-up dialog box. We first call the appropriate method for getting a reference to the window manager, used for creating the dialog box. We then call the CREATE_WINDOW method and specify the necessary title, window name, message mode, and the buttons to be displayed (through the BUTTON_KIND parameter). After the creation of the window, we need to show the dialog on the screen, which is done via the OPEN method of the IF_WD_WINDOW_MANAGER interface.

For the BUTTON_KIND, MESSAGE_TYPE, and DEFAULT_BUTTON parameters, the possible values that may be passed are shown in the following table:

Parameter	Possible Values
BUTTON_KIND	CO_BUTTONS_ABORTRETRYIGNORE
	CO_BUTTONS_CLOSE
	CO_BUTTON_OK
	CO_BUTTONS_OKCANCEL
	CO_BUTTONS_YESNO
	CO_BUTTONS_YES_NOCANCEL
MESSAGE_TYPE	CO_MSG_TYPE_ERROR
	CO_MSG_TYE_INFORMTION
	CO_MSG_TYPE_NONE
	CO_MSG_TYE_QUESTION
	CO_MSG_TYPE_STOP
	CO_MSG_TYPE_WARNING
DEFAULT_BUTTON	CO_BUTTON_ABORT
	CO_BUTTON_CANCEL
	CO_BUTTON_CLOSE
	CO_BUTTON_IGNORE
	CO_BUTTON_NO
	CO_BUTTON_NONE
	CO_BUTTON_OK
	CO_BUTTON_RETRY
	CO_BUTTON_YES

There's more...

Also, for calling the pop-up dialog box after the click of the button, we can make use of the Web Dynpro code wizard. While being in the editor for the code of the `OnActionbutton` `handler` method, navigate to **Edit | Web Dynpro Code Wizard**. On the general tab, select the **Generate Popup** option and enter the window name that embeds our view.

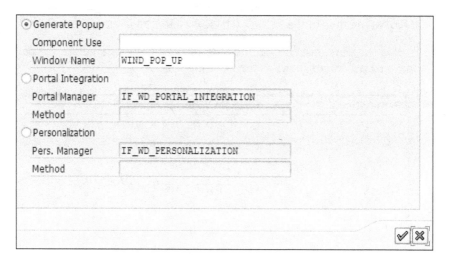

Simply press *Enter*. This will add the appropriate code.

Displaying Adobe forms in Web Dynpros

In this recipe, we will see how we can display an Adobe form within a Web Dynpro application. We will use one of the forms that we created in the *Creating nested tables* recipe in *Chapter 13, SAP Interactive Forms by Adobe*.

How to do it...

We will now see the required steps in detail:

1. We create a new Web Dynpro component. On the MAIN view, we create an interactive UI element. We name it INTERACTIVEUI.

2. Within the properties, the template source (that is, Adobe form) was set as
ZST8_NESTED_TABLES_EXAMPLE as used in the *Creating nested tables*
recipe in *Chapter 13, SAP Interactive Forms by Adobe*.

Property	Value	Binding
ID	INTERACTIVEUI	
additionalArchives		
contextMenuBehaviour	Inherit	
contextMenuId		
dataSource	MAIN.ZST8_NESTED_TABLES_E	
displayType	native	
enabled	☐	
height	300px	
jobProfile		
pdfSource		
readOnly	☐	
templateSource	ZST8_NESTED_TABLES_EXAMPLE	
tooltip		
visible	Visible	
width	300px	

We will also increase the height and width to 1500px instead of the default 300px.

3. After pressing *Enter*, a dialog box is displayed. This asks you whether context
nodes should be created within the view context node corresponding to the
context defined in the Adobe form. Click on the **Yes** button in order to generate
the context automatically.

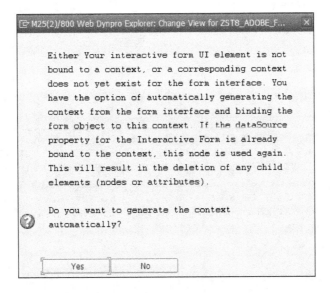

M25(2)/800 Web Dynpro Explorer: Change View for ZST8_ADOBE_F...

Either Your interactive form UI element is not
bound to a context, or a corresponding context
does not yet exist for the form interface. You
have the option of automatically generating the
context from the form interface and binding the
form object to this context. If the dataSource
property for the Interactive Form is already
bound to the context, this node is used again.
This will result in the deletion of any child
elements (nodes or attributes).

Do you want to generate the context
automatically?

Yes   No

4. This will generate appropriate context nodes within the Web Dynpro view corresponding to the context of the Adobe form. The two nodes EMPLOYEE_GRADES and EMPLOYEE_ADDRESS are generated in the CONTEXT MAIN window of the view in question.

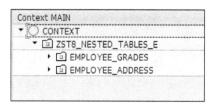

5. Next, we will write the code that is necessary to populate the data regarding the EMPLOYEE_GRADES and EMPLOYEE_ADDRESS nodes in the WDDOINIT method of the MAIN view. We use the Web Dynpro code wizard and choose the settings shown in the following screenshot (both for the EMPLOYEE_ADDRESS and the EMPLOYEE_GRADES nodes).

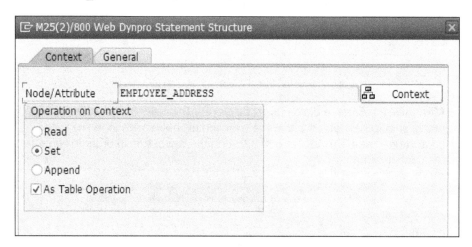

6. The main part of the added code for the EMPLOYEE_GRADES node is shown as follows:

```
DATA LO_ND_EMPLOYEE_GRADES TYPE REF TO IF_WD_CONTEXT_NODE.
DATA LT_EMPLOYEE_GRADES TYPE WD_THIS->ELEMENTS_EMPLOYEE_GRADES.
LO_ND_EMPLOYEE_GRADES = WD_CONTEXT->PATH_GET_NODE( PATH =
                      `ZST8_NESTED_TABLES_E.EMPLOYEE_GRADES`).
""" code to fill LT_EMPLOYEE_GRADES  not shown
LO_ND_EMPLOYEE_GRADES->BIND_TABLE(
     NEW_ITEMS = LT_EMPLOYEE_GRADES
     SET_INITIAL_ELEMENTS = ABAP_TRUE ).
```

How it works...

We first created an interactive UI element in our view layout. Then we linked it to our Adobe forms using the template source property. We then generated a context corresponding to the Adobe form in our view. The appropriate code was then added in the WDDOINIT view for populating the data context nodes EMPLOYEE_GRADES and EMPLOYEE_ADDRESS. Upon running the application, the data of the grades and addresses were passed on to the Adobe form context node.

The displayed PDF form opens in the browser as shown in the following screenshot:

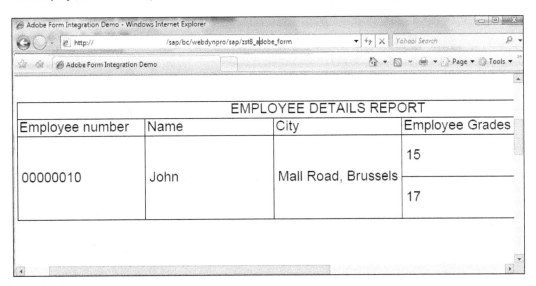

See also

- http://help.sap.com/saphelp_nw04s/helpdata/en/43/
  bccdcfe326332ee10000000a11466f/frameset.htm

- http://help.sap.com/erp2005_ehp_04/helpdata/en/6c/7aae42cd7fb61
  1e10000000a155106/frameset.htm

- http://help.sap.com/saphelp_nw04s/helpdata/en/35/447741b0d6157d
  e10000000a155106/frameset.htm

15
Floorplan Manager

In this chapter, we will see recipes involving **Floorplan Manager** (**FPM**) for **Web Dynpro applications**. We will look at:

- ▶ Creating applications based on OIF Floorplan design
- ▶ Changing header and ticket area at runtime
- ▶ Adding list GUIBBs to Floorplan applications
- ▶ Viewing structure of FPM applications
- ▶ Creating GAF applications
- ▶ Creating FPM applications using Application Creation Tool

Introduction

FPM may be simply defined as templates that allow us to create large, complex, and big Web Dynpro applications quickly and easily without the need for excessive programming. Using the Floorplan framework, interface views of multiple components may be combined together to form an application. The interface views, within the FPM arena, are termed as a **UI building blocks** (**UIBB**).

We first create an application based on one of the four supported Floorplan designs. Then we create the application and component configurations using the configuration editor. There are four types of Floorplans:

- ▶ **Object Instances Floorplan** (**OIF**)
- ▶ **Guided Activity Floorplan** (**GAF**)
- ▶ **Quick Activity Floorplan** (**QAP**)
- ▶ **Overview View Floorplan** (**OVP**)

Our main emphasis in this chapter will be on the OIF and GAF Floorplan designs.

Here is a brief introduction of the two:

> ▸ OIF: This Floorplan focuses on a particular object type such as an employee or sales order. It provides functionality such as `Create`, `Change`, `Display`, or `Delete`, and may consist of multiple tabs that provide input/output fields relevant to the given object instance (belonging to the object type in question).

> ▸ GAF: As the name indicates, the guided activity Floorplan allows you to perform a given task for an object over a number of steps (screens). The guided activity Floorplan provides a roadmap showing all the numbered steps as well as the current step highlighted for the user.

The **Identification Region** (**IDR**) is comprised of the application title. In addition, an optional Extended IDR consists of the ticket area on the left-hand side and the items area on the right-hand side. The ticket area may be configured while the items area may only be accessed through coding. The ticket area has **Ticket top** and **Ticket bottom** as shown in the following screenshot:

Creating applications based on OIF Floorplan design

In this recipe, we will see how we can create an application based on the OIF Floorplan. We will create the application configuration, then the IDR and the component configuration.

Getting ready

We will use the Web Dynpro component and application used in the *Integrating Adobe forms in Web Dynpro* recipe in *Chapter 14, Web Dynpro for ABAP*. However, we need to make certain changes in the component and its application in order for them to be used in the FPM design.

First, on the **Properties** tab of the created application, we will assign the FPM_OIF_COMPONENT component in the **Component** field and the FPM_WINDOW component in the **Interface View** field.

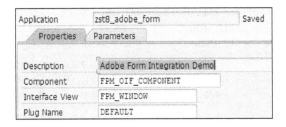

Next, at the component level, a change is also required. On the **Implemented Interfaces** tab, we will add the `IF_FPM_UI_BUILDING_BLOCK` component.

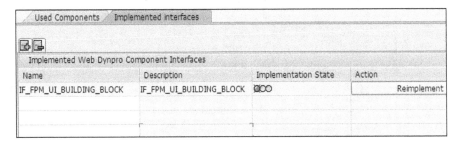

Then, click on the **Reimplement** button in the **Action** column. The **Implementation State** column should show a green signal. A message will appear saying that the interface was successfully implemented.

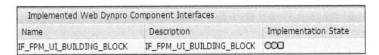

This adds a number of methods (related to the Floorplan design) to the component controller. Each method is called at a particular instance during the execution of the application. Each method serves a particular purpose and we can write coding within them in order to serve our requirement.

How to do it...

For creating an FPM OIF application, proceed as follows:

1. Call transaction SE80. In the left-hand pane, choose the **Web Dynpro Component** option in the list box and enter `FPM_OIF_COMPONENT` in the field provided. Then press *Enter*.

2. In the list that appears, under Web Dynpro applications, right-click our application `zst8_adobe_form`, and from the context menu that appears, choose the option **Create/Change Configuration**.

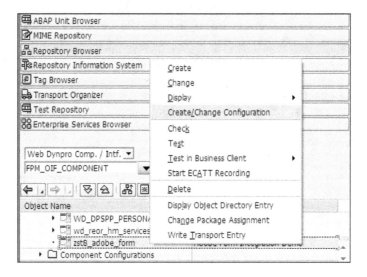

3. This will open the **Editor for the Web Dynpro ABAP Application Configuration** window. Enter a suitable ID in the **Configuration ID** field provided (in our case `ZST8_MY_OIF_DEMO`) and click the **Create** button.

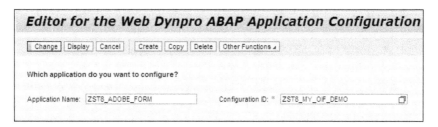

4. This leads you to the screen shown in the following screenshot:

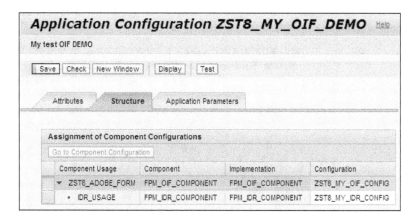

5. On the **Structure** tab, enter the name of the configuration components
    ZST8_MY_OIF_CONFIG and ZST8_MY_IDR_CONFIG in the fields provided.

6. First, select the OIF component row and click the **Go to Component Configuration**
    button. This will take you to the screen that looks like the following screenshot:

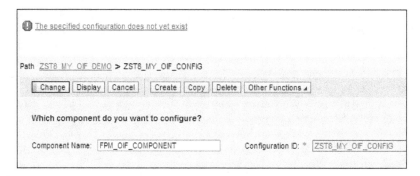

7. Since the component configuration does not exist, an error occurs. Click the
    Create button. The pop-up box appears as shown as follows:

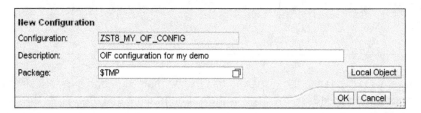

8. Enter suitable description and package (in our case local $TMP). Press the **OK** button.

9. The message appears, **The Configuration ZST8_MY_OIF_CONFIG has been created successfully**. Click the **Change** button.

10. This will lead you to the **Configuration Editor** window showing one **Main View** (**Main View 1**) having one **Subview** (**Subview 1 1**). On the left-hand pane, there is a tree showing the various components.

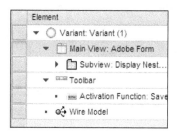

11. We will now assign a UIBB to our subview.

12. On the right-hand side is the detail screen for the object selected in the left-hand pane. Select the **Subview 1 1** option, and make sure the attributes appear in the lower part of the screen. Within the **Component** field, enter the name of the component that we are using (ZST8_ADOBE_FORM). Also, enter ZST8_WEB_DYNPRO in the **View** field, the respective window containing the view that we like to display in the subview at the execution of the application.

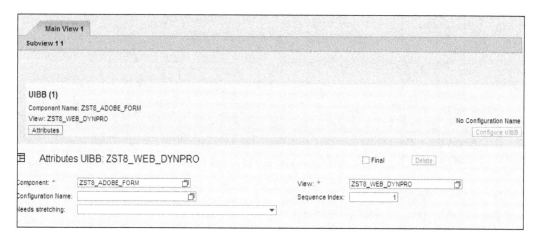

13. If we need to change the displayed text for the main view and subview, simply select the **Main View** or **Subview** node in the left-hand pane and then enter the new text in the **Main View** name attribute or **SubView** name attribute. Save your entries.

14. Now return to the application configuration screen. Now, we will create the IDR configuration. Select the row showing the **FPM_IDR_COMPONENT** component and click the **Go to Component Configuration** button. This will take you to the screen that looks like the following screenshot:

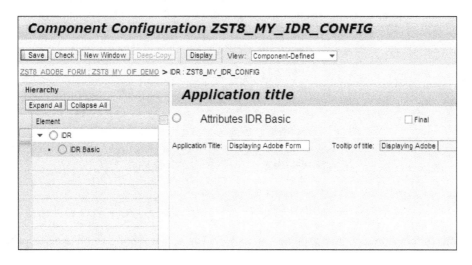

15. In the left-hand pane, click the **IDR Basic** node. On the right-hand side, enter the application title and the tooltip. Save your entries. You may click the **Check** button to check the consistency of your configuration.

How it works...

We created an application configuration based on OIF Floorplan. It comprised of the IDR configuration in which we specified the application title. We also created the component configuration of the component **FPM_OIF_COMPONENT** and within the view and subview we assigned the window (and view) that has been created earlier by us. You may add further subviews to the application. The views displayed within the subviews may be in different Web Dynpro components.

There's more...

On the left-hand side of the component configuration, click the **Add** button and select the **Initial Screen** option. You may then specify the component and view to be used as an initial screen. The **Initial Screen** window is displayed before the OIF application is displayed.

Similarly, we may add a confirmation screen as well. The confirmation screen is displayed at the end of the execution of the OIF application.

In addition, we need to make sure that the **Implemented Interfaces** tab on the used components have the interface **IF_FPM_UI_BUILDING_BLOCK** implemented, otherwise the error occurs as shown in the following screenshot:

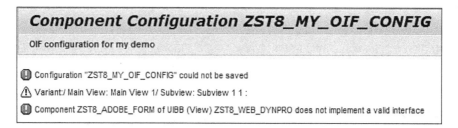

Changing header and ticket area at runtime

In this recipe, we will see how we can change the IDR header (title and ticket area) programmatically. In this case, the previously statically defined (through IDR configuration) ticket area and title are overridden. This concept applies to both the OIF and OVP Floorplans.

In this recipe, we will write the code for changing within the view (window) shown within a subview. When the particular subview is selected, the header title and ticket area will change. We will write the code in the component whose view is used as an UIBB in a subview. We will write the code in the respective view (WDDOINIT method).

How to do it...

For dynamically changing the IDR title and ticket area, proceed as follows:

1. First, we define an attribute at the component controller level by the name
   MY_FPM_IDR based on the type IF_FPM_IDR.

Component Controller	COMPONENTCONTROLLER	Active(revised)

Properties | Context | Attributes | Events | Methods

Attribute	Public	RefTo	Associated Type
WD_CONTEXT	☐	☑	IF_WD_CONTEXT_NODE
WD_THIS	☐	☑	IF_COMPONENTCONTROLLER
MYMESSMANAGER	☑	☑	IF_WD_MESSAGE_MANAGER
MY_FPM_IDR	☑	☑	IF_FPM_IDR

2. Next, we define a SET_IDR_TITLE_TICKET method in the component
   controller. Then, we will write the coding in the method. We first define a
   reference variable MY_FPM that point to the interface IF_FPM. We call the
   static method GET_INSTANCE of the CL_FPM_FACTORY class in order to
   create a reference to the FPM service object.

```
DATA : MY_FPM TYPE REF TO IF_FPM.
MY_FPM =  CL_FPM_FACTORY=>GET_INSTANCE ( ).
```

3. We then call the GET_SERVICE method with the constant attribute GC_KEY_IDR of
   the class CL_FPM_SERVICE_MANAGER. The result of the method is then assigned to
   MY_FPM_IDR attribute we defined in the first step.

```
WD_THIS->MY_FPM_IDR   ?= MY_FPM->GET_SERVICE (
    CL_FPM_SERVICE_MANAGER=>GC_KEY_IDR ).
```

4. We then call the SET_APPLICATION_TITLE method of the attribute MY_FPM_IDR.
   We pass the New Title and New Tooltip parameters for the IDR.

```
WD_THIS->MY_FPM_IDR->SET_APPLICATION_TITLE (
IV_TITLE = 'New Title '
IV_TITLE_TOOLTIP = 'New Tooltip' ).
```

5. We then call the `SET_TICKET` method for the reference `MY_FPM_IDR`. The necessary `Ticket top` and `Ticket bottom` texts are passed as values corresponding to necessary parameters.

```
TRY.
    WD_THIS->MY_FPM_IDR->SET_TICKET(
    IV_TOP = 'Ticket top '
    IV_BOTTOM = 'Ticket bottom   '
    IV_TOP_TOOLTIP = 'Top tooltip '
    IV_BOTTOM_TOOLTIP = 'bottom tooltip' ).

    CATCH CX_FPM_IDR.

ENDTRY.
```

6. We then need to write the code for calling the method `SET_IDR_TITLE_TICKET` from the `WDDOINIT` method of the view that is used in the UIBB of the subview.

```
DATA MYCOMPONENTCONTROLLER TYPE REF TO IG_COMPONENTCONTROLLER .

MYCOMPONENTCONTROLLER = WD_THIS->GET_COMPONENTCONTROLLER_CTR( ).
MYCOMPONENTCONTROLLER->SET_IDR_TITLE_TICKET( ).
```

By following these steps, we are accessing the IDR at runtime and specifying its displayed IDR title and ticket area text.

How it works...

We created a method `SET_IDR_TITLE_TICKET` at the component controller level that access the service object for accessing the IDR. Appropriate methods are called in order to set the application title, ticket top, and bottom. Next, this method is called from the `WDDOINIT` method of the view used in the UIBB of our OIF application.

When the application is run and the relevant subview is selected, the `WDDOINIT` method is called that calls the `SET_IDR_TITLE_TICKET` method of the component controller. The **New Title**, **Ticket top**, and **Ticket bottom** parameters are changed as shown in following screenshot:

Adding list GUIBBs to Floorplan applications

SAP provides a number of **Generic User Interface Building Blocks** (**GUIBB**) generic building blocks such as **Tabs UIBB**, **Form**, and **List UIBB**. These allow you to reuse them into your applications without programming from scratch. In this recipe, we will see how we can add a list GUIBB in our applications.

The GUIBB list must have an associated feeder class that provides the data that is displayed in the list. We will add the list GUIBB in OIF application created earlier. We will add the GUIBB list in a new subview within the component configuration.

Within the list, we will display the columns showing the employee information based on our previously created structure (in *Chapter 14, Web Dynpro for ABAP*) **ZST8_EMPLOYEE_ADDRESS** as shown in the following screenshot:

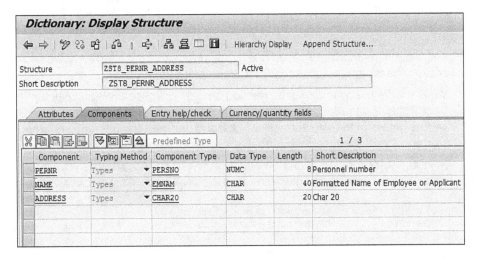

How to do it...

For adding the list GUIBB in our applications, proceed as follows:

1. We will first create the feeder class through transaction SE24. On the **Interfaces** tab, we will add two interfaces IF_FPM_GUIBB_LIST and IF_FPM_GUIBB_LIST_EXT interfaces (the IF_FPM_GIUBB interface will come by itself).

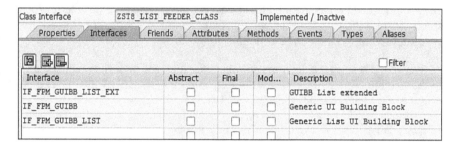

2. A number of methods are added due to the inclusion of the interfaces. We will write code in the two methods GET_DEFINITION and GET_DATA.

3. We first write the code within the method GET_DEFINITION. We first call the DESCRIBE_BY_NAME static method of the CL_ABAP_TYPEDESCR class in order to get the details of the structure ZST8_PERNR_ADDRESS. The reference returned is stored in the defined reference variable MYSTRUCTDESCR.

4. Next, the static method CREATE method of the CL_ABAP_TABLEDESCR class is called and the returned reference is stored in EO_FIELD_CATALOG.

```
DATA MYSTRUCTDESCR TYPE REF TO CL_ABAP_STRUCTDESCR.
MYSTRUCTDESCR ?= CL_ABAP_TYPEDESCR=>DESCRIBE_BY_NAME( 'ZST8_PERNR_ADDRESS' ).
EO_FIELD_CATALOG = CL_ABAP_TABLEDESCR=>CREATE( MYSTRUCTDESCR ).
```

5. Next, we call the GET_COMPONENTS method in order to get the components of our structure ZST8_PERNR_ADDRESS. The components returned in the internal table MY_COMPONENT_TAB. A loop is then run on the internal table. For each component, we set the properties as visible, read-only, and the column header to be used from the data dictionary definition. The property information is set using the structure WA_FIELD_DESCRIPTION which is then appended to the internal table (exporting parameter) ET_FIELD_DESCRIPTION.

```
DATA MY_COMPONENT_TAB TYPE ABAP_COMPONENT_TAB.
DATA WA_COMPONENT_TAB LIKE LINE OF MY_COMPONENT_TAB.
DATA WA_FIELD_DESCRIPTION TYPE FPMGB_S_LISTFIELD_DESCR.

MY_COMPONENT_TAB = MYSTRUCTDESCR->GET_COMPONENTS( ).
LOOP AT MY_COMPONENT_TAB INTO WA_COMPONENT_TAB.
  WA_FIELD_DESCRIPTION-NAME = WA_COMPONENT_TAB-NAME.
  WA_FIELD_DESCRIPTION-VISIBILITY = CL_WD_UIELEMENT=>E_VISIBLE-VISIBLE.
  WA_FIELD_DESCRIPTION-READ_ONLY = ABAP_TRUE.
  WA_FIELD_DESCRIPTION-HEADER_LABEL_BY_DDIC = ABAP_TRUE.
  APPEND WA_FIELD_DESCRIPTION TO ET_FIELD_DESCRIPTION.
ENDLOOP.
```

6. Within the GET_DATA method, for our requirement we only need to make very small code insertion. For simplicity sake, we assume that the data that is to be displayed in the list is available in the internal table IT_ADDRESS (the coding for fetching this data is not shown). The two lines to be inserted are shown as follows:

```
ct_data  =  it_address.
ev_data_changed = abap_true .
```

7. For all other methods, we will create empty implementations and save our code. Then save and activate your class.

8. Next, we will go to the configuration editor and will add a new subview to our application. We will then use the **Add UIBB** button on the right-hand side of the configuration editor screen and choose the option **Add List Component**.

9. For the **List UIBB (1)** window, within the attributes, we will enter a suitable configuration name (in our case ZST_LIST_CONFIG) and click the **Configure UIBB** button on the right-hand side of the screen (note the component **FPM_LIST_UIBB** and view **LIST_WINDOW** are inserted automatically).

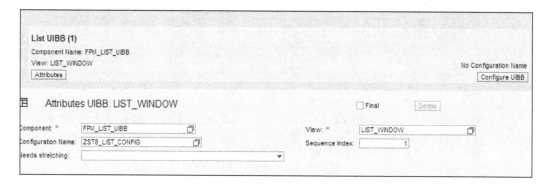

10. This will lead to the editor for the **Web Dynpro ABAP Component Configuration** window and will generate an error saying that the configuration does not exist.

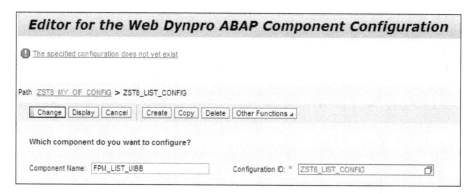

11. We will then click the **Create** button. A pop up appears that asks the feeder class to be used for the list configuration. Enter the name of the feeder class created in the first step. Click the **Edit Parameters** button.

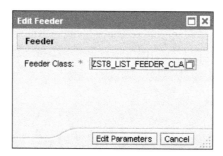

12. Since there are no parameters defined, the save pop up will appear and will ask us to save our configuration. This will then take us to the component configuration of our configuration ZST8_LIST_CONFIG.

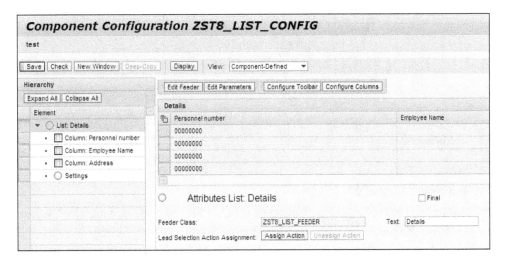

13. Then we will click the **Configure Columns** button. This will show the columns that we had set in the GET_DEFINITION method to be available for list configuration. We will use the **Add Columns** button in order to select the columns that we need to be shown in our list. We may change the header description also if we like and well as the displayed length and sequence.

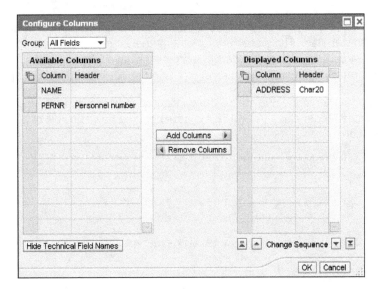

14. We set the description of the three fields in our structure as shown in the following screenshot:

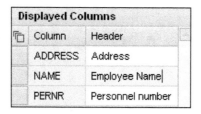

15. We save our configurations and then test the application configuration of our main application.

How it works...

We first define the feeder class using the transaction SE24. The code is written for the two important methods GET_DATA and GET_DEFINITION. Both these methods are called each time the GUIBB is processed.

The GET_DEFINITION method has two exporting parameters that are filled within the code that we have written. The list of columns that are to be made available in the configuration editor is specified in the exporting parameter EO_FIELD_CATALOG, whereas, the properties of each column is specified in the exporting parameter ET_FIELD_DESCRIPTION. The properties that are set include the column heading that may be later changed at the time of configuration.

Within the GET_DATA method that provides the data to be displayed, the exporting parameter CT_DATA is filled with data. The statement for setting the value of EV_DATA_CHANGE to ABAP_TRUE must be there. If not, the data will not be displayed, however, the list columns are displayed correctly upon application run.

The configuration is then done. We create the configuration of the list UIBB and assign it the newly created feeder class. The GUIBB is attached to a new subview of our existing application.

Upon executing the application, the list is displayed along with the data.

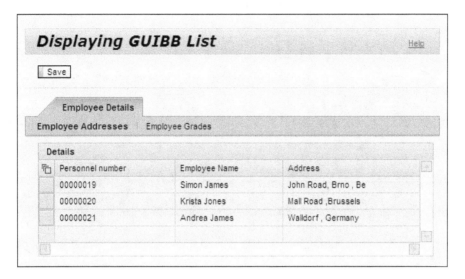

There's more...

There are other notable methods of the feeder class such as GET_PARAMETER_LIST, used to define parameters for your feeder class, the NEEDS_CONFIRMATION method that allows us to display a data loss dialog box, and the PROCESS_EVENT method that is used for handling any events triggered during the application execution.

At the minimal, coding must be entered in the mandatory methods GET_DEFINITION and GET_DATA.

Viewing structure of FPM applications

In this recipe, we will see how we can use a standard Web Dynpro component in order to view the entire structure of our FPM applications.

How to do it...

Follow these steps:

1. Call transaction SE80. In the left-hand pane, choose **Web Dynpro Component** from the list box and enter the component name FPM_CFG_HIERARCHY_BROWSER in the field provided. Click the **Display** button.

2. Then open the **Web Dynpro Applications** node and double-click the
   FPM_CFG_HIERARCHY_BROWSER application.

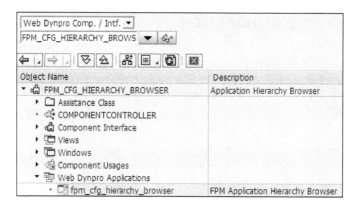

3. Then, choose the menu path: **Web Dynpro Application | Test | In Browser - Admin
   Mode**.

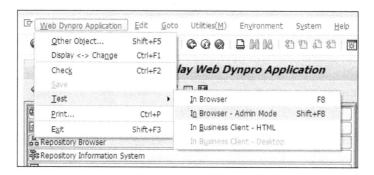

4. The browser will open and the screen will appear as follows:

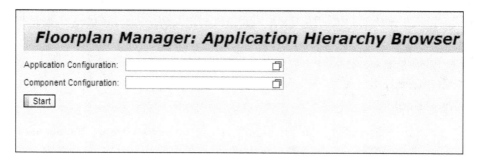

5. Enter the name in the **Application Configuration** field provided and click the **Start** button. We will use our already created application configuration `ZST8_MY_OIF_DEMO`.

6. The entire hierarchy of the application (and configuration) will be displayed in the next browser screen.

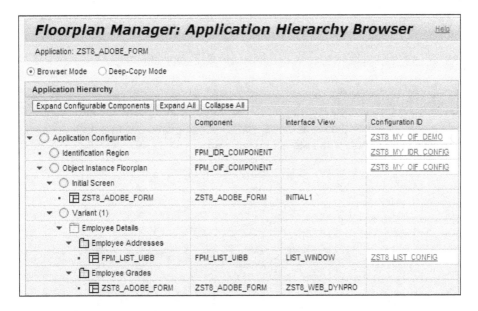

How it works...

We use a standard application to display the hierarchy of our FPM application. The IDR and the OIF details are shown. The configuration IDs of the various involved configurations are also displayed. The component used for the initial screen as well as the various subview and views details are displayed. If a GUIBB is used, (for example, list UIBB), the component name used along with the relevant configuration ID is displayed. We may click on a particular configuration ID to display. In a separate browser session, the details of its configuration are given.

See also

▶ http://www.sdn.sap.com/irj/scn/go/portal/prtroot/docs/library/
   uuid/c0a2b7c2-1598-2e10-45bc-c556df3b9576?QuickLink=index&overr
   idelayout=true&51591147228485

Creating GAF applications

In this recipe, we will see how we can develop and configure **Guided Activity Floorplan** (**GAF**) applications. By default, one single step is automatically added to the component configuration. We will create one main step (step 2) that will comprise of one substep. We will write coding that will display the substep after the **Next** button of the step 2 is clicked. There is no ticket area for a GAF application.

In this recipe, we will focus on the steps relevant to GAF applications.

Getting ready

We create a component by the name ZST8_GAF that comprised of views and windows shown in the following screenshot for the steps and substep:

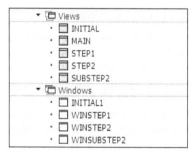

The defined application is based upon the component FPM_GAF_COMPONENT and interface view is FPM_WINDOW.

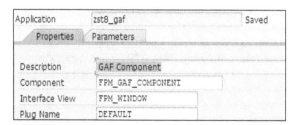

How to do it...

Follow these steps:

1. Within the configuration editor, one main step already exists. In addition, two toolbar buttons, **Previous** and **Next** buttons also exist.

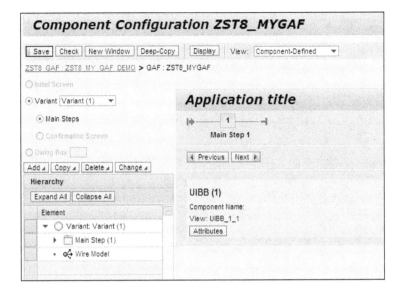

2. Select the main step and in the **Attributes UIBB: WINSTEP1** panel, assign the component and view as shown in following screenshot:

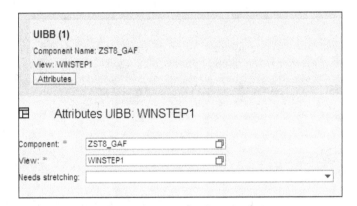

3. Then add one more main step using the **Add Main Step** button on the right-hand side of the screen. Assign the component and view appropriate values (**WINSTEP2**).

4. Then, select the **Main Step 2**, and add a substep using the **Add Substep** button. For the substep, enter the component and view name created earlier.

5. Also on the attributes of the **Next** button of **Main Step 2**, enter STEP2_NEXT in the **Event ID** field.

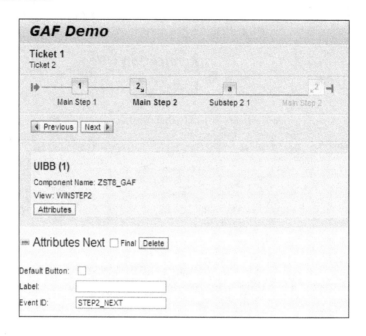

6. Next, we will create a new toolbar button on the **Substep2 1**. We will press the button **Add Toolbar Element**. The dialog appears as shown in the following screenshot:

7. Next, we need to know the substep variant parameter. Select the **Substep variant** node from the left-hand pane and then choose the menu **Change** and then click **Substep Variant Parameters**.

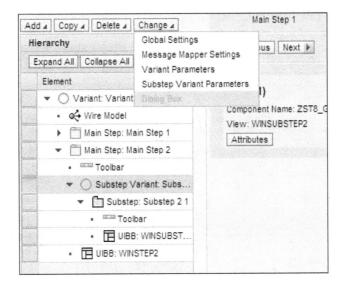

8. Note the value from the pop up that appears and then press **OK**.

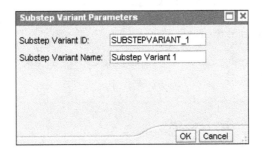

9. Save and activate your configurations.

10. Next, we will write the code for activating the substep. This code is written in the PROCESS_EVENT method of the component controller.

11. We use a CASE statement to make sure our added code runs for the **Next** button click of the MAINSTEP_2.

12. We call the CREATE_BY_ID method of the CL_FPM_EVENT class in order to create an event object.

13. Next, the SET_VALUE method is called in order to specify the event parameters. The method is called three times, for specifying the main step, the next active substep, and the substep variant having the values MAINSTEP_2, SUBSTEP_2_1 and SUBSTEPVARIANT_1 respectively.

14. Finally, we raise the event that we have created using the RAISE_EVENT method. The MY_EVENT object is passed for the parameter IO_EVENT.

```
 1  METHOD PROCESS_EVENT .
 2    CASE IO_EVENT->MV_EVENT_ID.
 3      WHEN 'STEP2_NEXT'.
 4        WD_THIS->FPM = CL_FPM_FACTORY=>GET_INSTANCE( ).
 5        DATA my_EVENT TYPE REF TO CL_FPM_EVENT.
 6        my_EVENT = CL_FPM_EVENT=>CREATE_BY_ID( CL_FPM_EVENT=>GC_EVENT_CHANGE_STEP ).
 7        my_EVENT->MO_EVENT_DATA->SET_VALUE( IV_KEY = CL_FPM_EVENT=>GC_EVENT_PARAM_MAINSTEP_ID
 8                                            IV_VALUE = 'MAINSTEP_2' ).
 9        my_EVENT->MO_EVENT_DATA->SET_VALUE( IV_KEY = CL_FPM_EVENT=>GC_EVENT_PARAM_SUBSTEP_ID
10                                            IV_VALUE = 'SUBSTEP_2_1' ).
11        my_EVENT->MO_EVENT_DATA->SET_VALUE( IV_KEY = CL_FPM_EVENT=>GC_EVENT_PARAM_SUBVARIANT_ID
12                                            IV_VALUE = 'SUBSTEPVARIANT_1' ).
13        WD_THIS->FPM->RAISE_EVENT( IO_EVENT = my_EVENT ).
14
15    ENDCASE.
16  ENDMETHOD.
```

How it works...

We created the GAF application configuration and component configuration. We created two main steps and one substep. By default, the substep is not active. We wrote the code for activating the substep at runtime. We also added a toolbar button **Return to Main Step** for returning from the substep to the main step.

Running the application configuration will display the GAF application. You may use the **Next** button to go to the next step.

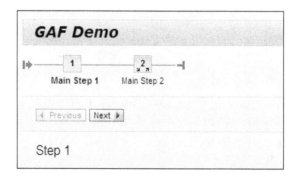

Creating FPM applications using Application Creation Tool

In this recipe, we will see how we can use a standard Web Dynpro application in order to create new FPM-based applications quickly and easily.

How to do it...

Follow these steps:

1. Call transaction SE80. Select the package from the list box. Enter APB_FPM_CONF in the field provided.

2. Open the Web Dynpro Applications folder. Right-click the **FM_CFG_APPL_CREATION_TOOL** component and then choose the **Test** option from the context menu that appears.

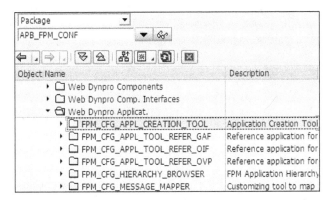

3. The **Application Creation Tool** window opens in a browser window.

4. Enter a suitable name for your application. Enter a description and choose from the list box the **Floorplan** type. Then click the **Propose** button.

5. The suggested configuration names are filled in the following table (screenshot) for the application, IDR, and component configuration.

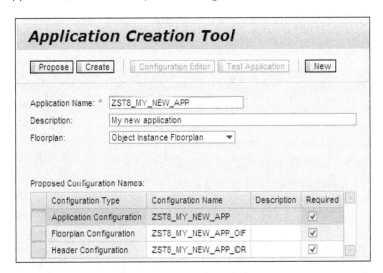

6. You enter description in the field provided and make sure the required checkbox is on.

7. Then click the **Create** button. The application will be created. Then we may select a particular configuration and then click the **Configuration Editor** button to go to the appropriate configuration.

How it works...

Application Creation Tool is a useful tool that allows you to quickly create an application and its various configurations involved quickly and easily from one screen and relieve us from the burden of creating each one by one manually. We may then also go directly to the configuration using the **Configuration Editor** button.

See also

- http://help.sap.com/erp2005_ehp_06/helpdata/en/08/1cd90cc855424 eb8177365a122a8b7/content.htm

- http://help.sap.com/saphelp_nw70ehp2/helpdata/en/15/ daf7c77c704c64ac8c8e48307e2bb0/content.htm

- http://help.sap.com/erp2005_ehp_06/helpdata/en/08/1cd90cc855424 eb8177365a122a8b7/content.htm

Index

creating, scripting used 230-232
error messages, adding 239, 240
working 232, 233
internal date type
date, converting into 73
internal tables
secondary indexes 93, 94
transformations, creating 175, 176
working 176

L

layout toolbar buttons
saving 51
working 51, 52
LIST_FROM_MEMORY function 199
LOOP statement 40

M

MESSAGE_TYPE parameter 261
multiselection parameter 110
mycheckbox method 63

N

navigation lists
about 248
creating 249-252
working 253, 254
nested tables
about 224, 225
creating 226, 227
working 227, 228

O

Object Instances Floorplan. *See* **OIF**
OIF 267, 268
OnActionbutton handler method 262
on_button_press method 58
on_click_checkbox method 64
Overview View Floorplan. *See* **OVP**
OVP 267

P

PDF object API
about 240
using 241
working 242
PDF output
Smart Form, converting to 124-126
persistent object
about 12
creating 13-16
working 17, 18
printed multiple forms
including, in single spool request 122-124
print preview
using 117-120
Print Preview option 119
program
running 199-202
program code
comments, removing 78, 79
program output
sending, as email 199-202
pseudo comments
used, for message suppressing 159, 160

Q

QAP 267
Quick Activity Floorplan. *See* **QAP**
quick code inspection
carrying out 150-152
working 152, 153

R

radio button selection
screen fields, changing 106-108
refresh method 63
regex
using, as IF statement 70, 71
regular expression 67, 68
regular expression operators, in ABAP
^ 68
?! 68

Where Clause block 35
WSDL 203

X

XML Spreadsheet 2003 format 182
XML stream 167

XSLT_TOOL 167
XSLT transformation 167

Z

ZST8MY_SPELL_AMOUNT method 222

Thank you for buying
SAP ABAP Advanced Cookbook

About Packt Publishing

Packt, pronounced 'packed', published its first book "*Mastering phpMyAdmin for Effective MySQL Management*" in April 2004 and subsequently continued to specialize in publishing highly focused books on specific technologies and solutions.

Our books and publications share the experiences of your fellow IT professionals in adapting and customizing today's systems, applications, and frameworks. Our solution-based books give you the knowledge and power to customize the software and technologies you're using to get the job done. Packt books are more specific and less general than the IT books you have seen in the past. Our unique business model allows us to bring you more focused information, giving you more of what you need to know, and less of what you don't.

Packt is a modern, yet unique publishing company, which focuses on producing quality, cutting-edge books for communities of developers, administrators, and newbies alike. For more information, please visit our website: www.PacktPub.com.

About Packt Enterprise

In 2010, Packt launched two new brands, Packt Enterprise and Packt Open Source, in order to continue its focus on specialization. This book is part of the Packt Enterprise brand, home to books published on enterprise software – software created by major vendors, including (but not limited to) IBM, Microsoft and Oracle, often for use in other corporations. Its titles will offer information relevant to a range of users of this software, including administrators, developers, architects, and end users.

Writing for Packt

We welcome all inquiries from people who are interested in authoring. Book proposals should be sent to author@packtpub.com. If your book idea is still at an early stage and you would like to discuss it first before writing a formal book proposal, contact us; one of our commissioning editors will get in touch with you.

We're not just looking for published authors; if you have strong technical skills but no writing experience, our experienced editors can help you develop a writing career, or simply get some additional reward for your expertise.

Mastering SQL Queries for SAP Business One

ISBN: 978-1-84968-236-7   Paperback: 352 pages

Utilize the power of SQL queries to bring Business Intelligence to your small medium-sized business

1. Practical SAP query examples from an SAP Business One expert

2. Detailed steps to create and troubleshoot SQL queries for Alerts, Approvals, Formatted Searches, and Crystal Reports

3. Understand the importance and benefit of keeping SQL queries simple and easy to understand

---

SAP BusinessObjects Dashboards 4.0 Cookbook

ISBN: 978-1-84968-178-0   Paperback: 352 pages

Over 90 simple and incredibly effective recipes for transforming your business data into exciting dashboards with SAP BusinessObjects Dashboards 4.0 Xcelcius

1. Learn valuable Dashboard Design best practices and tips through easy to follow recipes

2. Become skilled in using and configuring all Dashboard Design components

3. Learn how to apply Dynamic Visibility to enhance your dashboards

4. Get introduced to the most important add-ons available for Dashboard Design with the most up to date information for Dashboards 4.0

Please check **www.PacktPub.com** for information on our titles

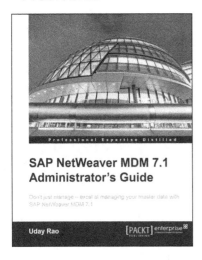

SAP NetWeaver MDM 7.1 Administrator's Guide

ISBN: 978-1-84968-214-5 Paperback: 336 pages

Don't just manager – excel at managing your master data with SAP NetWeaver MDM 7.1

1. Written in an easy-to-follow manner, and in simple language

2. Step-by-step procedures that take you from basic to advanced administration of SAP MDM in no time

3. Learn various techniques for effectively managing master data using SAP MDM 7.1 with illustrative screen shots

SAP Business ONE Implementation

ISBN: 978-1-84719-638-5 Paperback: 320 pages

Bring the power of SAP Enterprise Resource Planning to your small-to-midsize business

1. Get SAP B1 up and running quickly, optimize your business, inventory, and manage your warehouse

2. Understand how to run reports and take advantage of real-time information

3. Complete an express implementation from start to finish

4. Real-world examples with step-by-step explanations

Please check **www.PacktPub.com** for information on our titles